THE REAL GREY'S ANATOMY

THE REAL

GREY'S ANATOMY

A Behind-the-Scenes Look at the
Real Lives of Surgical Residents

ANDREW HOLTZ, M.P.H.

BERKLEY BOULEVARD, NEW YORK

THE BERKLEY PUBLISHING GROUP
Published by the Penguin Group
Penguin Group (USA) Inc.
375 Hudson Street, New York, New York 10014, USA
Penguin Group (Canada), 90 Eglinton Avenue East, Suite 700, Toronto, Ontario M4P 2Y3, Canada
(a division of Pearson Penguin Canada Inc.)
Penguin Books Ltd., 80 Strand, London WC2R 0RL, England
Penguin Group Ireland, 25 St. Stephen's Green, Dublin 2, Ireland (a division of Penguin Books Ltd.)
Penguin Group (Australia), 250 Camberwell Road, Camberwell, Victoria 3124, Australia
(a division of Pearson Australia Group Pty. Ltd.)
Penguin Books India Pvt. Ltd., 11 Community Centre, Panchsheel Park, New Delhi—110 017, India
Penguin Group (NZ), 67 Apollo Drive, Rosedale, North Shore 0632, New Zealand
(a division of Pearson New Zealand Ltd.)
Penguin Books (South Africa) (Pty.) Ltd., 24 Sturdee Avenue, Rosebank, Johannesburg 2196,
South Africa

Penguin Books Ltd., Registered Offices: 80 Strand, London WC2R 0RL, England

This book was not authorized, prepared, approved, licensed, or endorsed by any entity involved in creating or producing the *Grey's Anatomy* television series.

While the author has made every effort to provide accurate telephone numbers and Internet addresses at the time of publication, neither the publisher nor the author assumes any responsibility for errors, or for changes that occur after publication. Further the publisher does not have any control over and does not assume any responsibility for author or third-party websites or their content.

PRINTING HISTORY
Berkley Boulevard trade paperback edition / January 2010

Library of Congress Cataloging-in-Publication Data

Holtz, Andrew.
    The real Grey's anatomy : a behind-the-scenes look at the real lives of surgical residents / Andrew Holtz.
        p. cm.
    Includes bibliographical references and index.
    ISBN 978-0-425-23211-8
    1. Surgeons. 2. Residents (Medicine) I. Title.
    [DNLM: 1. Oregon Health & Science University. 2. Grey's anatomy (Television program) 3. Internship and Residency—Oregon—Personal Narratives. 4. Internship and Residency—United States—Personal Narratives. 5. Academic Medical Centers—Oregon—Personal Narratives. 6. Academic Medical Centers—United States—Personal Narratives. 7. General Surgery—Oregon—Personal Narratives. 8. General Surgery—United States—Personal Narratives. 9. Television—Oregon—Personal Narratives. 10. Television—United States—Personal Narratives. W 20 H758r 2010]
    RD27.34.H65 2010
    617.092'2—dc22

                                                                                    2009017586

PRINTED IN THE UNITED STATES OF AMERICA

10 9 8 7 6 5 4 3 2 1

To caregivers of all varieties,
especially to those who have always cared for and supported me:
my wife, Kelly Butler Holtz; our children, Aaron and Judy;
and my parents, Merriman and Carolyn Holtz

THANKS

This book would not have been possible without the support of John G. Hunter, M.D., Mackenzie Professor and Chairman of Surgery and Karen Deveney, M.D., Professor of Surgery, Vice Chair of Education and Residency Program Director at the Oregon Health & Science University (OHSU) in Portland. They agreed to open their program to me to help the public they serve better understand the work they and colleagues do every day and every night. The staff members who work with them, including Residency Coordinator Robin Alton, Pam Sidis, and Erin Anderson were always helpful.

Liana Haywood of the News and Publications staff deserves special notice for her persistent efforts to clear the way. Jim Newman and Tamara Hargens-Bradley both helped champion the project. Christine Decker's assistance was appreciated and will be missed.

Of course, the heart of this project is the team of residents and surgeons at OHSU. They allowed a visitor to shadow them, ask questions, page them, and pester them day and night. Here are the names of some who helped.

Attending Surgeons

John Barry, M.D.; Kevin Billingsley, M.D.; Bruce Ham, M.D.; John Ham, M.D.; Karen Kwong, M.D.; Greg Landry, M.D.; Tim Liem, M.D.; Robert Martindale, M.D.; John Mayberry, M.D.; Erica Mitchell, M.D.; Greg Moneta, M.D.; Richard Mullins, M.D.; Robert O'Rourke, M.D.; Susan Orloff, M.D.;

Stephen Rayhill, M.D.; Martin Schreiber, M.D.; Brett Sheppard, M.D.; Donn Spight, M.D.; Donald Trunkey, M.D.; Jennifer Watters, M.D.

Fellows

Charles Kim, M.D.; Renee Minjarez, M.D.; Aaron Partsafas, M.D.; David Shapiro, M.D.

Residents

Aric Aghayan, M.D.; Alexis Alexandridis, M.D.; Cyrus Ali, M.D.; Amir Azarbal, M.D.; Adam Baker, M.D.; James Ballard, M.D.; Jeff Barton, M.D.; Daniel Brickman, M.D.; Nathan Bronson, M.D.; Jeffery Brown, M.D.; Emily Bubbers, M.D.; Brian Caldwell, M.D.; Jimmy Chim, M.D.; David Cho, M.D.; Dara Christante, M.D.; Daniel Clayburgh, M.D.; Molly Cone, M.D.; Rachel Danczyk, M.D.; Birat Dhungel, M.D.; Raphael El Youssef, M.D.; Michelle Ellis, M.D.; Kristian Enestvedt, M.D.; Michael Englehart, M.D.; Loïc Fabricant, M.D.; Brian Farrell, M.D.; Megan Frost, M.D.; Guang Gao, M.D.; Arvin Gee, M.D.; Ryan Gertz, M.D.; Michael Grant, M.D.; Esther Han, M.D.; Karin Hardiman, M.D.; Adrienne Heckler, M.D.; Winnie Henderson, M.D.; Crystal Hessman, M.D.; Yin-Kan Hwee, M.D.; Shiney Isaac, M.D.; Terah Isaacson, M.D.; Brian Jones, M.D.; Jason Jundt, M.D.; Modjgan Keyghobadi, M.D.; Sajid Khan, M.D.; Laszlo Kiraly, M.D.; Chris Komanapalli, M.D.; Marcus Kret, M.D.; Sandeep Kumar, M.D.; Nicholas Kunio, M.D.; David Dae Lee, M.D.; Tim Lee, M.D.; Jessyka Lighthall, M.D.; Jean Lin, M.D.; Katrine Lofberg, M.D.; Carl Luem, M.D.; Alosh Madala, M.D.; Kristen Massimino, M.D.; Laura Matsen, M.D.; Lyudmila Morozova, M.D.; Melanie Morris, M.D.; Stephen Noble, M.D.; Pat O'Herron, M.D.; Marc Orlando, M.D.; Timothy Osborn, M.D.; Alan (Scott) Polackwich, M.D.; Glenda Quan, M.D.; Arun Raman, M.D.; Jennifer Rea, M.D.; Gordon Riha, M.D.; Mitchell Sally, M.D.; Kelli Salter, M.D.; Chitra Sambasivan, M.D.; MaryClare Sarff, M.D.; Scott Sklenicka, M.D.; Mary Sorensen, M.D.; Nick Spoerke, M.D.; Elliot Stephenson, M.D.; Ashley Stewart, M.D.; Jason Susong, M.D.; Julia Swanson,

M.D.; Nick Tadros, M.D.; Brandon Tieu, M.D.; Rakhee Urankar, M.D.; Phil Van, M.D.; Tammy Washut, M.D.; Charlotte Weeda, M.D.; Wei Wei, M.D.; Nathaniel Whitney, M.D.; Daniel Wieking, M.D.; Victor Wong, M.D.; Sharon Wright, M.D.; Lianjun Xu, M.D.; Douglas York, M.D.; Minhao Zhou, M.D.; Liyan Zhuang, M.D.; Karen Zink, M.D.

Melissa Johnson, M.D. (Emergency Medicine); Eric Reid, M.D. (Urology).

Medical Students

Jonah Attebery (MS3); Alalia Berry (MS3); Joshua Kornegay (MS3); Derek Leinenbach; Mara O'Brien Colbert; Kirstie Schneider (MS4); Ian White (MS4).

Others

Norman Cohen, M.D.; Nicole DiIorio, M.D.; Sydney Ey, Ph.D.; Robert Hendrickson, M.D.; J. Mark Kinzie, M.D., Ph.D.; Zachary Litvack, M.D.; Madison Macht, M.D.; Mary Moffit, Ph.D., R.N.; Doug Norman, M.D.; Thomas Yackel, M.D.

A wave of thanks also goes to those whose names I failed to record.

All I did for them in return was occasionally deliver some sutures to the scrub tech in the OR when the circulating nurse was busy.

AN APOLOGY

In this attempt to respond to the curiosity of fans of *Grey's Anatomy* and others, the book limits itself to the frame of reference of the show—that is, the experiences of surgery residents and the attending surgeons they are learning from. Looking at hospital care through this lens unfairly diminishes the role of nurses and others, without whom patients would be lost. I have written elsewhere about nurses, so I hope they will forgive me for not giving them their due prominence in this work.

A NOTE

The privacy of patients is protected by tradition, ethics, rules, and law. In connection with my status as a Clinical Instructor at OHSU, my observations of patient care will be used by OHSU as part of its educational and quality assessment and improvement activities. OHSU Legal Counsel Steve Conklin and Chief Privacy Officer Ronald Marcum, M.D., helped me do this work while protecting the trust and rights of patients.

To protect the privacy of patients certain descriptive details have been altered. The events described took place at various times during 2007–2009.

OREGON HEALTH & SCIENCE UNIVERSITY (OHSU)

OHSU is Oregon's only academic medical center. Perched on hills overlooking Portland, it is probably the only teaching hospital that offers staff and students a tram pass so they can shuttle between the main campus and a new clinic building on the Willamette riverfront several hundred feet below.

The hospital has more than 600 beds. The hospital and associated clinics serve about 200,000 patients who make more than 700,000 visits each year. There are about 12,000 employees.

The educational programs include about 2,400 students and almost 1,000 residents. The General Surgery residency program graduates 12 surgeons each year, making it one of the largest programs in the United States. (Indiana University graduates up to 12 general surgeons a year and the University of Texas Southwestern graduates up to 13 general surgeons each year.) Surgery residents work at not only the OHSU hospital but also the Portland VA Medical Center and several community hospitals in the Portland area.

CONTENTS

Introduction

Let's get the sex out of the way.

The first scene of the first episode of *Grey's Anatomy* opens with Meredith Grey and Derek Shepherd waking up in her living room after a one-night stand. They don't even know each other's names, much less that they will be working together at Seattle Grace Hospital. From that opening moment it is clear that the focus of the show is squarely on the personal lives and relationships of the main characters. Medicine, or more specifically hospital practice and the training of young surgeons, form the cauldron of stress and crisis and challenge in which the characters react and act, fight and love, achieve and stumble. "Grey's Anatomy" is a medical drama . . . with the emphasis on personal drama. Medicine merely provides the background.

The characters of Meredith Grey, Cristina Yang, Izzie Stevens, George O'Malley, and Alex Karev have just graduated from medical school. They are beginning their intern year in the Surgery Residency Program at Seattle Grace as the series gets under way. Surgery residency in a big-city hospital is a rich source of drama for several reasons. First, the hospital is full of patients facing death, pain, or loss in myriad forms. Second, the impact of surgery is often immediate. Patients frequently either improve or decline rapidly, rather than slowly making progress or failing during long-term drug therapy or other care. Third, the act of surgery is inherently dramatic. No matter how powerful a medicine might be, the act of writing a prescription or swallowing a pill cannot rival putting scalpel to skin. And fourth, young doctors who aspire to be surgeons must traverse a years'-long gauntlet of both intellectual and physical challenges. The hours are extensive, the scrutiny intense, the stakes daunting.

Grey's Anatomy is, of course, entertainment. The situations and personalities are exaggerated for dramatic effect. The intensity and pace exceed human endurance. And yet there are reflections of reality in the stories. The questions are, What is real? What is it like to be a resident learning to be a surgeon?

To find out, I spent months following surgery residents who, just like those on *Grey's Anatomy,* spend their days (and many nights) putting their medical education to use and finding out what it takes to become a surgeon. Like the fictional Seattle Grace Hospital, Oregon Health & Science University (OHSU) in Portland operates a teaching hospital in the Pacific Northwest. But while the OHSU hospital is similar in location and in function to Seattle Grace, it is planted firmly in the real world. That means patients don't pull through or pass away just in time for the closing credits. The ultimate outcomes of cases are not always clear; loose ends are not neatly tied up. For most patients, the causes and treatments of an ailment are unremarkable and routine. By the same token, the residents' days and nights in the hospital are marked by real successes and real failures involving real people, not merely the entrances and exits of actors between commercial breaks.

That's what this book is about: the crucible that is surgery residency . . . and how it shapes the lives of the people within it.

> General surgery is really on the upswing. I think partially that's the fault of a certain television show. That sort of thing was seen right after *ER* became popular. I think general surgery has been really glamorized.
> —INTERN LOÏC FABRICANT, M.D.

Fans of *Grey's Anatomy* will learn about the reflections of that intense reality that are seen in the flickering images of the immensely popular TV series. But stories from surgery residency are relevant to all, whether *Grey's*

Anatomy fans or not, because today's surgery residents will be operating on us, our families, and our friends.

We grant surgeons extraordinary trust and authority. They have license to cut and burn and sew and staple people in order to repair injury or mitigate disease. Interns like the young characters on *Grey's Anatomy* have their medical degrees already in hand. They are M.D.s with a limited license that allows them to diagnose and treat patients under supervision. It is the five or more years of residency that transforms them into surgeons.

> None of them have bags under their eyes. They all leave the hospital dressed cute, with their hair done and makeup on. That is so far away from the reality of interns. You are just dragging your butt, trying to stay alive. You don't have time to do your hair. You don't have time to put on makeup. Every surgery intern has bags under their eyes.
> —FOURTH-YEAR RESIDENT KAREN ZINK, M.D.

Everyone who sits down in front of the screen to watch the joys and pains of Meredith Grey and her fellow characters knows it is just a story. But most of us know very little about what happens on surgical wards or in operating rooms (ORs). Even if we have been through surgery or spent time waiting for a loved one to heal, we see the surgeons only fleetingly. What they do before they arrive at the bedside and after they leave is mostly unknown.

And so, as our eyes soak up the scenes of *Grey's Anatomy* cast in shades of blue scrubs and white coats, grayscale imaging scans, and brilliant OR lights and as our imaginations connect with the emotional heart of the stories, our attitudes and beliefs about surgery and medicine shift and adapt unconsciously. Media researchers have documented the power of medical shows, and they have even done experiments with episodes of *Grey's Anatomy*. For instance, one national survey study showed that a few brief scenes about a pregnant couple changed the attitudes about mother-to-child HIV transmission for millions of viewers.

But of course, people don't tune in to *Grey's Anatomy* to learn about surgery. Viewers want good stories about interesting characters. Even a medical detective series like *House* is really all about the lives, the dreams, the successes, and the disappointments of the central players. One distinction between medical shows like *House* or *ER* and *Grey's Anatomy* is the role medicine plays.

In *House,* medicine is front and center. The episodes open with patients struck by a mysterious malady, and throughout the show, viewers ask themselves, "What is the diagnosis?" and "How will the patient be saved?"

Grey's Anatomy episodes typically open and close with Meredith Grey and her friends, co-workers, and family. It is a medical drama, certainly. There are patients and diseases and trauma and treatments at Seattle Grace. Actors spout medical jargon. Blood spurts during operations. But where the disease is a virtual character in *House,* an antagonist to Dr. Gregory House, in *Grey's Anatomy* medicine and disease play much smaller roles. So in approaching the examination of this series, I took a somewhat different tack than in *The Medical Science of House, M.D.* That book focused on diagnoses and treatments. This book, like *Grey's Anatomy,* concentrates on the lives of surgery residents and the environment of a teaching hospital.

Finally, just to state what most fans may already know, the title *Grey's Anatomy* is a play on *Gray's Anatomy,* a classic textbook with over a thousand exquisitely detailed illustrations of the human body. The formal title is *Anatomy of the Human Body* by Henry Gray. It was first published in 1858 and has been used by generations of students and doctors seeking to understand the human body in order to relieve suffering and extend life.

Additional Reading

Gray, Henry. *Anatomy of the Human Body.* Bartleby.com, 1918 ed. Available at: www.bartleby.com/107. Accessed August 2009.

Holtz, Andrew. "Evidence-Based Television." *Oncology Times,* September 25, 2008. Available at: www.oncology-times.com/pt/re/oncotimes/pdfhandler.00130989-200809250-00008.pdf. Accessed August 2009.

Leonard, Jim. *Anatomy of Gray.* Hollywood, CA: Samuel French, 2006. For more information, see http://books.google.com/books?id=W58hCC0NyPgC or www.theaterreview.com/index.php3?maindata=proddetail&productionurl=1698. Both accessed August 2009.

Oregon Medical Board. Limited License Rule for Postgraduate Medical Education in the State of Oregon. Rule 847-010-0051. Available at http://arcweb.sos.state.or.us/rules/OARS_800/OAR_847/847_010.html. Accessed August 2009.

Rideout, Victoria. "Television as a Health Educator: A Case Study of Grey's Anatomy." A Kaiser Family Foundation Report. September 2008. Available at: www.kff.org/entmedia/7803.cfm. Accessed August 2009.

CHAPTER ONE

The First Day

"Rule number one: don't bother sucking up. I already hate you, that's not gonna change," chief resident Miranda Bailey told her new interns when she first met them in "A Hard Day's Night" (1-01).

Just a few days after the new class of interns began work in the Oregon Health & Science University (OHSU) hospital, a senior resident vented as he stomped into a physician workroom.

"An intern was screaming at me on the phone! She said, 'We're busy up here,'" he exclaimed. "Don't f---ing yell at me on the phone. It's just the fifth day and they're already freaking out. Where are we getting them these days? I should know better than try to be nice to interns."

That outburst is not the norm. Indeed, interns here remark about the relatively relaxed hierarchy. Still, tough days can lead to frayed nerves on both sides.

"You're interns, grunts, nobodies, bottom of the surgical food chain. You run labs, write orders, work every second night until you drop and don't complain," Bailey also told the interns right off the bat in the first episode of *Grey's Anatomy*.

Despite the generally comfortable relationships between newcomers and veterans here, interns are at the bottom. The only people they outrank are students.

"My sister said to me, 'You are being demoted today. You were a student, now you are an intern,'" says Laura Matsen, M.D., on her first day on the OHSU trauma service.

It started at 6:00 A.M. She is heading toward orthopedic surgery, but for the first year she'll rotate through different surgical services along with the general surgery residents. For her first rotation, she got trauma. But that doesn't mean she's hanging around the ambulance entrance waiting for the next car crash or assault patient. As the intern, her primary job is to help manage patients on the floor, while more senior residents and attendings spend much of their days in operating rooms.

Although she is part of a team of surgeons, the team is spread thin. As the new interns begin their year, other residents are taking vacation. Also, the chief resident on the trauma service is out sick. Yes, doctors get sick too. The next chief won't come on to the service for a few days, so they just have to juggle the workload.

By the way, unlike at Seattle Grace Hospital, there is not just one chief resident. Each service, such as trauma, transplant, and vascular, has chief residents that rotate through over the course of the year. Chiefs spend two months on a service. Midlevel residents rotate every month and a half. Interns change services every four weeks. This staggered schedule helps provide continuity for the patients; someone is always there who saw how things went the day before.

MATSEN'S DAY IS FILLED WITH QUESTIONS, SOME APOLOGIES, AND backtracking when she gets lost trying to get to an unfamiliar part of the hospital.

She is sent to talk to the wife of a patient, even though she hadn't been in on the operation. She has very little information; just where the patient is and that, as far as she knows, everything is fine. In response to questions, her most common responses are "I don't know" and "Check back in an hour."

Back in the workroom, Nurse Practitioner Lynn Eastes asks, "Did the wife know he was in surgery?"

"No," Matsen replies.

"How did you know she was the wife?"

"The receptionist in the waiting room told me it was the wife. I didn't check for a wedding ring."

"That's the job of an intern." Eastes says with a chuckle.

Another staffer chimes in with stories about patients who suddenly have multiple wives trying to visit. Or when the patient is a baby, it can seem like everyone is claiming to be the mother.

These are practical tips that weren't covered in the official medical school curriculum. Matsen listens closely, knowing the nurses and others here are her safety net. She may have the M.D., but they have the experience, and they know the details of how things work here.

Eastes leads Matsen through writing up discharge orders for a patient. They enter medications. There are notes telling this patient to keep his hand elevated and other advice. There are lists of tests that will be needed later and a schedule of recommended appointments. It's the kind of work that is meted out as punishment on *Grey's Anatomy*. And while documentation is not the most glamorous part of being a surgeon, look at it from the patient's perspective: it's vitally important. While you are in the hospital and after you leave, your chart, your notes, your orders are critical to making sure you get the right care at the right time.

Later in the day, as Matsen checks her work, she compares first-day experiences with another intern.

"Have you done any discharges?" she asks.

"One," he answers. "But it seemed too easy, so I probably did it wrong."

Like most interns, Matsen spends the bulk of her first day at a computer terminal, reviewing and updating notes. When her pager beeps with an alert about incoming trauma, she doesn't drop everything to dash to the Emergency Department, she stays on the floor to learn the "drudgery" that is essential to the care of the patients on her service. A couple of hours pass. One of the attending surgeons stops by on his way to check on patients. Matsen wants to go with him, but she stays to continue working on patient records.

Like everything in health care, entering medical orders is complicated.

Mistakes happen. After working on the computer for hours, Matsen runs down to the hospital café and brings back a sandwich. When she returns, the phone rings. Matsen answers and listens. "Sorry, I didn't see that other order, so I double-ordered. Thank you for bringing it to my attention," she tells the caller.

Matsen is barely off the phone when a nurse asks about putting a patient on a sliding scale. "Okay, I'll order the sliding scale," Matsen says. The nurse ducks back out of the workroom. She turns to another intern and asks, "A sliding scale is insulin, right?"

"That's the only thing that makes sense to me," he replies.

The phone rings again. The caller points out another slip. "Thank you. My apologies," Matsen replies. Later, there's another quick phone call to clear up a medication issue. "Oh, then I made a mistake. Cancel the solution."

There is just so much to learn. Pharmacists, nurses, and other physicians look over medical orders . . . and those entered by interns often get special attention, especially at the beginning of the new year.

The entire day isn't spent sitting at a computer. Besides patient rounds, Matsen does check on a few patients to answer their questions or reevaluate their care. She is asked by a nurse to check on a patient going through severe alcohol withdrawal. "Why is he on the trauma floor and not in intensive care?" she wonders. At the moment, the nurse practitioner, is away, so Matsen has no one right at hand to lean on. She goes to check the patient before calling a senior resident for advice.

"He is actively shaking. He is incoherent. Pulse one twenty-five. Oh two sat ninety [the blood oxygen saturation is 90 percent]," she tells the senior resident. He agrees the patient needs one-on-one care in the intensive care unit (ICU) and tells Matsen to make the arrangements.

"How do I do that?" she asks. One more new thing during a long day of firsts for her . . . and for every other intern in the hospital.

Another patient needs a chest tube removed. Matsen starts to go to the room. Then she stops. "There's a time to go fast and a time to go slow. This is a time to go slow," she says as she pages Eastes for help.

Many attendings say a key to succeeding at residency is to know what you know and don't know . . . when to take action and when to call for help. Calling too often means not learning enough. Calling too late could harm a patient.

Miranda Bailey bluntly stated her third and fourth rules to new interns on *Grey's Anatomy,* "If I'm sleeping, don't wake me unless your patient is actually dying. Rule number four: the dying patient better not be dead when I get there. Not only will you have killed someone, you would have woke me for no good reason. We clear?"

While senior residents and attendings don't actually want interns to always wait until a patient is near death before calling for help, they do want the interns to quickly gain a sense of the boundaries of their expertise.

Finally a question comes along that Matsen feels ready for: occupational therapy advice for a patient's shoulder. Matsen, aiming for a career in orthopedic surgery, goes to examine the patient. "This is more familiar territory," she says with apparent relief.

EARLY IN HIS INTERN YEAR, NICK TADROS, M.D., IS IN A PHYSICIANS' workroom. Tadros says that for now he is focusing on learning the system, how to order medications and other care for his patients. Learning more about medicine will come later.

"I went to do a platelet order at the VA [the Veteran's Administration Medical Center, which is connected to OHSU and shares residents]," Tadros says. "It seems like no big deal, but I still asked a lot of questions. I've got less confidence than when we were medical students, because then we knew someone was always checking our work."

As medical students, Tadros and his fellow interns were often asked how they would handle a particular situation and what tests or drugs they would order for a patient, but they didn't have the authority to actually enter orders for care. Now they do. While there are others watching them, especially the experienced nurses and the senior residents on the service, interns have the legal authority to prescribe drugs and other care. Residents have a limited license, which allows them to practice medicine as long as they are supervised in an approved training program.

Even with the supervision, Tadros and the other interns feel the weight of their expanded responsibility.

"Now if we give an order and no one checks it, they'll go ahead and do it," he points out. "It's kind of scary."

As his comment about scary responsibility hints, the primary reason physicians and surgeons are licensed is not because of the great benefits they can offer patients or the daunting complexity of the subject matter they are expected to master. To be sure, economic and professional factors helped drive the history of medical licensing: Having a license provides a market advantage. But for society, the key rationale for medical licensing is the potential for great harm inherent in many medical interventions. Medicines can poison. Scalpels can maim.

Think about what a surgeon does. She takes a knife and cuts people open. He drills through skulls. She removes vital organs. Under normal circumstances, these acts are crimes. But as with the police officer who shoots someone or a military pilot who drops a bomb, acts that would be criminal in most cases are permitted, based on the premise that failure to take these severe actions would likely lead to greater harm.

The terrible responsibility is conferred on young surgeons in dollops, with the bulk of an intern's time spent on routine chores. One intern points out that although she went into medicine in part because she didn't want an office job she now finds herself spending hours typing information into a computer in a tiny windowless room that is often crowded with more people than there are chairs. The reality is certainly far different from the TV depiction.

But then the routine is interrupted by a taste of what they are working toward. Senior resident Laszlo Kiraly, M.D., invites Tadros along as he goes to check on a patient in the operating room (OR). Karen Deveney, M.D., is removing the patient's colon. She specializes in colon, rectal, and gastrointestinal surgery. She is also the director of the Surgery Residency Program. Kiraly and Tadros have come to the OR because the patient had previous surgery that altered the connections between the patient's colon and the other organs in the abdomen.

The interns are joined by one of the surgeons who had been involved in the earlier surgery. The surgeons poke around in the patient's abdomen and confer about whether any special adaptation of the standard colon removal procedure is needed, in light of the previous surgery. The patient's bowel had been twisted. When the colon was removed it untwisted. As the surgeons inspect the organs and the results of the previous surgery, they look like they could be auto mechanics checking the coolant hoses and fuel lines in a customized engine. In the end they agree on a plan for anchoring the patient's bowel.

Tadros returns to his workroom. Although he didn't participate in the surgery, he is refreshed by the glimpse of surgeons in action.

CHAPTER TWO

The First Cut

Laura Matsen has just begun her intern year. She's in a trauma treatment bay in the Emergency Department, taking a look at a nasty cut on a patient's head. He's sitting quietly as though it didn't hurt at all.

"Are you stoic?" she asks, but he doesn't seem to know what she means.

"Are you on lots of pain medication?" He answers no.

"Does it hurt?"

"No, should it?"

Matsen uses a stapler to close the wound. It's longer than she expected.

When she finishes, she smiles. "That was the best part of the day!"

That's why surgery.

Two residents are talking about the next day's schedule as they close up a patient in the OR.

"We're doing a colonoscopy. If we find colon cancer, are we going to take it out?"

"Yes," the other resident replies. "But can we do it on Friday instead? I'm not here tomorrow."

Surgeons love surgery.

Surgeons eventually earn a wage that's more than adequate, though the hours for most are long. But you don't usually hear residents talk about the money, unless it's about their student loans, which may reach $200,000 by the time they finish. Residents do get paid, but with an 80-hour workweek, the salary works out to only about $10 an hour, if you take into account overtime rates.

2009–2010 OHSU RESIDENT SALARY SCHEDULE

Intern: $47,400

2nd year: $49,500

3rd year: $52,000

4th year: $54,500

5th year: $57,000

The first taste of surgery comes in medical school as the students rotate through various specialties in order to discover which ones they might want to devote a career to.

It's just after one o'clock in the morning. A patient has an abscess that needs to be drained. Laszlo Kiraly, chief resident tonight on the emergency general surgery service, reviews common types of bacterial infections with the medical students who are following the surgeons. Some bacteria smell fruity, others don't have a strong odor, and some just stink.

The team enters the OR. The patient is lying on his side, because the abscess is on his rear end. The medical students fumble with the sterile gowns. Once they are gowned and gloved, Kiraly hands a scalpel to one of the medical students and shows him where to cut.

He draws the scalpel in a straight line down the exposed skin. This is not a delicate operation. He has to cut through deep layers of tissue. Then the scalpel pierces open the abscess and pus flows strongly into a bucket. The medical student steps back as the surgeons go to work cleaning out the abscess.

"Fantastic!" the medical student exclaims. "That's the first time I've cut into a human who was alive. Well, except for making a cut in my son's finger to remove a splinter."

Kiraly says the case was a good one for a student. "You can't really mess up there, making a cut in the butt. There are no vital organs there. If you went in too deep, you'd just hit the pus. Med students often go through their six-week surgery rotation disengaged; but he'll remember this, even if . . . especially if . . . he doesn't go into surgery."

THAT FIRST CUT IS A MILESTONE ON A JOURNEY INTO RARE TERRITORY, AS Meredith Grey marvels in "Great Expectations" (3-13).

"And from the day we decide to become surgeons, we are filled with expectation. Expectations of the trails we will blaze, the people we will help, the difference we will make."

If anyone else takes a knife to another person, it's a criminal attack. But surgeons earn the privilege and responsibility of cutting people in order to help them.

LAURA MATSEN, M.D.

Status: Intern

Where from: Seattle. Medical school at Oregon Health & Science University

Why did you want to become a surgeon?
Laura Matsen is the daughter of an orthopedic surgeon, so she had long familiarity with the life of a surgeon. In fact, she says that when she was growing up, she didn't really understand what medical specialties were all about, because she saw everything from the perspective of the surgeons around her. "I can talk to my mom about what I had for lunch and talk to my dad about what operation I saw," she says.

What's the biggest difference between what you thought it would be like and the reality?

Matsen says her intern year has mostly matched her expectations, both good and bad. She says she often thinks of a comment a fellow medical student made about the level of endurance required.

"She said, 'It's amazing how bad you can feel.' I just try to remember that, because sometimes you are post-call or tired or stuff's not going well at home and you just feel so bad. And then I just tell myself, 'It's amazing how bad you can feel.' Then you recognize that this is not going to last forever, and then it gets better again. There definitely are lows, but I'm really excited about the responsibility that I have, a little scared sometimes, and excited about how much I get into the operating room."

Matsen is also heartened by the attitudes of the people she works with.

"How excited people are to teach you. Even if they know just a little bit more than you, they'll sit down with you and share their knowledge. That's cool."

Matsen says, like most interns, that she is growing more accustomed to the responsibilities of being an M.D.

"You put on a more confident front, but you're still asking a lot of questions. I'm asking my senior residents and I'm asking my attendings. Sometimes they don't even know. And sometimes your gut is right. This morning I told my attending, 'I'm really uncomfortable about this patient, something's not right,' and an hour later they were in Afib [atrial fibrillation]. We had been planning to discharge [the patient] that day. It was one of those situations where I thought, 'It's okay that I feel nervous about something sometimes.' That's good."

The attending surgeon called for the Rapid Response Team.

"It's nice when you see your attendings and your seniors calling for help," Matsen says. "Then you realize it's okay. We can't be experts in everything. It makes you really respect all of the specialties."

What do you want patients to know about what you do?

Matsen says that every day she encounters patients who equate "young female" with "nurse."

"I think partly it's because I look young, but it happens the majority of the time. When I walk into the room I try to say, 'I'm *Dr.* Matsen,' and then they start to ask me about their lunch tray."

She also sees patients who seem to expect the surgeons to be certain and infallible about what is going on with them.

"Last night I got called into patient's room. He was very upset, because he'd been told he had a fracture; and then he was being told he did not have a fracture. Really what he had was a dislocation and some small chip fractures." They relocated the joint and repaired the small chip fractures.

"It was very upsetting to him. The word *fracture* is like a brand, and he wanted to know whether he had one or not. And he was very unhappy that we didn't know whether he had one or not." Matsen says that as they explained things to him, he eventually understood why the original diagnosis shifted as the surgeons studied his case more closely.

Why did you select your specialty?
Matsen set out to follow her father's path into orthopedics. Although she does rotate through a variety of services along with the general surgery interns, she spends three months of her first year in her surgical homeland: orthopedics. She says that she feels more "on" when she's working the orthopedics service, both because she enjoys the specialty and because she really wants to live up to the expectations of the senior residents and attending surgeons.

"It's a lot more responsibility on ortho. I'm running all the consults [when physicians on other services need orthopedic diagnosis or treatment recommendations]. I'm the first person to go down to the emergency department to see a finger amputation or the first person to see a spine injury. There's always help and always backup that I can call, but they are often busy in surgery or in the clinic. So they are available, but it's more pressure [on me]."

CHAPTER THREE

Some Background

Residency—that is, young doctors going through a structured program of clinical training in a hospital—has existed in the United States for only a little more than a century. Johns Hopkins Hospital opened in Baltimore in 1889 with a medical education program that resembles what we are used to seeing today. And the surgeon who led the way at Hopkins was William Stewart Halsted, M.D. The former chief of surgery at Hopkins, John L. Cameron, M.D., has made a study of Halsted.

"All surgeons were self-trained or learned by way of an apprenticeship, and few spent more than one or two years in a hospital setting. Halsted introduced a system in which medical school graduates entered a university-sponsored, hospital-based surgical training program that, over a several-year period of increasing responsibility slowly led to the training of young surgeons who were well versed in anatomy, pathology, bacteriology, and physiology. The training program culminated in a final period of near-total independence and autonomous activity. This system of training surgeons spread slowly to other hospitals in Baltimore and eventually throughout the entire country. It is this method for training surgeons introduced by Halsted that probably is more responsible than any other single factor for the incredible productivity that has placed the United States in the forefront of surgical science throughout the world," Cameron wrote in *Annals of Surgery*.

Now there are more than 8,000 residency programs that are accredited by the Accreditation Council for Graduate Medical Education (ACGME). Several hundred of the programs train young surgeons.

Residency is not just a continuation of medical school. Certainly residents have to learn a lot of facts, but they mostly learn by doing.

The goal of a surgical residency program is to prepare the resident to function as a qualified practitioner of surgery at the advanced level of performance expected of a board-certified specialist. The education of surgeons in the practice of general surgery encompasses both didactic instruction in the basic and clinical sciences of surgical diseases and conditions, as well as education in procedural skills and operative techniques. The educational process must lead to the acquisition of an appropriate fund of knowledge and technical skills, the ability to integrate the acquired knowledge into the clinical situation, and the development of surgical judgment.

—ACGME PROGRAM REQUIREMENTS FOR
GRADUATE MEDICAL EDUCATION IN SURGERY

"We don't teach surgeons, we create opportunities for them to safely learn," is how trauma surgeon Richard Mullins, M.D., describes what happens in the hospital.

Another surgeon, Donn Spight, M.D., explains that the residents progress through several stages. The process starts with understanding the basic steps of a procedure—for instance, what a surgeon does to take out a gallbladder without damaging the liver, common bile duct, and other nearby tissues. The next step is doing some and then all of the actual surgery. Of course, at first new surgeons are tentative and use all of their concentration on each cut and suture. Finally, the knowledge about what to do and the physical experience of doing it come together, so that like an experienced musician, the surgeon doesn't have to consciously think about each maneuver.

"You can turn up the iPod a bit," John Hunter, M.D., says to the circulating nurse as he works on a patient's esophagus with surgery fellow Charles Kim, M.D. "You can highlight a song and adjust the playback level," Kim suggests. They go on to chat about a recent surgery meeting and other topics. They *are* paying attention to the surgery, but as long as things proceed routinely, they can also talk about other things.

"It is necessary to reach that level because everyone's anatomy is different, there are hurdles that are thrown in front of you, and challenges within the operating room. For example, somebody has a reaction to one of the medications while you are performing surgery, somebody gets hypotensive, or something else happens, you need to be able to handle that task at the same time as continuing to execute the functions of the operation. Certainly, if you are focused on understanding what the operation is, you're never going to get there. If you are trying to master the physical task of getting it done, you're never going to get there," Spight says.

But in addition to the technical skills of surgery, there is the broader, and harder to define, goal of learning how to think like a surgeon.

He also points to the things beyond technical skill that go into making a good surgeon.

"There is the gestalt of decision making," says Aaron Partsafas, M.D. He recently completed residency. "Is the patient facing something 'bad' or 'not bad'? You just get a sense for it. I don't think you can teach it. Some have it. Some develop it. Some don't."

Additional Reading

Accreditation Council for Graduate Medical Education. For general information, see www.acgme.org. For "ACGME Program Requirements for Graduate Medical Education in Surgery," see www.acgme.org/acWebsite/downloads/RRC_progReq/440_general_surgery_01012008_u08102008.pdf. Both accessed August 2009.

American Medical Association. "FREIDA Online," a database of accredited graduate medical education programs, is available at: www.ama-assn.org/ama/pub/education-careers/graduate-medical-education/freida-online.shtml. Accessed August 2009.

Cameron, J. L. "William Stewart Halsted. Our Surgical Heritage." *Annals of Surgery* 225, no. 5 (1997): 445–458. Available at: www.pubmedcentral.nih.gov/articlerender.fcgi?artid=1190776. Accessed August 2009.

CHAPTER FOUR

Codes and Trauma

Before new interns take their places in the hospital, they have to pass Advanced Cardiac Life Support (ACLS) certification . . . running a code.

In the second episode of *Grey's Anatomy*, "The First Cut Is the Deepest," George O'Malley is assigned to respond to cardiac arrests and other codes. In response to his first page, he runs down the hall, rushing to a trauma bay.

"I'm Dr. O'Malley," he says. "I'll be running this code. What do we got?"

"We have a fifty-seven-year-old male. C-systole," answers a staffer who has started chest compressions.

George calls for the defibrillator paddles. "Charge me to two hundred please," he says as he attempts to shock the patient's heart back into a normal rhythm.

During the episode, he responds to page after page, but things don't work out the way he had hoped.

"Lost five patients on the code team today. I feel like the Angel of Death," George moans.

Yang shoots back: "George, ninety-five percent of all code patients can't be revived. Most of them are seriously dead before you get there."

That dismal fact, which George apparently didn't know, is drilled into interns before their first day on the job.

"The patients are already dead. You can't kill them, so relax." That's how one of the instructors starts a class about responding to a code. The point of emphasizing the high failure rate of resuscitation attempts is not to be cavalier about the patient's life but rather to try to counteract the storm of anxiety that floods the mind of a young doctor when suddenly thrust into the responsibility of running a code so that he or she can think clearly in a stressful situation.

"When a code is called, the first thing is your pulse goes up and your brain doesn't work as well," the instructor continues. "The first pulse you should take is your own." In other words, take a deep breath and calm down, because even though the odds the patient will survive are slim, the odds are even worse if the doctor in charge isn't thinking smoothly.

Other tips include:

Think out loud. There will be a team responding, at least some of the others will have much more experience. Talking about the options and the plan gives everyone a chance to chime in, offer suggestions, catch potential errors.

Keep it simple. That's the only way to remember things in an emergency.

Again the instructors remind the interns that responding to a code is emotionally strenuous. They need to take care of themselves so that they can then take care of the patient. And remember, most patients will not survive a code, no matter how much experience the physician in charge has. It's best to think about the situation as having no downside. Don't worry about what might go wrong. Don't worry about hurting the patient. Then methodically go through the steps, so that after it's over, no matter the outcome, you feel good about what you did.

Then the class runs through a few scenarios with a mannequin and an electrocardiograph (ECG or EKG) designed to display various heart rhythms. One of them, pulseless electrical activity (PEA) often looks like normal sinus rhythm, but there is no pulse. Blood is not actually being pumped. In order to decide the best treatment, the team has to decide what the likely cause might be.

Because advanced cardiac life support situations are inherently high stress, there are several memory aids, mnemonics, that help responders remember the key steps. For instance, the **5 Hs and 5 Ts:**

Hypovolemia [low blood volume]

Hypoxia [low oxygen]

Hydrogen ion [acidosis]

Hyper/hypokalemia [high or low potassium level in the blood] (or other metabolic problem)

Hypothermia [low body temperature]

Tablets [drug OD, accidents]

Tamponade (cardiac) [blood pooling and putting pressure on the heart]

Tension pneumothorax [buildup of air outside the lungs]

Thrombosis (coronary) [blood clot in the heart]

Thrombosis (pulmonary) [blood clot in the lungs]

The interns in the class quickly run down the list and if one of the Hs or Ts seems to be a likely problem in the current scenario, they explain how they would try to reverse it. They've all studied these problems in medical school and reviewed the material for this ACLS certification course. Still, being put on the spot, even in a simulation, is stressful.

"It's a lot harder to think of things when you're in charge," one intern says.

Being in charge is a new role for the interns, who were medical students just days earlier. Learning to be in charge is just as important as knowing the difference between the signs of tamponade and hypovolemia.

"If you are leading the code . . . Lead," urges an instructor. In a number of scenes of *Grey's Anatomy* a character yells out for "someone" to do something. That's a recipe for confusion and inaction in a real crisis. The interns are told to be decisive and specific. "I'd like *you* to handle the airway. I'd like *you* to do compressions," and so on. And if enough people are on hand, the leader does not jump in to do the intubation or chest compressions or injections. The leader's job is to think and direct.

After a day of instruction and practice, the interns return for "Megacode" testing. As each intern takes a turn leading a code, the EKG tosses them a challenging heart rhythm to decipher and treat. The interns are supposed to treat the mannequins as if they were real patients. That includes asking questions if the patient is conscious.

During one scenario, the female intern leading the code suddenly begins to stumble and pause as she asks the patient about his medical history, including what medications he is taking, in case any of them might be contributing to the abnormal heart rhythm or might interact with drugs used to treat heart problems. There's a question the intern keeps dancing around. Finally, out it comes: "Are you taking anything like Viagra?" In other words, is the patient being treated for erectile dysfunction? She'll learn to get over the embarrassment of being personal with patients, especially when a life may be on the line.

The interns have been well prepared and get through the Advanced Cardiac Life Support certification without major problems, other than with a few sweaty brows.

"I had been worried yesterday," one said just before his test. "I'm not as worried today. But . . . still, I wonder about when it's real."

The calming message the interns kept hearing—that patients who are coding can't be hurt—is echoed by trauma surgeons when they talk about the challenges that come their way. On the other hand, the saves can be exhilarating.

"I had a lady one time that was stabbed in the heart. She had tamponade, blood was collecting around her heart, so her heart couldn't beat," says trauma surgeon Martin Schreiber, M.D. "She came in with blown pupils, like a dead person. We immediately opened her chest, opened the pericardium, let the blood out. Her heart starts beating as she wakes up. Then she walks out of the hospital five days later.

"There is nothing that dramatic in any other kind of medicine. That's why I was attracted to, first, surgery, and then trauma."

But what about those cases in which a patient comes in badly injured and you can't pull out a save?

THE PATIENT WAS IN A ROLLOVER CRASH. NO SEATBELT. THE AMBU-lance crew had not been able to intubate him—that is, get a large tube down into his windpipe to help him breath. This was one of the cases seen in "Let the Truth Sting" (4-03). Meredith Grey wants intern Lexie Grey to give it a try.

"You know how to intubate?" Meredith asks.

"Uh, I've never done it," Lexie answers.

Meredith prompts Lexie through the steps. "Visualize the cords, pull straight up, watch the tube go through the cords."

Lexie struggles to get the tube down the patient's throat. A nurse calls out that the oxygen level in his blood in dropping. Eventually it's obvious the patient is dead.

"That wasn't bad," Meredith says.

"What?!"

"That wasn't bad for your first intubation."

"Is that some kind of joke? The guy is dead. He died."

"He was dead when he came in here. He was dead on the scene. He was dead for fifteen minutes in the ambulance. He was dead before I asked you to intubate." Meredith points out. But the answer doesn't satisfy Lexie. "You're pretty cavalier, don't you think? I mean, they brought him here for help," she shoots back.

DOESN'T THE RISK OF QUICKLY LOSING A PATIENT TAKE A TOLL?

"That's the interesting thing about trauma," Schreiber explains. "In trauma, the patient's already hurt. They've been in a motor vehicle crash.

They've been shot. They've been stabbed. They come to you hurt. And you can only make them better.

"If you have an aortic aneurysm, your aorta ruptures, you're going to die. So you're standing in the way of that person dying. Sure complications can occur, but there's no complication worse than death, which is where they're headed. So if you stop the bleeding and you save the patient, you've done a great thing, it's a really wonderful thing. If you've done the best you can and the patient dies; well, you did the best you could, they had a fatal disease."

Schreiber says that means that in a way there's really less downside risk for trauma surgeons than for surgeons who perform elective surgeries. Even though elective surgeries rarely go wrong, sometimes they do.

"If you do an elective hernia repair on a patient . . . that person comes in, frequently very, very healthy, maybe a young patient. If something goes wrong, you could make them sterile, and that's a big deal, that is a huge complication," Schreiber points out. "Or if you are doing an elective gallbladder operation. Someone comes in, they've got a little intermittent pain when they eat, in the right upper quadrant (of their abdomen). Their gallbladder's hurting them. You go to do an elective operation. You take out their gallbladder . . . and you cut their common bile duct . . . you've hurt the patient."

The burden of responsibility placed on a surgeon is linked to the expectations. When death is a likely outcome, any other outcome feels like success. But when a procedure has a very low complication or death rate, then harsh fingers may be pointed when things go wrong.

IT HAPPENED TO MEREDITH GREY IN "THE OTHER SIDE OF THIS LIFE" (3-23). Her father's second wife was hit with a series of unlikely problems and complications that turned a routine case in a fatal direction.

"We . . . We did everything . . . we could," Grey tells her father after his wife has died.

"You . . . You said it was really simple and that it was this . . . small thing."

"It was."

His grief and anger overwhelm him. He slaps her.

"She had the hiccups. She came here . . . because . . . because she trusted you. I trusted you," he cries.

TRAUMA SURGEONS MAY BE SPARED DIFFICULT QUESTIONS WHEN THEY can't save a badly injured patient, but they often have questions of their patients . . . and they don't always get clear answers.

In "Didn't We Almost Have It All?" (3-25), Derek Shepherd is removing an ice ax from the head of a mountain climber. The man's climbing partners said he was impaled by accident during a fall, but in the operating room Shepherd sees that the wound doesn't match the story.

At the weekly conference of the OHSU trauma service, chief resident Laszlo Kiraly presents a case—and some questions. The patient reported being attacked and stabbed by an intruder, but pieces of the story didn't seem to add up for the paramedics who first responded. They passed along their questions to trauma surgeons when they delivered the patient to the Emergency Department.

Although a sharp tool was imbedded in the patient, most of the wounds appeared to be only skin deep, not what you would expect from a violent, criminal attack, Kiraly tells his colleagues. Even the deepest wound did not cause as much damage as they first thought it might have. The attending surgeon says the patient was squirming like a child. As they looked into the patient's history, they found notes on psychiatric treatment. They began to suspect the wounds might be self-inflicted.

Regardless of the cause, the injuries needed attention. A CT scan showed little hidden damage. The wounds would probably heal on their own, so the treatment plan for the physical issues was simple observation. The psychiatric issues needed attention. Even though the patient wanted to leave, the doctors ordered a psychiatric hold so the patient could be monitored and evaluated for a couple of days.

All sorts of stories are told by people who roll in on ambulance gurneys.

Kiraly recalls another time, when a patient told them that all he knew was that he woke up from the party with a table leg stuck into his body.

GEORGE O'MALLEY IS TRYING TO FIGURE OUT WHAT'S GOING ON WITH a teenage patient in "Begin the Begin" (2-13). The girl has an enlarged lymph node. But as he rolls up her sleeve to draw some blood, O'Malley notices cut marks on the girl's wrist. Although his assignment is to work on a straightforward physical diagnosis, he struggles with whether and how to delve into possible psychiatric problems.

ON A WARM EVENING IN THE EMERGENCY DEPARTMENT, A PATIENT IS BEING treated after he was found hanging. At least that's the story the patient's friend told: that there had been an argument, that the patient was alone for just a few minutes when he was discovered. But the trauma team wonders if they are getting the full story. Maybe the friends were together. Maybe the asphyxiation wasn't from an attempted suicide.

The patient's care can proceed for now without getting final answers, so the questions are put aside for the moment.

Another puzzling case has the team wondering about physical and mental mysteries. A young patient has air inside her skull in places it doesn't belong. There may be a tear in her esophagus, but it is not obvious. The patient's explanations are vague and don't lead them to the precise cause of the problem. They pour over scans of her head and talk through the various mechanisms without coming to a conclusion.

When the case is reviewed later, an attending surgeon says, "The patient needed someone to go in and talk to her and get the real story. Just one person to go in and say, 'Let's go over the story.'"

Making a diagnosis frequently involves more than simply a thorough knowledge of organs and bones and blood vessels; surgeons sometimes wish they could be mind readers, too. This patient appeared to be stable, and the surgeons predicted the air in her body would probably be reabsorbed without doing any harm, so they let the patient leave. In this case, the exact nature and circumstances of the puzzling injury will remain a mystery.

BEING A TRAUMA PATIENT IS NO FUN. SOMETIMES PATIENTS ARE MORE UPSET about certain medical interventions than about the original injury itself.

"I had a patient who said he would rather die than get a catheter into his bladder," recalls chief resident Michael Englehart, M.D. "He had rib fractures and I warned him that if he wasn't breathing deeply, he could develop pneumonia. He needed an epidural for pain control, which means you have to put a catheter into the bladder also. Sure enough, he ended up in the ICU. I had to really pressure him before he relented and accepted a catheter."

And there's a standard part of the trauma evaluation that often catches patients by surprise. Along with checking the neck and spine and limbs for fractures, looking at the pupil response, and simply talking to the patient to assess his or her condition, there is a routine check for anal tone. A lax sphincter may point to a spinal injury. The simple test involves inserting a gloved finger into the patient's anus.

As one trauma surgeon noted after caring for a patient who had been injured doing something silly on a weekend night, "If more people knew about the finger up the butt check, they'd be more careful."

Additional Reading

American Heart Association. For more information about the Advanced Cardiovascular Life Support course, see www.americanheart.org/presenter .jhtml?identifier=3011972. For preparation materials for the ACLS certification, see www.acls.net. Both accessed August 2009.

CHAPTER FIVE

Unexpected

A defining moment found intern Ashley Stewart, M.D., one day on the pediatric surgery service.

A little girl died. She had a serious illness, but everyone on the team thought she would pull through. When Stewart reviews how the girl's death affected her, two things stand out. Her doctor's armor was pierced. She felt the death as a person, not as a provider. But also, her inner certitude that surgery is right for her became stronger than ever.

"That was very odd, because we failed," she says, her voice reflecting puzzlement at the apparent contradiction. "That little girl died. And surgery couldn't make it better." She pauses as the recollection chokes her voice. "I don't know why, in that situation, I felt like, 'This is what I should be doing.'"

She and her attending were paged: trouble with patient. Come stat.

The girl's illness depleted the platelets in her blood, disrupting clotting and turning any bleeding into a potentially life-threatening emergency.

"By the time we got there . . . we realized that the bleeding wasn't controlled; she wasn't able to stop herself from bleeding, so we had to cut her chest open and shove a lot of sterile towels in there. We couldn't see the source of the bleeding."

She says an emergency surgery team wasn't immediately available. "Right before she stopped having a heartbeat and before her lungs filled with blood, we went to the OR, at the last minute, and we were trying to resuscitate her there."

Other surgeons arrived to help. But their efforts were not enough. After the attending called the time of death, Stewart says she felt the impact.

"Up until that point I was really fine. I was just kind of doing my job and wanting to do the best that I could. But after that, everyone left the room, and it was just me and the nurse, and I didn't know what to do."

Cleaning the girl's small body fell to Stewart.

"I didn't feel like a doctor anymore. I felt like a mother, even though I've never had children. Looking at this child's body and realizing that she had died. I don't know how to describe it other than that. Feeling her little spirit. I could feel it. It sounds really crazy, but I could feel her in the room with me. And then cleaning up her little chubby arms, cleaning up the blood, trying to put her back together for her mom; it was something I will never forget," Stewart says.

"It happens all the time; because there're risks with everything we do, especially as surgeons. So I can objectively understand it, but it didn't change the fact that a mom came to the hospital with a baby and left without one. It was really, really hard. It's like a light switch went off, and I wasn't a doctor anymore, I was a person, a woman holding this child." Stewart pauses as the memory grips her.

She says she was hypervigilant for the rest of her pediatric surgery rotation; constantly nervous about something going wrong with each young patient.

"I didn't sleep for about a month, just picturing her body a lot, trying to come to terms with the fact that this kid was sick, but she was going to be okay, but she died."

Stewart says she spoke with family and friends about her feelings, and then sought out the counselors at the OHSU Resident Wellness Program.

What helped her most was a conversation with Surgery Residency Program Director Karen Deveney. Stewart says Deveney helped her sort through her feelings and put the incident in context.

Pediatric surgery is one of the specialties Stewart has been considering as a career. Despite this terrible experience, she says she's glad she'll have another chance to do another rotation on the service to see if it seems right for her, after some time has passed.

Stewart says she is comfortable with death, but this little girl was different.

"I had seen a lot of people die, but with this little girl, I could *feel* her die; that was the difference." And yet she also felt affirmation. "The other overwhelming sensation with this was realizing that I was exactly where I wanted to be. It was really, really hard. It's still really hard. I still have a hard time talking about it, but I wouldn't have wanted to be anywhere else. I knew I was where I needed to be. That was also very clear.

"I think it's kind of a rite of passage, I guess. I'm sure that everybody has experiences like that, that have that effect on them. It's an important part of our career and our training."

Despite the wrenching experience, Stewart says she believes things happen for a reason, even though she doesn't have complete control.

"It's good that I don't forget about it. I don't think I should. I think it's those cases that remind you how important your job is and how you have to be on the ball. You have to be prepared all the time. It's overwhelming, but it's a really good object lesson, a painful object lesson."

Equally important is learning to manage her natural human response; learning to be comfortable, professional, and effective in the midst of chaos, especially when everything you know and everything you do simply isn't enough. Dealing with failure is an essential skill for anyone who aspires to become a surgeon. And Stewart says this little girl's death is a milestone on her path.

"I knew that I was in the right place and doing the right things."

CHAPTER SIX

Flame On

It was an initial incision that started off like any other. The resident was using a Bovie electrosurgery knife to steadily slice through the patient's skin and the underlying layers of tissue. The surgeons weren't sure exactly what they would find when they opened up the patient's abdominal cavity. CT scans and the patient's symptoms pointed to something, perhaps an infection, near the spleen.

The man had been admitted for problems that didn't have anything to do with his spleen, at least as far as the doctors could tell. The evening before, he had appeared to be doing well. A surgeon who examined him noted some chest pain, but there was no indication of anything new and dangerous developing. Things took a turn during the night. They had considered using interventional radiology—working through a small puncture, guided by the scans—to place a drain near what looked like an abscess.

"But his vital signs forced our hand," said one surgeon. They decided they needed to open him up to get a direct look at the problem. Everything was routine as the resident continued to cut.

Then the hot spark from the Bovie sliced through the inner layer of tissue . . . and there was a flame.

A greenish jet of flame, just an inch or two tall, flared from the opening, like a natural Bunsen burner. When gas in the patient's abdomen was released, it ignited in the combination of room air and the Bovie spark.

The flame lasted just a few seconds.

"Did you see that?" one startled observer asked the person next to her, as though seeking confirmation of a sight that didn't seem quite real. "Yes, I saw it," the second person confirmed.

The resident had jerked back when the flame appeared, but now that it was out, he leaned in again to continue expanding the incision. The attending surgeon grabbed his hand to pull the Bovie away. There could still be more gas leaking out.

The patient appeared uninjured and the surgery continued, without the Bovie electrosurgery device.

As startling as the flame was to everyone in the operation room, patients do on rare occasions breathe fire. The attending surgeon in this case recalled a case in which he was working on the patient's rear end. A common and natural puff of gas—*flatus* is the technical term doctors tend to use—caught fire. It singed a towel.

Reports in the medical literature document electrosurgery or electrocautery (the use of a Bovie or similar device to seal small blood vessels) igniting gases coming from a patient. Some of the fires occur when enriched oxygen leaks from a patient's airway during surgery. Indeed, besides electrosurgery devices, operating rooms contain powerful lights and other equipment that can ignite oxygen and other flammable gases. In contrast to a small, brief eruption of a patient's natural gases, fires from flammable gas lines and tanks are potentially lethal.

No harm occurred in this case, and the operation proceeded after only a brief delay. Later, the resident talked about the incident during rounds. "It was a learning point: not to use electrocautery when there is free gas in the abdomen." Indeed. The story raced through the hospital. During a café break well past midnight, sleep-deprived residents joked about bringing marshmallows to the OR in case it happened again.

Additional Reading

American Society of Anesthesiologists. "Practice Advisory for the Prevention and Management of Operating Room Fires." *Anethesiology,* 108, no. 5 (2008): 786–801. Available at: www.guideline.gov/summary/summary.aspx?doc_id=12547. Accessed August 2009.

ECRI. "Only You Can Prevent Surgical Fires." Available at: www.mdsr.ecri.org/static/surgical_fire_poster.pdf. Accessed August 2009.

Errando, Carlos L.; García-Covisa, Nuria; Del-Rosario, Elia; Peiró, Celsa M. "Infrequent Case of Fire in the Operating Room during Open Surgery of a Tracheobronchopleural Fistula." *Journal of Cardiothoracic and Vascular Anesthesia,* 19, no. 4 (2005): 556–557. Available at: www.jcvaonline.com/article/PIIS1053077004002563/fulltext. Accessed August 2009.

Greilich, Philip E.; Greilich, Nancy B.; Froelich, Edward G. "Intraabdominal Fire during Laparoscopic Cholecystectomy [Case Report]" *Anesthesiology,* 83, no. 4 (1995): 871–874. Available at: www.anesthesiology.org/pt/re/anes/fulltext.00000542-199510000-00031.htm. Accessed August 2009.

CHAPTER SEVEN

Hospitals Never Close

In "Begin the Begin" (2-13), Seattle Grace's Chief of Surgery, Richard Webber announced, "There were too many mistakes made last year. Fatigue played too big a role. Exceeding eighty hours per week will not be tolerated."

On October 24, 1940, a 40-hour workweek became the legal standard in the United States for most workers paid an hourly wage. But it was 63 years later, on July 1, 2003, that the accrediting body for medical residency programs in the United States declared: "Starting today, all 7,800 residency programs in the United States must comply with the Accreditation Council for Graduate Medical Education's duty hours standards, which limit resident duty hours to a maximum of 80 hours a week and set other restrictions on duty hours."

Although 80 hours is double what most people consider a normal workweek, in residency programs, particularly in surgery programs, the new standard represented a dramatic reduction in the number of hours residents were in the hospital.

Jennifer Watters, M.D., was midway through her residency when the 80-hour workweek took effect.

"When I was an intern, it was very typical to work a hundred and twenty hours a week, if not more. There were certainly some months where it was more like a hundred and thirty hours. And as an intern I had my two weeks of vacation, and I had nine other days that I didn't come to the hospital. A pretty marked difference."

Watters figures that with additional days off and vacation time that are part of the new standard, today's residents are out of the hospital 40 days more a year than when she was an intern. But don't for a minute think that the duty hour limits have made residency easy. In some ways, fewer hours make the days harder. Watters points out that although she was physically in the hospital more hours than today's residents, there were breaks in the action.

"And in that downtime between doing things, I think there was more opportunity for teaching. I can remember my upper-level residents and attendings sitting down with us at nine o'clock at night, while we're waiting to do our last case or whatever, teaching us for twenty minutes or half an hour about some topic. Or going around together, seeing patients in the hospital and doing some teaching at each bedside," she recalls. "And I think a lot of that is gone, simply because now you are working for eighty hours. You're cramming it all into less time. I remember there being more leisure in the day, despite being here more."

As Bailey recalled her intern year in "Begin the Begin" (2-13): "No one enforced an 80-hour workweek when I was an intern. One hundred ten, one hundred twenty hours suited me just fine. I learned more because I worked more."

Even though the thing surgery residents want to do most is spend time in the OR, doing or at least watching surgery, that is what often gets cut first in order to limit hours, especially for interns.

"It used to be the whole team was always there," Watters says. I remember as a medical student the general rule was: If the team is operating, everybody's operating. I can remember, as a med student, standing in cases and it would be all the students and all the residents on the team standing in the OR while the chief [resident] and the attending operated. And then they were asking you questions through the whole operation, pumping you for information, checking your anatomy. And now that just doesn't happen, because all those bodies need to be working."

* * *

IT'S GROWING LATE AS FOURTH-YEAR UROLOGY RESIDENT ERIC REID, M.D., makes his way to OR 17. A kidney is coming in. He will help prepare it for transplant.

"I told the patient the kidney would be ready around four P.M.," Reid says. But five o'clock and six o'clock have come and gone. This is one way the hours add up. At 7:00 P.M., the hallway outside the OR is deserted; most of the rooms are done for the day. But Reid is just getting started with this transplant. He prepares the "back table." That's the sterile table where the donated kidney will be checked and made ready to be implanted.

The attending surgeon, Stephen Rayhill, M.D., arrives. They double-check to make sure the blood type and other parameters of the kidney are a match to the recipient. Rayhill quizzes Reid about the upcoming procedure and checks the records in the computer about the source of the kidney. A mismatch could be dangerous or even lethal to the recipient. Finally, he is satisfied that the kidney is the right one, and will be going into the right patient.

"Okay. We will accept this one," Rayhill says.

A nurse independently rechecks the organ number and blood type against the case records.

Then the back table work gets under way. Reid begins to trim fat off the kidney.

"Stay a bit farther away when doing the front," Rayhill cautions, "in case there is an artery." They locate the adrenal gland on the top of the kidney. Rayhill teases loose the ends of tiny blood vessels and then directs Reid how and where to tie them off so they won't cause a problem with the main blood vessels that will deliver the patient's blood to the kidney and then send cleaned blood back out.

"Too long and it might allow a clot to form," Rayhill says. "Too close in and the knot might affect the main vessel."

As the recipient is rolled into the OR, nurses and the anesthesiologist make light banter while going about their pre-op tasks. "We're going to get you a brand-new kidney," one says with a smile. The two surgeons stay focused on the kidney, making sure the key blood vessels are ready to be mated to the patient's arteries and veins.

Then one more surgeon appears. Elizabeth Evans, M.D.[1] is the surgery intern on the kidney transplant team this month. Her primary duty is monitoring patients waiting for or recovering from surgery; getting to the OR is a rare treat.

So is everything all quiet on the patient floor? "Shhh!" she says, worried about jinxing her escape. "We don't say that." She is practically shaking with excitement at seeing her first transplant since she became a doctor. When she came into the OR, she wrote her name on the whiteboard by the door that lists the key staff working this case. "It's the first time I've put my name on the resident line, rather than the student line, for a transplant."

Evans steps in to help Rayhill arrange the patient where he wants her. He's looking for the flex point, where the middle of the table can rotate to raise or lower the patient's midsection. "Where do you want it and why?" Evans asks, looking for insight to his technique. "We want to flex her back a bit. It gives us more room to work in," Rayhill replies.

Then as he takes a closer look at the table, he says in annoyance, "She's on the table backward! Who uses it backward?" "Neuro," says a nurse. That explains it: setting up to work on the brain is different from arranging things to suit a kidney transplant.

Evans tempts the fates by scrubbing in. She'll get to be closer and more involved in this procedure, but it'll take longer to respond if there's an urgent problem on the patient floor. But she wants to be close to the action tonight and pick up all the surgery tips she can. "I keep my index finger nail a bit long. It helps to apply pressure on knots," Rayhill tells her.

The patient's abdomen is open, but not exactly where a kidney naturally sits. Instead of swapping out a dysfunctional kidney for a new organ in the same spot, the surgeons will connect the donated kidney to an artery and vein that normally feed the leg. The kidney still will do its job of filtering blood and this spot is easier to get to. Also, it is close to the bladder, so it is easier to connect the ureter, the tube that carries urine out of the kidney.

The kidney is cold and gray as they lift it out of its protective ice bath and test-fit it into its new home. Putting the kidney back in the ice bath,

[1] Name changed by request.

the surgeons work on isolating the blood vessels they will connect to it. Again the kidney placement is tested. They trim the cuff off the end of an artery and check again. The patient's vein is clamped and the cut is made where the kidney's vein will be attached.

Rayhill turns to Evans. "You can help suction as well." Now she's doing more than just watching.

Two hours have passed since Evans left her post on the patient floor. Rayhill's pager beeps. The circulating nurse tells him there's a question about fluids for a patient. "Why didn't they call the resident?" he asks, not used to being interrupted for this sort of routine question. "Uhh, that would be me," Evans points out. She is scrubbed in, so one person holds the phone to her ear while another holds her notes where she can read them.

At the end of the call, Evans gives the floor nurse her name and pager, so that the next call won't bother the attending surgeon. But then the circulating nurse points out that now the people on the floor will page her directly, perhaps even after her shift is over. "Tell them to page the resident on-call," the nurse advises. "Oh, good point," Evans says.

Pulled back to the reality of a floor full of patients that are her responsibility, Evans reluctantly takes off her sterile gown and gloves in order to get back on the computer and phone that are an intern's primary work tools. She stays in the OR, trying to maintain a connection to the surgery, even as patient lab results and calls from nurses claim her attention.

Midway through the fourth hour of the transplant procedure, Eric Reid is suturing together the blood vessel connections between patient and kidney. Elizabeth Evans calls across the room to get his advice on a patient who may be dehydrated.

And then the final blood vessel is connected. The kidney turns from gray to pink. "Hey, Mr. Kidney!" Reid says. There's a flurry of activity. Blood is leaking. The surgeons call for "four by four" sponges to soak it up. In contrast to the cold, dead appearance it had just a moment ago, the kidney is bright red and full, glowing with life. The surgeons use electro-cautery to zap the bleeding capillaries.

But rather than being part of the climax of the transplant, Evans is tied to the phone, asking about a patient's magnesium levels and conferring with Reid about whether to order replacement magnesium. Evans's pager beeps while she is still on the phone. Another patient has a low phosphate level. "I'm not sure what to do in a renal transplant case," she tells Reid. "Give phosphate and check the renal function," he replies.

Evans is in residency to learn surgery, but even though she is just a few feet from a woman receiving a new kidney—and freedom from dialysis machines—Evans is tethered to her intern duties. Still, the evening is a highlight for her.

"I took my own time to go to the OR. I could have gone home. I was on home call that night," she says later. "But by staying a bit later, and juggling pages and documentation work in the OR, I got to see a patient's transplant, rather than just care for them on the floor without ever seeing them get their kidney."

UNDER THE 80-HOUR WORKWEEK RULE, TAKING TIME FOR ONE THING MAY mean leaving something else undone. Before the rule, residents often sacrificed their sleep.

"You get to a point where you are so exhausted that you almost don't care anymore about the patient's feelings. You're like, 'let's just get 'em in, get 'em out, the quicker, the better, dead or discharged, one way or the other they are off my list,'" says one young surgeon who was an intern under the old rules. "I can remember as an intern thinking, 'Oh, my God, have I completely made the biggest mistake of my life by becoming a physician? Because I shouldn't be a doctor if I feel this way about my patients, right?'"

"That sounds awful," the surgeon says after reflecting on these words. "You can't possibly resent people who are simply sick and in the hospital." Extreme exhaustion allows doubts and dark thoughts to break unbidden into the mind, expressions of utter fatigue, not actual beliefs. The 80-hour workweek helps prevent residents from being utterly consumed by work, so at the end of their shifts they can still think straight and feel humanely about their patients and don't regret their choice to become a surgeon.

Karen Zink, M.D. started her residency just after the 80-hour rule.

"It forces you to be more efficient. I think it's a really good thing. You'll hear a variety of opinions about whether it's good or not, but once you've been up for a certain amount of time, you don't have the ability to think straight. You're not going to be as effective for your patients. And you're not going to learn things. If your brain's so tired you can hardly remember your own name, you're not going to remember a darn thing you see or learn."

The 80-hour workweek was a long time coming. One of the key events that brought attention to the potential risks of fatigued residents took place when most of today's residents were infants. On the evening of March 4, 1984, Libby Zion was admitted to New York Hospital (now New York–Presbyterian Hospital) in Manhattan. The college freshman was agitated and apparently disoriented. During the night she was prescribed several drugs and restrained. The next morning, Zion suffered a cardiac arrest and died.

The cause of her death was the subject of lawsuits for many years, but key facts and the public advocacy of her father prompted scrutiny of the long work hours of residents and the amount of supervision given to young doctors. The residents caring for her had been on duty for more than 18 hours when critical decisions about drugs and other actions were taken.

The hours and working conditions of residents had been set by the training programs. The state of New York led the nation in restricting work hours and imposing other limits on residents in 1998. The national standard for resident duty hours set by the ACGME came more than 19 years after Zion's death. She was just 18.

THE INTERNS ARE WARNED TO COMPLY WITH THE RULES. "YOU CANNOT exceed eighty hours per week, averaged over four weeks. You cannot exceed thirty hours consecutively. There's no averaging here: thirty hours and one minute is a violation. Neurosurgery has already violated once. Someone worked thirty-three hours."

Each resident should get four days off every four weeks. A day off means 24 consecutive hours outside of the hospital. Residents are supposed to get at least 10 hours off between shifts, but that's not mandatory, as long as the shifts don't add up to more than 80 hours in a week.

A duty hour rule violation is not like a parking ticket, with a specific penalty imposed, but the reports go into the file of the institution. Too many violations can jeopardize the accreditation of a medical school. And without accreditation, a school cannot survive.

Are duty hour limits being strictly enforced? Surveys indicate that compliance with the new standards is high, but not perfect. The residents are told that, of course, they must never abandon a patient, even if staying means going over the 30-hour shift or 80-hour week limits. They are told that some violations are expected and should be documented.

"As I've watched this unfold, I find that the more junior members of the team adhere to the eighty-hour workweek very diligently. I think that the more senior members of the team, even though I always ask them if they are under eighty hours, probably are less diligent about some of their work hours. I think that comes with ownership of the patient. When you are an intern, you're far removed, but when you've done the operation on this person, and they are not doing well or their family members are there and want to talk, it's hard to go home," says faculty member Brett Sheppard, M.D.

But even some interns say they are stuck between finishing their work and staying within the requirement to work no more than 80 hours a week. "That's what we're logging, but not what we're doing," one says.

"Other services will report you, if you undercount your hours," a presenter says to residents gathered for the weekly intern conference. "We have already had to put some services on probation and threaten to take away their residents."

A chief resident offers advice for juggling the duty hour limits and the intense demands to stay longer and do more.

"Chiefs and attendings know about the hours, but they are also thinking about ten other things besides your hours," he says. "So you have to tell them when you are getting close to your limit, warn them in advance." He urges them to find ways to do their work more efficiently. "But eventually we will max out the savings from efficiencies," he admits. Honestly recording duty hours, even when they exceed the limits, will help efforts to find long-term solutions. "We need data and evidence in order to support a request for help."

And the interns are reminded that all the rules come second to patient safety, that they should never leave unless someone is there to take over.

"We know there will be violations [of the duty hour limits.] Just document it with an explanation."

*   *   *

EVEN WHEN THEY DO CLOCK OUT ON TIME, THE RESIDENTS AREN'T DONE with work. Even the official guidance says, "Duty hours do not include reading, studying, and preparation time spent away from the hospital." So instead of sacking out, when residents go home from the hospital they may just hit the books.

And then there's "home call." That's when residents are on call but aren't always in the hospital. If they have to get up in the middle of the night to answer a phone call with a question about a patient's care, it doesn't count toward their work hours unless they actually go to the hospital to see the patient. Even then, the time spent getting to and from the hospital doesn't count.

"They call it *home* call," one intern remarks, "But I'm not smart enough to know what's going on, so I always come in."

Nevertheless, residents are in the hospital less than they once were. The former chief of the department of surgery, Donald Trunkey, M.D., recalls that when he was an intern, he would work 36 hours straight, get 12 hours off and then come back for another 36-hour shift.

"One hundred twenty hours was probably my average workweek. It was a rite of passage. Was it in the best interests of the patient? No," Trunkey says.

THE CLEAR-CUT NATURE OF ORTHOPEDICS THAT APPEALS TO INTERN Laura Matsen also helps her deal with the heavy demands of residency.

"I like simplification, and it really does simplify my life. I work here thirteen to sixteen hours. I work out one to two hours. And then I eat and sleep. And it's really nice. Yes, I'm not seeing a lot of my friends, but it's also kind of fulfilling. It's solid. It's what you do every day."

Matsen wrote a note about how she responds to the long hours of an on-call shift.

I finish a 32-hour shift and 30 minutes of weights, convinced that I need to lift weights before I leave the hospital, and pull on my running shoes and start the seven-mile jaunt uphill home. Something about call takes more than a marathon out of my legs, which I've known since taking my first call with OBGYN two years ago. . . . I get frustrated that I just sleep when I return home from call, and so I decide that one way to guarantee exercise is to run to the hospital Saturday morning so that a run is the only way to get to my bed on Sunday afternoon. Outside the hospital, I tighten the camelback which holds my pager, cell phone, and list of patients, turn on my iPod shuffle to some Lyle Lovett. It is a joy to exit the hospital at 3 P.M., but the bright sun is confusing after being up all night.

I crash into bed at home after a shower and two bowls of cereal. Before I want to hear it, my 4 A.M. alarm is going off. Repeat: rise, shower, cereal, coffee, unplug phone, bike bag, unlock garage, swing door up, pull bike out, cycle up hill, and then down, down, down hill, enter the hospital, rinse off my sweat, print out my list, write down the vitals and labs for our patients.

And so begins another shift.

OVERNIGHT SHIFTS PLAY HAVOC WITH THE BODY'S RHYTHMS.

At one o'clock, things are quiet, and the trauma team is talking about going to the café. But it's not 1:00 P.M., it's the middle of the night.

"One A.M. is the lowest point. It's weird to eat a meal," says Terah Isaacson, M.D., as she chats with chief resident Michael Englehart.

"I eat lunch when I wake up. It's all screwed up," he agrees. He says he tries to stay awake until 9:00 A.M. after he goes home from the night shift. "I try to see my daughter and wife. Then they try to keep the house quiet or they go out while I sleep during day."

Isaacson picks up the phone to respond to a page from another member of the trauma team. "What's the food plan?" she asks. They gather in the café shortly after two in the morning. The residents are giddy with sleep deprivation and out-of-sync body clocks. The conversation rambles through stories of former residents and where they've ended up. For once, a meal break is not interrupted by an incoming trauma or an urgent page from the floor.

*   *   *

SO, HAVE THE DUTY HOUR RESTRICTIONS WORKED? IT SEEMS OBVIOUS THAT patients would be better off under the care of residents who are working shorter hours. However, it has not been easy to prove the effect of the new rules on errors or general patient safety.

A recent review by the ACGME reported: "Numerous studies have attempted to assess the impact of resident work-hour reductions on patient outcomes, but the net effect remains unclear." Part of the explanation is that with each resident working fewer hours, there may be fewer people on hand to care for patients, unless more people are hired, which means spending more, even though the amount of care being provided and the amount of money coming in to the hospital stays the same.

Also, when shifts are shorter, there are more handoffs from one team to the next. And with each handoff comes a risk of miscommunication if the notes put in a patient's chart aren't clear enough or leave out key information. More than half the residents at a Massachusetts hospital who responded to a research survey reported that a patient had been harmed by a problem related to handoffs during their last rotation.

INTERN RYAN GERTZ, M.D., SAYS HE ACTUALLY LIKES TO BE ON CALL overnight in the hospital. "Because then you really get to know the patients and what they've been through," rather than relying on notes in the computer or what the resident on the last shift told him hours earlier, he says. A survey of internal medicine residents done a year after the 80-hour workweek took effect echoed Gertz's concern, with many residents saying they had to leave the hospital when their shift was over, even though they preferred to stay because they believed they could provide better care than the resident being handed the case.

Former Chief Trunkey says the increased number of handoffs is the one serious concern he has about limited work hour rules for residents.

> The one downside that has me concerned is this whole issue of con-
> tinuity of care. . . . We don't have a perfect answer to that yet, but my

idea is that there is going to have to be a shift overlap and the two teams will have to go and make rounds, talk to the family, and I think you could do all of this in an hour. And then that way you maintain the continuity of care, but most importantly, you maintain the continuity with the family; because there is nothing more frustrating to a family than not getting information. You've got to give them information. It's important that the team be there together so that there are no misunderstandings and you are all singing from the same hymnal.

Of course, creating those overlaps will probably mean lengthening some work shifts . . . and that extra time will have to be cut somewhere else.

There are some hopeful signs. Some studies indicate that when errors do happen, they are less likely to be linked to fatigue. And it appears that most programs have adapted to the shorter work hours without simply making each resident cover more patients.

THOUGH LIFE FOR SURGERY RESIDENTS SEEMS TO BE IMPROVING, IT IS STILL tough enough to scare off some medical students.

During one night on call with the trauma service, three medical students take a meal break. They wonder aloud if surgery is right for them. They aren't sure they could handle the hours or even if they would want to try.

"You never have less than a thirteen-hour day and then up to thirty hours when you are on call," one of the students points out. It's not just the time in the hospital, it's also the additional hours needed to study and prepare. They compare notes on the different surgery services. Some are more supportive than others.

"They offered lots of help," one of the students says of the residents on a service she worked with recently. "They will quiz you and help you study." But she says that when she asked residents on another service about study time, they didn't seem to care.

"I wonder if we'll ever learn how to function while exhausted."

LONG, HARD WORKWEEKS ARE NOT JUST ABOUT PATIENT SAFETY. EXTREME fatigue can put the safety of residents and others at risk also.

In "Damage Case" (2-24), Yang is beaming. "Three ambulances are coming in full of bloody, broken car crash victims, all of whom need to be cut open. So I'm cheer, cheer, cheerful!" But one of the patients, the one who caused the crash, turns out to be an intern at another hospital. He had been driving home after a 30-hour shift. "I fell asleep for . . . a second behind the wheel. I closed my eyes for a second at the red light. A second."

Crashes on the way home from a long shift are a real hazard. One study of thousands of interns found that working a long shift more than doubled the chances of having a crash and increased the risk of a near-miss by almost sixfold.

During orientation, the new interns heard from a sleep expert who said, "Make sure you are not harmed and that you don't harm others." He told them to go online to see the car crash videos at www.drowsydriving .org. He urged them to take a nap before getting behind the wheel.

WHILE MUCH OF THE RESEARCH INTO THE 80-HOUR WEEK HAS FOCUSED ON "hard" outcomes, such as treatment errors, patient deaths, or car crashes involving weary residents, there are other effects, too.

In "Kung Fu Fighting" (4-06), Izzie Stevens and George O'Malley are on the verge of having sex when Izzie breaks down crying.

"I'm exhausted! Every bone . . . and every muscle in my body . . . aches. And I don't think I can do this. I don't . . . It's not that I don't want to, because I do. I really, really do. It's just that I . . . I just spent six and a half hours on my feet in surgery, and I can barely hold myself up, and I'm just so tired!"

For residents who want to have children, long hours and exhaustion are formidable barriers.

"I think without the eighty-hour workweek . . . uh, I mean . . . not to be crude, but first you have to have sex so you can have a baby. And I think being here less gives you opportunities to do other things in life," Jennifer Watters says with a chuckle. She and her husband, who was an internal medicine resident at the time, decided to have their first child when she was doing a year of research, which meant she didn't have to spend every waking moment in the hospital. They embarked on their second pregnancy during her final year of residency, after the 80-hour rule took effect.

"I don't think I would have even entertained the idea of being pregnant as a resident when I was working one twenty, one thirty hours a week. It was not something that I thought we would do while I was still a resident. I thought we would wait. When they enacted the eighty-hour workweek . . . maybe it speaks to my level of personal insanity"—she chuckles—"but I said, 'Hey, maybe we can do this now. If they're going to let me work forty hours less a week, maybe I can have a baby in there.'"

While Watters did put the additional hours outside the hospital to fruitful use, she says today's residents, just a few years her juniors, will have a different experience than she did.

"I think there was a sense of 'at least we're all in it together' when everybody was just always here. Now maybe the camaraderie is more friendly, because I think residents actually have a chance to see each other socially outside of here."

Brett Sheppard, now Watters's fellow faculty member, also points to camaraderie and other intangibles that develop during long days and nights in the hospital.

"I think some junior residents miss some things, so their learning is delayed," Sheppard says. "The intangibles of being here for a hundred hours or whatever, working with your team and seeing all these things that go by, you don't get. So, yes, you can pass the written test, but you don't have the richness of that intangible experience."

"Part of it is the camaraderie, the team spirit that you develop from being here so many hours with people. They become your family. So you miss a certain amount of that bonding experience."

And Sheppard points out that although today's residents do take call, frequently working up to 30 hours at a stretch, they still won't pile up the sheer quantity of experiences their predecessors did.

"There's a lot going on at night in the hospital. People are spiking fevers, people are coding, people are sick. There's a lot of experience that you miss out on by not being here and seeing that."

*   *   *

"I'm fortunate. Most of the world doesn't wake up at four a.m. happy to go to work and to be part of a team," intern Loïc Fabricant, M.D., says. "I worked Monday night overnight at one hospital, got off at six A.M. and then came straight here. I worked until three thirty P.M. I was a zombie. But I have to say that it all melts away when I'm with the patient. Outside of the patient's room you have to deal with all the BS, but when I'm with the patient everything else just melts away. It's a reminder that I made a good career decision."

Trunkey sees the work hour limits as part of a larger trend of surgery residency programs doing more to recognize that residents have lives outside the hospital. He points to a surgery program in Australia. "If you are a woman, you are allowed seven years to finish the program, you get time off to be a parent, you get time off to have children," he says.

"So there's been an absolute paradigm shift in residency training. Has it been good? Yes," Trunkey says. "I think the residents get better supervision now. I think they can have a reasonable lifestyle. And they can certainly recognize now, better than they could when I was doing this, that you have to spend time with your family and your children. You can't be married to your medical career completely."

Trunkey welcomes the trend toward shift work in medicine.

"I think that's clearly where we are headed. We are going to be doing shift work. And the positive side of that is it's going to bring more women into surgery, because they'll do twelve or thirteen twelve-hour shifts a month, and that will give them almost half their time off, and they'll have time to be a professional, and they'll have time to be a parent," he says. "I think it'll be good for the men because maybe they can share some of the home duties."

But some worry that something may be lost.

"I don't want it to become just a job," vascular surgery fellow Aaron Partsafas says. "The eighty-hour restriction is okay, but any shorter and it wouldn't require the same commitment or devotion."

Additional Reading

Accreditation Council for Graduate Medical Education. "ACGME Duty Hours
    Standards Now in Effect for All Residency Programs." Chicago: ACGM, 2003.
    Available at: www.acgme.org/acWebsite/newsReleases/newsRel_07_01_03
    .pdf. Accessed August 2009.
Barger, Laura K.; Cade, Brian E.; Ayas, Najib T.; Cronin, John W.; Rosner, Bernard; Speizer,
    Frank E.; Czeisler, Charles A. "Extended Work Shifts and the Risk of Motor Vehicle
    Crashes Among Interns," *New England Journal of Medicine,* 352 (2005): 125–134.
    Available at: http://content.nejm.org/cgi/content/full/352/2/125. Accessed August 2009.
"Compliance with Duty Hour Requirements Remains High Four Years after Intro-
    duction of Common Standards." *Medical News Today,* February 11, 2008. Avail-
    able at: www.medicalnewstoday.com/articles/96889.php. Accessed August 2009.
Goitein, Lara; Shanafelt, Tait D.; Wipf, Joyce E; Slatore, Christopher G.; Back,
    Anthony L. "The Effects of Work-Hour Limitations on Resident Well-Being,
    Patient Care, and Education in an Internal Medicine Residency Program."
    Archives of Internal Medicine, 165 (2005): 2601–2606. Available at: http://
    archinte.ama-assn.org/cgi/content/full/165/22/2601. Accessed August 2009.
Iglehart, John K. "Revisiting Duty-Hour Limits: IOM Recommendations for
    Patient Safety and Resident Education." *New England Journal of Medicine,*
    359 (2008): 2633–2635. Available at: http://content.nejm.org/cgi/content/
    full/359/25/2633. Accessed August 2009.
Jagsi, Reshma; Weinstein, Debra F.; Shapiro, Jo; Kitch, Barrett T.; Dorer, David;
    Weissman, Joel S. "The Accreditation Council for Graduate Medical Education's
    Limits on Residents' Work Hours and Patient Safety." *Archives of Internal Medi-
    cine,* 168, no. 5 (2008): 493–500. Available at: http://archinte.ama-assn.org/cgi/
    content/full/168/5/493. Accessed August 2009.
Kitch, B. T.; Cooper, J. B.; Zapol, W. M.; Marder, J. E.; Karson, A.; Hutter, M.;
    Campbell, E. G. "Handoffs Causing Patient Harm: A Survey of Medical and
    Surgical House Staff." *Joint Commission Journal on Quality and Patient Safety,* 34,
    no. 10 (2008): 563–570. Available at: www.ingentaconnect.com/content/jcaho/
    jcjqs/2008/00000034/00000010/art00001. Accessed August 2009.
Lerner, Barron H. "A Case That Shook Medicine: How One Man's Rage Over
    His Daughter's Death Sped Reform of Doctor Training." *Washington Post,*
    November 28, 2006. Available at: www.washingtonpost.com/wp-dyn/content/
    article/2006/11/24/AR2006112400985.html. Accessed August 2009.
"Libby Zion" [Obituary]. *New York Times,* March 6, 1984. Available at: www
    .nytimes.com/1984/03/06/obituaries/libby-zion.html?sec=&spon=&partner=per
    malink&exprod=permalink. Accessed August 2009.
U.S. Department of Labor. The Fair Labor Standards Act of 1938, as Amended. WH
    Publication 1318, rev. ed. Washington, DC: U.S. Department of Labor, 2004. For
    more on the establishment of the 40-hour workweek, see www.osha.gov/pls/epub/
    wageindex.download?p_file=F15794/FairLaborStandAct.pdf. Accessed August 2009.

CHAPTER EIGHT

Holidays

When most people have the day off, residents are in the hospital.

Christmas

"Do you happen to know what time of year neurosurgeons are the busiest, Dr. Stevens?" Derek Shepherd asked Izzie Stevens during a brain operation in "Grandma Got Run Over by a Reindeer" (2-12).

"No, there's a time of year?" she responded.

"Well, there's no hard or fast rule, but brain injuries tend to pile up around the holidays. Like our friend here. Folks fall of their roofs while they string up lights or they go skating for the first time in a decade, break their heads open. And every year people drive through blizzards to get to parties where they kiss germ-infected strangers under poisonous mistletoe and then they get so drunk they smash their heads against their windshield on their way home. Like I said, there's no hard or fast rule."

There are spikes in deaths around the Christmas and New Year's holidays. In one study, researchers found that deaths were almost 5 percent higher than expected around those two holidays.

"There are multiple explanations for this association, including the possibility that holiday-induced delays in seeking treatment play a role in producing the twin holiday spikes," the study authors wrote.

They looked at death statistics over a span of 26 years stretching from the summer of 1973 to the summer of 2001. The holiday spikes were seen every year except two; 1973 and 1981. The researchers speculated that perhaps the fact that fewer people traveled over the holidays during the oil embargo in 1973 and the recession of 1981 may explain the lack of death spikes in those years.

IT'S VERY EARLY CHRISTMAS MORNING. MOST PEOPLE ARE HOME WITH their families. Some parents are being roused by eager children who can't wait any longer to start opening presents. Other people are sleeping in after attending midnight church services.

In the surgical intensive care unit, third-year resident Sajid Khan, M.D., is pre-rounding just as he would on any other day, checking lab reports that came in during the night, quickly sifting through data in the computer and the bulging patient binders to look for warnings of downturns or signs of improvement. Maybe some of his patients can be transferred out to a regular patient floor today.

Staffing is about the same as any other day. Illness doesn't take holidays, but there are fewer patients than usual, just 7 of the 13 beds are occupied. People postpone elective surgeries around holidays. The soft sounds of ventilators and beeps of monitors mingle with the quiet conversations of nurses and doctors.

"He's grumpy," a nurse tells Khan as he looks over the patient's chart.

Khan smiles. "Appropriately so. He's here on Christmas."

The nurse says she celebrated Christmas a week early because she knew she'd be working the holiday. Another doctor chimes in that he's worked most Christmases since he graduated from medical school, but he doesn't mind. He took a day off for Thanksgiving, so it evens out.

Khan goes in to the room of a woman who has had a tough time recovering from emergency surgery. She's been in the ICU for a month. The patient's nurse asks the doctor about possibly changing some of her medications. Khan tells him that he's reluctant to make changes. He's not the patient's primary physician.

Holidays have some benefits. Because the number of patients in the ICU is lower than normal, Khan finishes his pre-rounds a bit early and has time to pop down to the cafeteria before meeting the rest of the day-time team for full morning rounds. "It's the first time I've been able to sit and eat before rounds," Khan says.

But the break is not long. At 7:00 A.M. he dashes back up the stairs. "Merry Christmas," Chief Resident Aaron Partsafas greets him. It's his first day back from vacation. He says he opened presents with his son before coming to work, but because it was so early, they had to carry him to the tree and wake him. How many parents are up before their kids on Christmas morning?

Rounds start with good news. The emergency medicine resident on the team says one of their patients suddenly improved overnight. "I didn't think he would recover. But he suddenly started communicating. It made my day. I had to run and tell someone as it was happening," she beamed.

It looks to be a light day. There is only one scheduled surgical procedure. And there was only one new patient admitted overnight; the driver of a car that went off the road. They note that alcohol doesn't appear to have been a factor in the crash; a notable exception in the season of holiday celebrations. With the low patient count, the team is hoping to let one of the residents leave early. She has family visiting for the holiday.

The team heads out on the floor. The nurses station is decorated with hanging stars and a little tree. Gift bags sit on the counter. The staff is giving "Secret Santa" gifts. The window to each patient room is decorated with a stocking.

They spend almost 20 minutes huddled around the bed of a patient who had been found unconscious on the ground. A nurse exclaims, "Oh, wow!" but not because of a medical emergency. It's the Christmas dawn: the Cascade Mountains are silhouetted along the eastern horizon by rich purple light that steadily lightens toward pink.

When one of the surgeons takes a knife in his hand, it's not to perform an incision on a patient, but rather to slice a homemade cheesecake. "The best part of being here on a holiday is all the food," he says. His cake cutting, however, looks a bit sloppy.

"It's actually easier being here at the hospital on Christmas," a relative of one of the patients remarks. "People are nice. Everyone here is in a good mood."

The family has been at the hospital every day for three weeks. The patient's crisis hit suddenly. "If it weren't for this illness we'd be splitting the day between the homes of family members." They have still been cooking up their favorite holiday foods, but then they've put them in the freezer. They'll thaw them and celebrate when their loved one is back at home.

Meanwhile, a chime announces the birth of a baby. Happy occurrences also don't take holidays.

New Year's Eve . . . and Day

This New Year's Eve has been busy for Sajid Khan. He's been involved in the care of six or seven trauma cases and it's still hours until midnight. During a lull, he rushes to catch up on his patient notes and then heads next door to the call room to take a break while he can. "I have a sense it's gonna get busy again," Khan says.

Half an hour later he rises from his power nap to check on a few patients. Tonight he shares the responsibility for almost 20 patients in intensive care. It's a heavy load. And while parties around the world countdown toward midnight, inside the intensive care unit there is almost no sense that this night is different from any other. Some nurses share a bottle of sparkling cider in a break room. But without looking at a clock you wouldn't be able to tell the new year had begun.

A couple of hours past midnight, the pace of care slows enough for Khan to again catch up on making notes about the treatments and plans for his patients. There's even time to check e-mail and do some reading . . . residents always need to read to keep up with medical research and prepare for evaluations and exams.

Just when it seems the night may pass without further incident, new trauma cases begin arriving. At 3:35 A.M. word comes of two transfers from community hospitals. And then the pagers buzz again and again, three more trauma cases arriving, including a shooting victim. Suddenly the Emergency Department trauma bays are filling up. A curtain is pulled across one room so that it can take two patients at once.

As one patient is rolled in from the ambulance entrance, the PA system announces another will be there in three minutes. Khan and senior resident Renee Minjarez, M.D., talk about the incoming cases as they walk toward Emergency. As they enter a stairwell, Minjarez doubles back to go help out with a surgery. "It's an unusual trauma night," she says. Khan continues down. "It's just me and Renee from the trauma team. Everyone else is in the OR. We do the best we can. There's no way we can get to it all, but there's no option," Khan says.

"Once I was sure [the first patient] was more stable, then the other patient rolled in. I made a quick assessment. You have to try to be everywhere at once," Khan says later, recalling how he shuttled between rooms in the ER. "There was more help needed in the other room, so I dashed over to the other room."

An hour later, Khan is back in the ICU. As he checks on one of the patients admitted earlier in the night, his pager announces yet another trauma case arriving at the Emergency Department. "I'm going to try to get there when I can," he says. But he never does, leaving that case to others on the trauma and emergency medicine teams.

Khan says toward the end of the night he was going "a hundred miles an hour" to keep up with the trauma cases rolling in.

"It always seems like it will be impossible to get the work done, but somehow you have to find a way to get it done, and somehow it does get done," he says.

Just before 7:00 A.M., the team gathers in their workroom to review the night and prepare to hand the patients over to the day shift. "What a night it turned out to be," Khan says. "I was just trying to make sure nothing was missed."

"Oh, man, I am tired," says one of the attending surgeons. He'd been operating almost all night long and still had another operation to get back to. "The sky opened up on us this morning."

Reflecting back on the last night of one year and the first morning of the next, Khan says it was incredibly busy, but it went the way it was supposed to. "Everything worked out fine. When we rounded in the morning, everything was set the way it should have been set. Patient care was not compromised," Khan says. In part, he says that is because no one was working alone. Khan recalls one of the attendings noticing things he had not seen right away. "She picked up a couple of things. There are different levels of people following things. One person is going to miss something, but if you have different people approaching it from different angles that usually cleans up whatever could be messed up."

Fourth of July

"Want to go see the fireworks?" trauma surgeon Jennifer Watters asks around. It's about 10:00 P.M. There's no crisis in the Emergency Department at the moment. "Maybe we could take a computer on wheels to the viewpoint, just in case," she smiles.

She leads a group of residents and students through the hospital to get to a good vantage point.

"Urgent fireworks consult," Watters calls out to nurses as the group makes a shortcut through a ward to get to a patio overlook facing toward several fireworks displays. The patio is packed with staff, families, and patients. Some of the patients are in wheelchairs. Some are connected to rolling IV stands. Some have oxygen tanks. Especially the youngest patients don't want to miss a good fireworks show just because they are in the hospital.

"It's my first time outside since five this morning," one of the residents says. A couple of them share a candy bar as they watch the explosions.

Down below, traffic has come to a halt on a freeway bridge across the river. "Don't have a stroke or an MI [heart attack] on the east side on the Fourth of July," Watters says as she looks down at the traffic jam that would stymie any ambulance.

Not all the fireworks are from official shows. The sizable bursts appearing over backyards and side streets across the city show that many people have more holiday enthusiasm than obedience to the law. "Are any of you brave enough to set off your own fireworks like these people?" Watters asks. She is not. "I can barely do sparklers." Every day, trauma surgeons see the damage done when things go wrong.

Watters says that just the day before she found her daughter leaning out a second-floor window at home. "I'd like to have big nets all around the house," she jokes.

The crowd on the balcony gives a loud round of applause to the firework show's grand finale. As the people shuffle back into the hospital, one of the residents turns to Watters. "Thanks for grabbing us," she says. Without an attending to lead the way, the residents probably wouldn't have taken advantage of even this brief escape.

The team checks a couple of patients in intensive care. Watters takes a moment to snack on some of the potluck offerings in a break room by the nurses station. As on other holidays, these treats are a way to mark special days, even though the call schedule continues uninterrupted.

It's been a fairly routine night, even a bit on the quiet side. The trauma cases have been typical for midsummer and not particularly holiday related.

A man who crashed his ATV (all-terrain vehicle) is brought in from a rural part of the state. "Automatic trauma victim" is what some surgeons call the off-road vehicles, because of the steady flow of injuries they cause.

People hurt in a couple of other small motor vehicle crashes arrive close together. A man riding a motor scooter about 50 mph slid on some gravel. It looks like he just fractured his wrist and got banged up a bit. The firefighters who bring him in say he was wearing a helmet and didn't seem to have any head problems.

A boy who tried to jump his motorbike crashed into a rock. They do a CT scan of his head just in case. He, too, was wearing a helmet. His injuries also appear minor.

Just before midnight, a sort-of fireworks-related injury arrives at the Emergency Department. The man was looking up at the fireworks. But then he felt lightheaded and fell down some concrete steps. Another trauma case arrives soon after. It is also not the kind of fireworks injury you might expect on this holiday. The man has a steak knife in his eye. A trauma nurse remarks that it is the fourth seriously damaged eye they've dealt with tonight. "Eyeballs are the theme of the night," she says.

Even as it appears this holiday will pass easily, an anesthesiologist working on a relatively minor operation says, "I really hope a massive trauma doesn't come in while were doing this case." He's wary of what mishaps the Fourth of July celebrations might yet produce. "I'm still waiting to see what the cat will drag in," he says.

Additional Reading

Phillips, David P.; Jarvinen, Jason R.; Abramson Ian S.; Phillips, Rosalie R. "Cardiac Mortality Is Higher Around Christmas and New Year's Than at Any Other Time: The Holidays As a Risk Factor for Death." *Circulation,* 110 (2004): 3781–3788. Available at: http://circ.ahajournals.org/cgi/content/full/110/25/3781. Accessed August 2009.

CHAPTER NINE

Truth in a Bottle

"People get stupid. People get violent. People get hurt," Miranda Bailey says with a smile as she explains why she likes working holiday nights in "Thanks for the Memories" (2-09).

"And that's a good thing because?" Meredith Grey asks her.

"Surgeries, Grey! Lots and lots of surgeries."

"I never thought of that."

"The stupidity of the human race, Grey. Be thankful for that," Bailey tells Grey.

THE YOUNG MAN HAD TOLD HIS PARENTS HE HAD CRASHED HIS MOTOR-cycle. He admitted a different story to the trauma team.

He had been drinking with his buddies. They decided to break beer bottles over their heads. He noticed the fingers on his left hand weren't working right. But he didn't think much about it at the time and went to bed.

When he woke up his left arm wasn't working. That got his attention.

So he went to the ER. Then his left leg went weak. A CT scan showed bleeding inside his skull putting pressure on his brain.

Although the man had been breaking bottles on his head, the trauma doctors didn't think the blows would have been hard enough to cause this kind of bleeding. Maybe there was some existing problem, perhaps a malformation of blood vessels. An arteriovenous malformation (AVM) could have been sitting unnoticed, possibly since he was born, not causing any problems until the beer bottle blows broke it open.

"Ooh." That's the reaction when an MRI scan of the patient's brain appears on the screen. The effect of the bleeding is dramatic. However, a cerebral angiogram, showing the blood flow in the brain, does not show any signs of a blood vessel abnormality. The AVM theory goes to the side. Maybe the beer bottle story, like the motorcycle crash, is not the real explanation. Could there be a third story?

On his fourth day in the hospital, he starts coughing up thick, frothy sputum. No one knows why brain injuries sometimes trigger this reaction, but it happens.

The patient's treatment continues, even though the doctors don't really know why this man's brain started to bleed.

CHAPTER TEN

Match Day

Eighty-hour weeks . . . holidays included. Years and years of training. Sometimes watching patients die. And yet medical students clamor for residency appointments. It's typical for them to apply to a couple dozen residency programs and then visit a dozen programs around the country. The interviewing process involves tours and meetings with a program's current residents and faculty. Looking back on the process, residents say it's nerve-wracking, tiring, and fun.

Students invited to interview generally all meet the basic requirements for a program: they are smart and have passed key tests and other evaluations. So program visits have a lot to do with getting a sense for whether a student and program would be a good fit for each other.

Nick Tadros says that when he went to visit residency programs around the country, he saw the process was about much more than test scores or program prestige. "[It's about] where you really fit in, just on a person-to-person level with the residents and faculty."

Loïc Fabricant says he began to notice that the residents would hit him with the tough questions, while the program chief would usually give a sales pitch extolling the highlights of his or her program. "I did get the sense that a lot of the people make an assessment of you in just seconds; that they've decided what you are about by the time they've finished shaking your hand."

When it comes to the application process, there's one major difference between residency programs and most other types of schools. Medical students don't get acceptance or rejection letters from each residency program they applied to; instead, they get matched to a single program, just one.

Half a century ago, major medical education organizations decided to coordinate their residency application schedules. They created a private, not-for-profit corporation, the National Resident Matching Program (NRMP). Under the current system, there are three major steps: registration, ranking, and results. After registering and visiting programs, medical students rank the programs they would like to attend. In turn, the residency programs rank applicants. Then the computer software at the National Resident Matching Program goes to work matching a resident to each open spot.

Ranking is serious business. The matching agreement is a binding contract. Except in unusual circumstances, residents have to go to the program they are matched to. They can't say, "Oh, I've changed my mind, I'd rather go to my second choice program." Like many medical students, Tadros says he ranked the programs he liked, put the list aside, came back to it, made some changes and then thought about it more, right up to the submission deadline, trying to answer the ultimate question: Would he really be happy spending five years or more in any of the programs he ranked?

For each medical specialty, match results are revealed at the same time across the nation. "Match Day" for general surgery residency programs is during the third week of March. Although residents can go online to find out their fates, most medical schools hold some sort of Match Day event.

At OHSU, a couple of hundred medical students, friends, family, and faculty gather in a large meeting space in the library building. There is a light breakfast buffet on a table by floor-to-ceiling windows that look across to the VA and children's hospitals. Nervous laughter floats above the conversations. At the east end of the atrium, the doors to a small room are locked. Through the glass wall, students can see a table covered with neat rows of sealed envelopes, envelopes that hold their futures.

"It's literally the most nervous I've ever been in my life," recalls resident Mitch Sally, M.D. While waiting to learn the news in the envelopes, the lives of the students have been on hold. Tadros says he and his wife put off buying a kitchen table, in case they had to suddenly move across the country. They couldn't respond to a family wedding invitation, because they might have to pack up their house that weekend.

The students ask each other how things will work. Will their names be called or will there just be a mad rush to grab envelopes? At some schools elsewhere in the country, at this very moment other medical students are sitting in assembly halls waiting for their matches to be announced for all to hear. The OHSU students don't have to face that prospect of public revelation. Once they get their envelopes they can open them here or take them away to open in private whenever they build up enough nerve.

The results are released at 1:00 P.M. eastern time, 10:00 A.M. here on the West Coast. A few minutes before the hour, Tadros says he is "surviving." He adds that he treated himself to an hour-and-a-half massage the day before. Still, he had a rough night and woke early, worrying about where he would be matched and whether he'd ranked programs in the right order.

Two minutes to go. A woman calls for everyone's attention.

"The envelopes are arranged in alphabetical order, A in the upper left down to Z in this corner," she announces. "An e-mail with your matches will go out tomorrow. If you don't want your results to be listed, contact the office today." Then she adds, "Army and Air Force information is on the back table." A bit of laughter runs through the crowd. The military services aren't part of the National Resident Matching Program, so they provide an option for students who aren't offered a match.

Then the doors are opened. The students push forward. It's not a mob scene, but they grab envelopes as quickly as they can. Over and over throughout the room, the big question echoes, "Where are you going?" The noise level spikes as students cheer and holler and high-five each other.

Tadros tears his envelope open right away. "OHSU. I'm staying here," he tells his friends. He is happy to continue in a program where he feels comfortable, and relieved to know he and his wife don't have to sell their house and move. "It was scary. I'm excited, I guess. I don't know." It's all too much to process right away. His wife couldn't take time off work. He calls her. "Hey, babe. Yeah, OHSU," he tells her, smiling. She asks him what's going on there. "It's fantastic. Everyone's screaming and everything." He fills her in on how some of their medical school friends fared. "I've got to find Loïc. I'll call you back in a little bit and let you know the updates."

Loïc Fabricant picks up his envelope, but doesn't open it right away. He works his way through the crowd to find his girlfriend. They step out on the balcony, standing alone together to learn the critical news. Fabricant opens the envelope. He smiles. They hug and kiss.

When the couple returns to their friends, Fabricant announces he, too, is staying at OHSU. He gives Tadros a hug, happy that they'll get to continue their friendship through the tough years of residency.

They find another medical school classmate. "I had been freaking out about my ranking list. I'm very happy I got OHSU," says Jessyka Lighthall. It's a relief after a rough morning. "I was too nauseated to eat breakfast. Then I had a surgery. We were all cramped into a small OR. It was done at nine forty-five A.M. [just 15 minutes before the results are released]. I dashed over, parked illegally, and ran down here."

Fabricant echoes her relief. "I'm so relaxed now," he says. "I had been having lots of dreams, like about not finding my envelope. I didn't really realize just how stressed I had been until now, with all the stress relieved."

As Fabricant is talking, Tadros turns to greet a friend. "I'm staying here," he tells her. She jumps and hugs him.

Another classmate gets news she is moving to Denver. That's where she wanted to go, and she'd had a good feeling about her chances. "It has been 'probably' for so long, it's weird that now it's real and official," she says.

One couple gets confirmation that they are both going to Seattle. They've been so busy preparing for the move that they are just now wearing green St. Patrick's Day outfits, three days after the event.

Twenty minutes after the hour, the swell of excitement is ebbing.

People are filtering out. Yet 13 envelopes remain unclaimed, arranged on the table in three neat rows. Perhaps these students could not break away from their patients. Or maybe they preferred not to get such momentous news in public.

There will be celebrations. But for some of the students, the stress has been so great that quiet relaxation is all they have in mind.

"People say, 'Oh, you should go out and have fun after Match Day.' But I was just wrecked, I was exhausted," Mitch Sally recalls. "We all got into where we wanted to go, we were all very happy, but none of us really felt like staying out late and drinking a lot or that sort of typical thing. It's intense."

Almost a year later, in the spring of his intern year, Loïc Fabricant still looks back with amazement at Match Day. "That was a defining moment," he says. And while he got good news, he says, "Not everyone got what they wanted."

NICK TADROS, M.D.

Status: Intern

Where from: Portland. Medical school at Oregon Health & Science University

Why did you want to become a surgeon?
During medical school, Tadros was attracted to the instant gratification that surgery can offer. "Instead of treating something with drugs for years, you just cut it out." He saw that surgeons also take care of the other medical needs of their patients, so they get to sample the best of both worlds.

Part way through his intern year, Tadros still thinks he picked the right path. "Medicine rounds give me the heebie-jeebies," he says. The pace of medicine seems too slow. The flip side is the sense that surgeons don't get to know their patients as well. But Tadros says he's already seen exceptions to that rule. During a surgery rotation in medical school, Tadros helped treat a woman with necrotizing fasciitis, the so-called flesh-eating bacteria. She needed frequent surgeries over several weeks to control the spread of the infection.

"People always say that in surgery you don't get to know your patients, there is no continuity, you're just operating and sending them out the door, but I really got to know this patient, and very intimately. Obviously, when you are operating on someone three times a week, you are physically seeing all of them, and you are really getting to know the depths of how this disease is treated. She had been in the hospital for a month when I came on the service and then she stayed after I left the service as well," he says. "She was the only patient who ever cried when I told her I was leaving the service. It meant a lot to me. It was interesting to me that it happened on my surgery rotation, not on family medicine, not on pediatrics."

As an intern, Tadros has also seen that while relationships with surgery patients may not be long lasting, they are intense.

"Surgeons do really get very close with their patients. Even though we don't see them for a long time, we see them at extreme times. It's a super intense experience." And it forms a bond. "I took an appendix out of a farmer, and he sent me syrup from his farm."

What's the biggest difference between what you thought it would be like and the reality?

In an interview during his final months of medical school, Tadros predicted that residency would be amazing but also overwhelming.

"My biggest fear is that I'm going to get so consumed during residency that I'm not going to have time for anything besides being a doctor," he said. But he also knew that it probably wouldn't be as all-consuming as it was for earlier generations of residents. "It's definitely a different mind-set than it was ten or twenty years ago, before the eighty-hour workweek."

Now that he is well into his intern year, Tadros sees there are days off. On a recent one, he went to a wedding. His brother has a birthday coming up, and his schedule will allow him to attend. So he is finding there is a life outside of the hospital. Still, the demands leave him drained.

"Last Friday I went out with friends, but by nine thirty P.M. I was all worn out," he says. "Usually on my day off, I just sleep and watch

TV. I'm getting lazy." He chuckles. Tadros says he wishes he could get together with friends more often, but with all the residents having different schedules it's rare to find time off together.

Time is a funny thing during residency, there never seems to be enough and yet for an intern, residency can appear to stretch forever into the future.

"Sometimes it seems hopeless, if I think too far ahead, if I'm on call and exhausted and the next day off is two weeks away. And when I look at all the rotations ahead of me, it seems like there's no end," Tadros says. "But then I can also look at it and see that I'm almost a third of the way through my intern year. Then it doesn't seem so bad."

What do you want patients to know about what you do?
Tadros mentions uncertainty and pain. "Patients expect us to know more than we do," he says. Of course, interns have a lot to learn, but even experienced surgeons can't always predict exactly how things will go. And as for the pain, it's not gratuitous. When he urges a patient to get up and walk after surgery, Tadros says he certainly isn't trying to cause them pain "But if you get too concerned about the discomfort you're causing, you might not do what needs to be done. For example, putting in an NG [nasogastric] tube, it's not comfortable, but may be necessary."

Even though, the perspective of a patient and a surgeon are very different, there are moments when they overlap.

"I got blood drawn for a life insurance policy," Tadros says. "It was normal, but my liver function test results were almost out of the normal range. I was thinking about how that affected me, even though it was still normal. Something like that helps me understand a little bit more about how families freak out about abnormal values that we take in stride. I almost felt like a patient for a minute."

What specialty are you most interested in?
"I'm still undecided about specialties. I like general surgery, but there are lifestyle issues. If you're going into something like colorectal surgery, you're not gonna have any emergencies. Same thing with plastic surgery," he says. "I love surgery for sure, but so far no subspecialty has jumped out at me."

If you could go back in time to tell your younger self about surgery residency, what would you say?

"Looking back, if I knew what med school was going to be like, I'm not sure I would've done it. Sometimes it's better not to know what it's gonna be like." Tadros says he was warned. "Some of my college professors asked, 'Are you sure this is what you want to do?' And I said, 'Why not?' Sometimes some naïveté is good."

Indeed, he says that despite the heavy demands, he's glad he chose medicine; in part because he couldn't imagine doing a job that wasn't demanding or that didn't offer the variety of options.

"The beauty of medicine is that there is something for everyone. You can work two hundred hours a week or thirty hours a week. You can talk to people or not talk to people. I can't think of another job with the same range of opportunities, from administrator to working in a free clinic. When I was in medical school, I knew people who wanted to do everything from breast augmentation to working in Africa. There's a huge range."

This afternoon offers a rare opportunity. All is quiet, and Nick Tadros is getting out of the hospital early.

"I was looking forward to seeing the sun, but it's cloudy out." Tadros shrugs. "Oh well, even if it's not good weather, at least it's weather."

LOÏC FABRICANT, M.D.

Status: Intern

Where from: Eugene, Oregon. Medical school at Oregon Health & Science University

Why did you want to become a surgeon?

Fabricant was a peer educator in high school. He helped teach other teens about eating disorders, sexually transmitted disease, and other health issues that challenge adolescents. Even at that early stage, he was attracted to surgery.

"It sounded like a cool thing. At that point I decided I wanted to be a surgeon, because it sounded really cool and glamorous, not because I necessarily knew what it really meant," Fabricant says.

While still in high school Fabricant shadowed some doctors, got to observe a couple of operations, and that cemented his interest in surgery and his preference for intervening with his hands, rather than relying on a prescription pad and other medical therapies.

"Foremost is the ability to fix something. You do that in medicine in some ways, but you don't get to have this tangible result and resolution to a problem that you get as a surgeon. So for somebody like myself who's come up doing a lot of construction, working in the outdoors, and doing things with my hands and enjoying that process, it's really appealing to be able to touch someone in the most intimate kind of way and fix the problem."

Fabricant says that being a physician who uses medicine to help manage someone's blood pressure over a decade is really important, but it's not the same thing as surgery. When he was doing a surgery rotation in medical school, he helped manage the care of a teenager who missed her senior prom because she was having surgery to remove stomach cancer.

"It was really heartbreaking," Fabricant recalls. "But we got her healthy and out of the hospital and back to school. I got an e-mail from her about a year later. It was a very heartfelt letter thanking me for my role in her care, which really meant a lot. Here she had been someone really sick, somebody who had a lot of years left, and we fixed the problem."

What's the biggest difference between what you thought it would be like and the reality?

During his final weeks of medical school, Fabricant thought about how things would be different once he started residency.

"As students, we've worked with the team and we've been there when the team was there, so we've worked the hours and observed the interns and what they are going through. So I think that more than anyone else we've got a very good sense of what we are coming up against, but I don't think anything is going to really brace me for having to make decisions for patients, having to manage a list of twenty or thirty patients, maybe some of whom I have never seen before. So I think maybe I have some idea of what it's going to be like, but I'm prepared for the fact that I really don't have a clue what's going to happen."

Fast forward several months to halfway through his intern year and Fabricant says he's more sure than ever that he made the right career decision, despite some grueling days when he's wondered about what he's gotten himself into.

"That's usually when you've been there sixteen hours and it's nine P.M. and you know you have to be back the next morning at four forty-five, which happens pretty often. That's usually when I start to feel like, 'Man, what am I doing?' But inevitably when I get up the next morning, I'm still excited to come to work. I think that's the real indicator that this was a good choice."

As an intern, the opportunities to actually perform surgery are often scarce. And most of the procedures they do get are ones that more senior surgeons don't want. Fabricant says he's drained a lot of abscesses in patients who are IV drug users. But every now and then a cool case comes along that reminds him what he's working toward.

For instance, he had a chance to scrub in as the primary assistant to John Mayberry, M.D., as they explored the abdomen of a patient who was having problems after a hernia repair.

"It was just a couple of open sores on his belly that Dr. Mayberry thought were granulomas [small areas of inflammation] around the stitches. They were probably about ten inches apart. We dove in thinking that these were separate lesions; maybe there were two stitches there that the body had reactions to."

But as they opened the patient, they wondered aloud if the sores might be somehow related. Then when they looked inside, they found a piece of mesh that had rolled up and was scarring the abdominal wall.

"As we started to dissect each one of them, we discovered they were the two ends of that curled mesh. Indeed, they actually were one problem. It was a good case that reinforced the excitement of surgery; that you don't necessarily know what you're getting into, and that you have to be careful, yet decisive, in figuring out what is going on."

What do you want patients to know about what you do?
Fabricant says being a surgeon is not just a matter of great dexterity or mastering the mechanics of or science behind an operation. He says you'll often hear surgeons say that anyone could be taught to do an operation, but not everyone could be a good surgeon.

"What makes a great surgeon is the ability to make good decisions, to know when to operate and maybe more importantly when not to operate, know when your patient after an operation is really sick or is just recovering normally. That judgment, that tempered judgment, is what makes a great surgeon," Fabricant says. "But I don't think people want to know about that either, because it will maybe lay bare the kind of gray areas that we have so much of in medicine."

And he says there's a big difference between how surgeons are often portrayed and what the daily routine is really like.

"It's not nearly as glamorous as you might think. And it's an incredible amount of hard work from the beginning, even just to get into med school. The whole path is just an incredible amount of hard work. I think that more than anything I wish that people understood that in medicine there are rarely black and white situations. There are a lot of judgment calls. The human element plays a big role; both the patient as a human and the provider as a human."

What specialty are you most interested in?
So far, Fabricant says the variety of general surgery remains appealing.

"Being able to attack just about any issue is something that's very appealing about general surgery. I have some aspirations to work overseas eventually, do relief work; and you are the most useful and versatile type of physician, being able to operate, but also manage sick people."

Halfway through his intern year, he says that choice looks like the right one.

"It's caught my eye most because of the variety, the range of surgical problems, the uncertainty about what every day holds. I really like that no two days are the same."

Additional Reading

National Resident Matching Program (NRMP). For more information, see www.nrmp.org.

CHAPTER ELEVEN

Bad News

Patients don't always get better.

In the very first episode of *Grey's Anatomy,* George O'Malley has to tell a woman that her husband had just died. He is uncertain how to deliver the bad news. Not surprising, since it's his first day as an intern. He fumbles with the words and then blurts out, "Tony died." George starts to offer a hug. The woman stiffens and backs away. It doesn't go well.

Even the most experienced characters appear to struggle and fumble when telling patients or families that things may not turn out all right.

Chief Webber seems caught off-guard when the wife of a patient asks him for news.

"My husband. I was wondering if there was any news because you look so worried. And I heard this doctor saying that even though that girl's got her finger on the tear in his heart, that my husband is losing blood. Every second he's losing blood. Which means he could die? He could die? I ask because I know you'll tell me the truth because you look so worried," the wife asks.

"Mrs. Carlson . . ." Chief Webber hesitates as if unsure how much truth to give her. "Yes, it's possible he could bleed out and die if we don't operate soon."

She nods. "Okay. Okay. Thank you for telling me the truth." She begins to cry. "I'll just . . . I'll just go wait over here."

Chief Webber lets her walk away without another word.

People go to doctors for care and healing. But often cure and full recovery are not possible. While medical schools hammer textbooks full of biomedical minutiae into the brains of students, only recently have medical educators begun to pay more attention to the communication skills that are put to the test when the outlook is grim. One review of medical education noted that physicians have to deliver bad news almost every day, but most of them have never had any formal training in how to do it. The review authors urged that students and residents need many opportunities to watch, think about, discuss and practice the communication skills necessary to give patients bad news without compounding their pain.

Chief Resident Laszlo Kiraly and third-year resident Terah Isaacson walk from the physicians workroom to the alcove waiting area where three family members sit. The family members had already been told that things looked bad for their relative but that a neurology specialist was going to examine her.

The talk in the workroom moments before had been blunt. The woman had a severe traumatic brain injury. When Isaacson told one of the senior residents that the neurology specialist was not yet ready to give up any pretense that recovery was possible, the senior resident was aghast.

"Neuro isn't talking comfort care yet," Isaacson said.

"What? Her brain is herniated everywhere!" the other resident shot back.

"How hard am I going to work to keep this woman alive?" Isaacson asked her senior resident.

"You're not."

When the day shift team arrived, Isaacson briefed them on the woman who had arrived in the middle of the night. They all knew there was no chance of recovery. But the ventilator was still moving air into the patient's lungs. Her heart was still beating. And the family had yet to tell them to remove the machines.

"They are waiting for another family member to arrive," Isaacson said. "I'm not going to do chest compressions," she added, referring to a potential CPR attempt if the patient's heart stopped before the family decided to halt all support.

"I'm not," agreed Kiraly. "That's assault."

"Just be supportive," the attending surgeon advised. "If something happens, tell them she didn't make it."

Everyone in the room had been through similar situations many times before. But they also knew that for the family members this was an unfamiliar and terrible ordeal. They wouldn't talk to the family the way they do to each other. When Isaacson and Kiraly go to meet with family members, they have to decide how to balance sympathy and honesty, how to strip away any remaining hope without being cruel.

The ACGME core competencies document states that: "Residents must demonstrate interpersonal and communication skills that result in the effective exchange of information and collaboration with patients, their families, and health professionals."

A survey of surgery residents in one program found that the residents said they were comfortable talking with patients and families about informed consent and the results of operations. They said they were almost as comfortable talking about bad news, but when it came to discussing do not resuscitate (DNR) orders and making a transition to comfort care, most residents said they were not comfortable. And while residents get constant feedback from faculty during operations, only a third of the residents responding to this survey said they received helpful feedback from faculty on their communication skills. Part of the problem is that even if attending surgeons are masters in the OR, not all have mastered patient communication. "Some faculty have no business teaching communication skills," read one comment from a resident.

The challenges are not unique to surgery. A survey of medical residents found that most began delivering bad news to patients when they were students or interns, but rarely was there any planning or faculty involvement in the events. The researchers concluded that, "In spite of their inexperience, many do not appear to receive adequate guidance or support during their earliest formative experiences."

The patient's son had told the nurses to change his mother's status to DNR. The likely outcome was probably clear to him. But Kiraly and

Isaacson now had the task of sitting with him to confirm that indeed there were no more options, alternatives, or even the slimmest chances of a turnaround. The surgeons sat down next to the family members in the hallway waiting area. It was quiet.

"We can't do anything," Kiraly said. "The brain injury is severe. If we took out her breathing tube she might go quickly, maybe in minutes." He tried to answer questions about the cause, though he had little solid information. The woman had arrived from another hospital just hours earlier. He tried to deflect "What if?" questions about the woman's initial care. "Even if we were watching from the beginning, we might not be able to do anything about it. Sometimes these bleeds start and can't be stopped."

The son's eyes teared up, yet he seemed resigned. "I feel she's already gone." He told the doctors that other family members were still on the way to the hospital.

"We can maintain her breathing tube," Kiraly said. "But something might happen."

Looking ahead to the final steps, Kiraly warned the son, "I'm not sure if you'll want to be there when we remove the breathing tube."

"Is it disturbing?" the son asked.

"It can be."

"I'm not sure I want that to be the last memory," the son said. He talked about what had happened to his mother. It was the kind of information that could be critical to the care of a trauma patient just coming in the door of the emergency department, how the trauma had occurred, how the patient was acting just after the injury, the kind of details that Kiraly and Isaacson would have scrutinized and weighed in order to help develop a treatment plan. But this woman could no longer be helped. The information would not change anything.

Yet Kiraly and Isaacson listened attentively. After all, they were still providing care, not to the patient, but to her family. The treatment was no longer medicine or surgery; it was listening and communicating.

"UH, THIS ONE'S BEING DISCHARGED TO HOSPICE?" INTERN NORMAN Shales asked Meredith Grey in "The Heart of the Matter" (4-04)

"When there's nothing else we can do," Grey replied.

"So we have to tell someone they're dying?"

"Don't worry. I'll teach you the protocol. . . . So when giving a patient the bad news, you want to be polite and detached, but not cold."

"How can you be detached, but not cold?"

"You show that you care without actually allowing yourself to care, because if you get too emotional, then they get scared, and then they get emotional, and that's bad," Grey said.

ACTUALLY, PATIENTS AND FAMILY MEMBERS DO GET EMOTIONAL. IT'S ONLY natural and expected. And it's not that the residents have to learn to not care but rather to care without being overwhelmed, to feel without letting the feelings interfere with the work. Sometimes a tear is shed, but after a pause the surgeon must continue on, because there are other patients and families waiting. And like a cop or firefighter or any other professional who is a witness to tragedy, residents have to learn to avoid carrying home the emotional trauma like some psychological infection.

Cancer surgeons get more than their share of practice delivering bad news to patients. In many cases, cancer is not cured. Surgery may help a patient live longer or better, perhaps for years, but often the disease eventually returns. And sometimes when a surgeon takes a look inside a patient, it is obvious that the disease has spread beyond containment.

Kevin Billingsley, M.D., chief of the division of surgical oncology at OHSU, says not too long ago he inserted a laparoscope into the abdomen of a woman who had a suspicious mass near her stomach.

"I put a scope into her abdomen and looked around to assess the extent of disease and confirm that it was cancer. What I found was that it was cancer and that it had spread all over her abdomen. Not only did she have cancer, but it was incurable and in fact would be best described as terminal," he says.

The woman was barely middle-aged. After the procedure, his next task was to give her the news. Billingsley says often doctors are too quick to just toss the bad news to a patient. He's developed an approach he thinks works better.

"Not sailing into a room and dropping a bomb on someone, but sitting down, creating a quiet space, and the sense that they have your full attention; and then starting not with, 'Let me give you this news,' but 'Let me probe what understanding you have already and then we'll work from there.' "

That's what he tried to do with this particular woman.

"I think I said something to the effect of, 'Let's start off by having you tell me what you understand about what's going on with your stomach and your abdomen.' She told me, 'I know I have a tumor in my stomach, but I don't know much more about it than that.'" he says. "So I said to her, 'Yes, you are right. There is this tumor. And in the procedure today what I found was that this is a cancer . . . and I wish I were giving you other news . . . but that's what the biopsy showed us. And unfortunately the cancer has left the stomach and is in other places around the abdomen.'"

"What she said was, 'Yes, I understand. I had a sense that that might be the case.' "

After getting such shattering news, Billingsley says patients rarely ask: "Am I going to die?"

"What they want to know is: 'What next? What are we going to do about it?' That's when I usually have to explain that this is not a problem we can cure with surgery and we probably won't be able to cure it completely at all. What we need to focus on is providing treatment that will suppress or control the disease as well as possible for as long as possible."

Surgeons rarely have to break the news to patients that they have cancer. After all, typically they are referred to a surgical oncologist by a primary physician or medical oncologist who has already given the patient at least a preliminary diagnosis. When surgical oncologists have to deliver bad news, it is usually about the recurrence or spread of cancer. Then the task is to discuss what the patient wants when cure is unlikely.

"This is a conversation that surgical oncologists have a lot," Billingsley says. "Part of the job is counseling people about what is reasonable and what really is going to help them. Because most patients who develop progressive disease get to a point where they could keep taking chemotherapy, but it's not likely to make them live longer or better."

The medical facts are only the starting point of the discussion. What really matters are the desires and values of the individual.

"Some people want to be treated indefinitely. They want to go down guns blazing. And other people say, 'You know, I don't see a lot of benefit to this at this point. I'm going to stop therapy and focus on other things. And live out the rest of my life with as much comfort and dignity as possible."

As vital as these decisions are, until recently residents received little or no formal training in how to conduct the discussions leading up to them. Of course, it is almost always the task of the attending surgeon to deliver the most critical news to a patient or family. Traditionally, residents have been expected to just absorb key lessons and techniques by watching. But now, more programs, including at OHSU, include doctor-patient communication in skills labs and then test residents using volunteers who act as standardized patients.

"This is a difficult area. There is very little formal curricula designed to address these issues. My hope, particularly with my senior residents, is that they spend enough time observing me doing this that they are aware enough and astute enough that they pick up the elements of my style that they think are effective and will work for them," Billingsley says. "I look back on my own training and I was fortunate to have two or three key mentors. I watched how they talked to patients and I took a lot away from that. That made the difference for me."

Intern Loïc Fabricant says it's tough being at the bottom of the hierarchy; patients ask questions that he can't answer. He is even hesitant to tell them everything he's heard, because he's not in charge. Things can change without him even knowing about it, and then he could be stuck trying to explain what happened to confused and angry patients and families. But he is glad he is not yet expected to be the bearer of devastating news. He has had to alert family members to unexpected problems, but it will be years before the ultimate responsibility is thrust upon him. For now, he listens, watches, and tries to learn.

"I don't know if it's something you can teach," Fabricant says, while noting that his skills labs do not include any specific training in delivering difficult news. "I just observe what I see the attendings do and try to integrate what I can."

Fabricant has thought about what he's seen so far. He says it seems best to be really direct; don't tease or dance around a tough fact.

"That makes sense, but it's harder to actually do than it seems," he says. "You have to be both compassionate and direct. One attending I admire makes his first statement something like, 'I don't BS, I'm just gonna tell you how things are.'"

Fabricant says he's seen that there is more to it than just what words to say. Body language and the setting are both important.

"Be in a quiet place. Sit down with the family. Be close. So you aren't towering over them. Speak in a low tone of voice."

The responses he has seen run the gamut; from older veterans who have been through a lot in life and seem to act as though they just lost a small bet, to family members who explode in anger.

"They may direct it at you," Fabricant says. "It's understandable, but it does make it hard to foster compassion. So what I do is step away and try to defuse the situation. Then I'll come back later. They always become more reasonable after they've had time to digest the news."

Death is not the only bad news. There are the nasty surprises. It's one thing to be told before a procedure that there are no guarantees of a good outcome; it's quite another to be faced with the sudden reality that the situation has taken a turn for the worse.

OHSU surgeons take cases that other surgeons in the region decide are beyond the scope of their skills or their institutions' capabilities. Typically those referrals are based on a diagnosis of a severe or complex condition or after an initial surgery has either failed to resolve the health issue or has created new problems. But sometimes a surgeon at another hospital starts something he or she can't finish. Then it can be up to the team here not only to finish the job but to talk with confused, frightened, and possibly angry patients and families.

It is midafternoon. Second-year resident Gordon Riha, M.D., is preparing to assist on a procedure when one of his senior residents alerts him that another patient is on the way. The patient was supposed to get a straightforward repair at another hospital to prevent a blood vessel aneurysm from bursting. But when surgeons at the small-town hospital opened up the elderly patient and saw the location and extent of the bulging weakness in a major blood vessel, they closed her back up and called for an emergency helicopter ambulance transfer to a larger hospital. One hospital had declined to take the case. It then fell into the hands of the vascular surgeons here.

The attending surgeon on the current case stops in to see how the preparations are going. They tell him about the incoming transfer. "Is it one of those where they open and then go, 'Oops'?" he asks. "I hate that," a nurse chimes in. "If only they would cry uncle sooner."

Riha is paged to the intensive care unit to see the new patient. As he hurries down the hallway, he talks about how he seems to attract cases where there is trouble. "You hear residents talk about their clouds, white clouds, clear clouds. Well, I've got the biggest, blackest cloud you'll ever find!"

He checks the OR schedule to find a room for an urgent operation. He has an intern fill in for him on the procedure he was originally supposed to help with. The new arrival has the staff stretched thin. He quizzes the helicopter ambulance nurse about the patient's vital signs. Her blood pressure is low, but stable.

As the lead person on the team reviewing this new case, his tasks include admitting the patient, checking her medications, and ordering additional blood tests. He reviews the notes sent by the surgeon who started the aneurysm repair. The notes say little beyond recording that after the operation was under way, the surgeon decided that the aneurysm looked more challenging than her hospital could comfortably deal with.

Riha briefs the attending surgeon who may take on the case. The surgeon shakes his head, vexed at having this unfinished surgery thrust upon his team. "We need to take her back to the OR and fix it. The longer we wait, the harder it'll be."

Riha also has to contact the patient's family to let them know where she is now and to get consent for further treatment. Though it's clear that the surgeons here are not impressed with the surgeon who handed off this case, Riha points out that they don't know all the details; so he says that when he briefs the family, he'll explain the situation diplomatically.

Soon visitors arrive, anxious and full of questions. They say they were told the original surgeon found an infection and decided to send the patient to OHSU.

"Yes, that's what we heard," Riha says.

"Is it riskier now?" one family member asks about the outlook for additional surgery on the aneurysm.

"Yes, it's higher up," Riha explains the location of the aneurysm makes the procedure trickier. "There is also a risk of other bleeding, infection, damage to the bowel and other organs."

"So basically what we heard from the other doctor before?"

"Yeah, there's also the possible risk of an extended hospital stay and death."

"When will you operate?"

"Tonight."

"You could take her now?"

Riha explains that the surgeon who will be doing their relative's case is finishing up another procedure now and will get to her in a couple of hours. Then he gets to the legalities of consent.

"Is her husband the one with power of attorney?"

"Well, he's the husband."

"We need to get consent for the surgery."

After speaking with the family members, Riha returns to working on the patient's medical records. His fingers are flying over the computer keyboard; there is a lot of information to enter and time is short. Despite typing as fast as he can, Riha is also trying to be careful. He knows that in cases like this, where things don't go as expected, what he puts in the record may be closely scrutinized by people reviewing the management of the situation.

Vascular surgery fellow Renee Minjarez comes to check on the situation. She looks at the brief notes the original surgeon sent along with the patient. "That's it?" she asks Riha.

"Yeah."

But when she goes to talk to the patient's family, she doesn't go into her initial impression of the other surgeon's work. She sticks to the key points they need to know about what will happen next and the risks the patient may face. She reiterates the small, but real, risk of death that Riha had warned them of.

"I don't want a vegetable back," a family member says.

"We don't either," Minjarez reassures them with a little nervous laugh, as she cautions them that the operation could take all night. The patient is elderly and, like many her age, has been treated for multiple chronic conditions. Sometimes patients like her can be fragile.

Minjarez and Riha go to the OR to prepare for the urgent procedure. They review images of the patient's aneurysm and make a plan to put a tube graft in place to prevent the weakened blood vessel wall from bursting. As she looks at the scans and considers the medical history of the woman they will be operating on, Minjarez sighs with doubt about the odds of success. "It's going to be a mess," she says.

Her harsh assessment certainly sounds different from the more qualified tone she had when speaking to the patient's family members. But then communicating with colleagues is a different matter from speaking to patients or relatives. In the OR, she has to focus on all the things that could go wrong and plan for problems large and small; focusing on the downside is a critical part of proper preparation. With patients and families, the task is different. She must be accurate and honest; but patients and families are already afraid, so highlighting the dangers can just frighten without informing. Despite the grave concerns Minjarez expresses to her colleagues, the surgeons agree that it is best for the patient to move ahead with the operation . . . and that's what the family members were told.

About four hours after the patient arrived, Minjarez begins the operation. Shortly, attending surgeon Timothy Liem, M.D., joins her. "I want the incision to go up much higher," Liem tells Minjarez. The higher-than-expected location of the aneurysm is one of the factors that prompted the patient's sudden transfer. "Do you feel the aorta?" he asks her. "The aneurysm is high. We have to clamp above the renal artery."

They carefully work to get clear access to the weakened aorta. Liem uses a sizing guide to select the right diameter polyester graft to match the woman's aorta. "Twenty-two by eleven, get a twenty-two by eleven," he tells the nurse. As they approach the critical part of the procedure, Liem barks out a series of orders for equipment he wants to have ready. The nurse scrambles to get everything set.

About an hour into the procedure, they clamp the aorta.

"Scissors, scissors! Gotta have them ready!" Liem says.

They remove the diseased aorta. "It's very close to the renal artery," Minjarez notes. They are working as fast as possible, quickly tossing instruments down before grabbing the next tool. Minjarez quickly sutures. Then Liem calls for the graft, scissors, and 3-0 sutures. He cuts the graft to the correct length. "Where do you want it?" Minjarez asks. "On the side," Liem says. But as she starts to put the graft in position, he interrupts. "The side! You are too anterior [toward the patient's front]."

"The liver is ischemic," Liem warns, referring to the fact that while they have the vessel clamped, vital organs are deprived of fresh blood. They keep a sharp eye on the clamp time. There is a blizzard of activity. Minjarez stitches as Liem supervises. "That's the right visualization. Very nice job," he tells her.

The OR phone rings. "Dr. Liem, the family is on the phone, is there any update?" the nurse calls out. "I can't talk right now!" Liem answers.

"We're operating!" Minjarez adds.

Liem tells the anesthesiologist that they plan to release the clamp in five minutes.

A few more stitches and the upper clamp comes off, blood again flows to vital organs, but now it passes through a protective sheath instead of an unstable aneurysm.

"Okay. Released. What was the time?" Liem asks.

"On at ten twelve, off at ten thirty-six," the nurse answers. The blood flow was interrupted for 24 minutes.

"That was the hardest part," Liem says. After another half hour of work, a lower clamp is also released, restoring blood flow to the left leg. The mood in the OR relaxes. Fifteen minutes later, blood is again flowing to the right leg.

Another family member calls the OR. "They need to have one representative," Liem tells the nurse. "She's doing okay. I'll come out and talk to them." Then to others in the OR he adds, "Don't call when we are operating on the aorta."

One of the first questions is whether the interruption in blood supply damaged the patient's kidneys. "I've got another ten of urine," the anesthesiologist announces.

"You got more urine?" Liem responds. It's a hopeful sign. He feels the patient's feet to check for blood flow. "Palpable blood pressure to the right," he says. Another good sign.

Everything appears to have gone well. After first meeting the family members in tense circumstances, explaining the uncertain situation and the risks ahead, it is looking like they will be able to deliver a more upbeat report after the surgery is done. Nevertheless, Minjarez is looking for potential trouble ahead.

"I'm going to use interrupted eights to close the wound," she says, referring to a type of stitch. "She's on steroids. She's elderly. It's a setup for wound failure. Maybe it's my chronic pessimism, but really, if we use an interrupted stitch then, when we have wound failure, it doesn't come all apart when we go in to repair it."

After three and a half hours of surgery, the patient is rolled back to the intensive care unit.

Minjarez catches up with the rest of the team as they do rounds on other patients. Although the procedure went far better than her worst-case predictions, she alerts them to serious risks ahead. She expects to see problems with healing because of the woman's age and prior medical treatment. The case has taken its toll.

"I must be a glutton for punishment," Minjarez says. "I really need a day to recover after a day like today, but I won't get it. I'll try to carve out some time for myself soon," she promises.

Additional Reading

Accreditation Council for Graduate Medical Education. "Common Program Require-ments: General Competencies." Chicago: ACGM, 2007. Available at: www.acgme.org/outcome/comp/GeneralCompetenciesStandards21307.pdf. Accessed August 2009.

Hutul, Olivia A.; Carpenter, Robert O.; Tarpley, John L.; Lomis, K. D. "Missed Oppor-tunities: A Descriptive Assessment of Teaching and Attitudes Regarding Communi-cation Skills in a Surgical Residency." *Current Surgery,* 63, no. 6 (2006): 401–409.

Orlander, Jay D.; Fincke, B. Graeme; Hermanns, David; Johnson, Gregory A. "Medi-cal Residents' First Clearly Remembered Experiences of Giving Bad News." Jour-nal of *General Internal Medicine,* 17, no. 11 (2002): 817–894. Available at: www3.interscience.wiley.com/journal/120132617/abstract. Accessed August 2009.

Rosenbaum, M. E.; Ferguson, K. J.; Lobas, J. G. "Teaching Medical Students and Residents Skills for Delivering Bad News: A Review of Strategies." *Academic Medicine,* 79, no. 2 (2004): 107–117. Available at: www.ncbi.nlm.nih.gov/pubmed/14744709. Accessed August 2009.

CHAPTER TWELVE

Amputation

In "My Favorite Mistake" (3 19), Cristina Yang amputates the foot of a man with diabetes. When she first confronts him with the fact that he has a life-threatening infection, the patient pleads with her to not take his foot, to find some other way, but there isn't one.

Similar scenarios are common on the vascular surgery service. Intern Loïc Fabricant recalls having to tell a man that he would probably lose both his feet. He says the man was in denial; he would appear to understand the plan and then later act as if he hadn't heard the devastating news. Fabricant says some patients cry openly when told they will lose a toe or a foot, while others try to hide their grief and fear.

"I have seen a lot of tears," Fabricant says. "Sometimes it's obvious. But there were a couple of ladies I had to give bad news to about losing toes or feet. They seemed to take it fine. Then I noticed that they are crying, but they are trying to tough it out."

As in the case on *Grey's Anatomy,* diabetes is frequently the reason limbs are amputated. Among the many problems the disease causes is damage to blood vessels. Then the compromised blood flow leads to tissue damage or interferes with wound healing. Disruption of normal blood flow within the muscle of the heart is one reason people with diabetes have higher rates of heart disease. Toes and feet, which are at the end of the line of the body's system of blood vessels, are also early victims of the effects of diabetes.

In the pre-op area, intern Ashley Stewart reviews a planned toe amputation with fourth-year resident Karen Zink.

"She was crying after you left this morning. She was upset," Stewart says. Zink asks for more details. "She's afraid of losing her toe. She's afraid she won't be able to walk."

"She'll be able to walk after physical therapy and with good shoes," Zink reassures her.

The fear and resistance of patients to losing a foot or even one toe are understandable. Who wouldn't despair, at least for a time, when faced with amputation? And yet considered in coldly rational terms, when calculating the health impact of a surgical procedure, the amputation of a toe is really no greater a loss than the removal of a spleen or a stretch of intestine. Yet the reactions of patients facing excision of an internal organ are often muted by comparison.

The difference really isn't surprising. Body image powerfully affects our sense of ourselves. Even if we know in our heads that a surgery has rearranged our internal plumbing, that awareness is nothing compared to the jolt of a missing toe or finger or foot. And so, in addition to learning the mechanics of a procedure, Stewart experiences the emotional dimensions of the task before her.

Toe amputations are intern territory; the kind of procedure that helps them build initial experience. Before going to the OR, Zink talks Stewart through the major steps: an incision going all the way around the toe, cutting all the way to and then through the bone, and trimming the bone back enough so that the skin can be closed over the wound.

In the OR, Stewart works with the nurses and anesthesiologist to prepare the patient before the attending surgeon arrives. Although she is playing a key role in this procedure, she says that in general the vascular surgery service doesn't offer interns much time in the OR. The patients, who have diabetes, peripheral vascular disease, or other problems related to blood flow, are so ill and usually have so many different problems that interns are constantly busy responding to pages about urgent issues.

"Thursdays and Fridays are crazy," Stewart says. "All the senior residents and attendings are in the OR, so the intern is running around trying to manage cases and communicate with the people in the OR. It gets hairy. We get pages like: 'The patient's hand is blue.' It will fall off if we don't deal with it soon, there's only a limited amount of time to respond."

In addition to dealing with the patients who are in the hospital for vascular surgery, the team also gets called in to deal with blood vessel issues in the patients on other services. "Some weeks I can't believe the workload," Stewart says.

Stewart double-checks that the patient has received antibiotics. As the nurses numb the patient's foot and prepare the sterile drapes, they chat with Stewart about their favorite TV shows and books. The scrub nurse is a fan of the Inspector Lynley mystery series on *Masterpiece Theater*. Stewart says she's read many of the books the series is based on. "I'm trying to read them all in order," she says. "But I haven't read any in a while." Intern year and leisure reading don't go together.

After she scrubs in, Stewart leads the OR team through the pause to confirm the correct patient is getting the correct procedure. "We are doing a left great toe amputation," she says.

"*Right* toe!" the team calls out.

"Right great toe," she confirms.

The correct toe is the one that was exposed and prepared, but the slip of the tongue is a small reminder that people make mistakes, and that's why safety nets and crosschecks are critical in the OR.

Dr. Gregory Moneta, the chief of the vascular service, is the attending surgeon for this procedure, but today he is also teaching and guiding, so rather than jumping right into the procedure, he begins with a question.

"How do you want to do it?" he asks Stewart.

"An incision here," she replies. With a marking pen she traces a line around the toe.

"If you do it there, you won't have enough skin to close," Moneta notes. He takes the pen and draws a new line. "Do you have a fifteen knife?" he asks the scrub nurse. She hands Stewart the scalpel. "Use the knife cutting toward you," he advises. "You'll have better control."

Stewart cuts along the line that Moneta drew, prying skin and tissue away to expose bone.

She slips. A small snap is heard. "Oooh," she says.

"Got an 'Oooh,'" Moneta responds. "It's okay at this point." There's no harm done.

The operation proceeds. Stewart trades her scalpel for a set of large clippers. She squeezes hard and snips off the diseased toe as if she were pruning a branch. Now the task is to clean the wound and make sure there is nothing left that could cause a pressure point and possible further tissue damage. Taking up the knife again, Stewart works as Moneta supervises. "Keep your fingers away from the sharp stuff." "There's a little dog ear," he says, as they check the skin flap that will be closed over the wound. He helps snip out rough spots. Stewart cauterizes small bleeds. Then as Moneta points the way, Stewart begins to close the wound. Slowly, a bit uncertainly at first, she inserts the needle into the under layer of the skin. Moneta demonstrates the first outer layer suture. Then as Stewart makes the next suture, he says, "Not too tight." And offers a rhyming reminder: "Close, don't necrose."

Stewart asks about which style of knot to use. "Is it okay to instrument-tie? It wasn't where I came from."

Moneta doesn't answer her question right away. "Some attendings put a question limit on residents," he says. "You need to learn to make decisions on your own. If you always ask, then you won't have to decide. And anyway, didn't I just do it?" he says, pointing out that he had used the instrument-tie technique. "Yes, but aren't the rules different for you than for me?" she tosses back. "Of course," he admits. "I had a resident that I put on a question limit. 'You are on a question limit,' I told him. He said, 'What?' 'That's one.'"

Stewart continues suturing the skin together. "That's much more efficient. You actually look like you know what you are doing," Moneta says. The suturing completed, Stewart squeezes and checks the wound. It's taken less than an hour and the lesson included more than just the proper techniques of cutting and suturing but also minimizing errors, working as a team, making decisions, and confronting the jarring loss of a toe damaged by diabetes.

Of course, anyone facing amputation wishes it didn't have to happen. Surgery is the last resort. Each year in the United States, about 70,000 people lose a toe or foot or leg to diabetes. Diabetes damages blood vessels and without healthy blood flow, tissue weakens and begins to die. Sores that won't heal can harbor infections.

In recent years the number of people with diabetes has grown dramatically. Most of the growth in new cases is linked to obesity. So ultimately, reducing the number of amputations may depend on how the nation grapples with issues of nutrition and physical activity.

But even after someone has developed diabetes, whether due to obesity or other causes, the risk of losing a limb can be reduced. For example, the Madigan Army Medical Center in Tacoma, Washington, created a Limb Preservation Service. Team members used a combination of education (for both patients and staff), aggressive management of diabetes, and alert care for skin ulcers and other complications. The Limb Preservation Service reported that over a four-year period, even though the number of cases of diabetes reported grew by almost 50 percent, the number of lower-extremity amputations declined dramatically from 33 in 1999 to just 9 in 2003.

Additional Reading

Driver, Vickie R.; Madsen, Jeff; Goodman, Russell A. "Reducing Amputation Rates in Patients with Diabetes at a Military Medical Center." *Diabetes Care,* 28 (2005): 248–253. Available at: http://care.diabetesjournals.org/cgi/content/full/28/2/248. Accessed August 2009.

CHAPTER THIRTEEN

Communication

Communicating with patients is about much more than just delivering bad news. Most of the time, it's about little things, updates on lab results, scheduling procedures, planning to go home. But to patients in a hospital, every little detail carries weight.

Intern Emily Bubbers, M.D., says she has seen how the machinery of health care can charge ahead, leaving patients to wonder what's going on around them.

"I've learned that we forget to tell patients what we're actually doing to them in the hospital. We make plans, and we go ahead and use them, and we don't tell them. And then two days later, you walk in and you start explaining something to them, and they go, 'Oh! That's nice that you told me.'"

A lack of communication can breed fear and anger.

In "Life During Wartime" (5-06) a girl with a tumor that other surgeons had said was inoperable is undergoing an extreme procedure. The girl's father is waiting for word. He corners Chief Webber.

"I just needed an update," the father says. But Chief Webber doesn't want to be interrupted.

"It's not important that you get an update right now, sir. What's important is: the best doctors in this hospital are focused on your daughter. Calls don't help us focus. Interruptions don't help us focus," the chief declares.

"I'm sorry, I know we have been underfoot sometimes, but we have been to a lot of hospitals, and hospitals are not easy places to get information. In fact, a lot of times it's impossible to even get a doctor to talk to you or to get the doctors to talk to each other. And I don't know if it's neglect, or their egos getting in the way, and I don't care. We're just trying to take care of our little girl. She's ten. She's scared. And she's sick. We are doing whatever we can."

The father's plea seems to jolt Chief Webber into remembering that his primary duty is to provide care to patients and that includes keeping parents informed about how their little girl is doing.

"Don't ever stop taking care of her like that," the chief says softly.

Not every question involves life or death. Intern Marcus Kret, M.D., says sometimes patients request the darndest things.

"A patient brought me a form from the DMV [department of motor vehicles]," Kret recalls. "I had no clue what to do with it. She started talking about how her husband needed a form signed. I told her that her condition didn't have anything to do with her driving, but she kept asking me about the DMV form."

Even when the questions directly relate to surgical care or recovery, residents often enter the situation with little or no background. When hit with questions they don't have answers for, they have to learn how to say more than "I don't know," without saying more than they know.

Kret gets called to the room of a patient. The patient is eager to begin eating, but before he can try taking that step toward recovery, a speech therapist has to evaluate his ability to swallow. But the therapist hasn't come by today, and so family members pepper Kret with questions about how long they will have to wait. It's clear they are annoyed.

"I'm not sure why the therapist has not been by to see him," is all Kret can offer as a response. "I can call."

"It's pretty important, right?" asks the patient's daughter.

"Yes, but it'll take time for him to make progress." Kret moves the conversation around to something he does know about: the man's general condition. "Let's run through the time course. I'll start up top. Is there still some confusion?" Kret asks them.

"Yes."

"Any pain?"

"No."

"How about his heart and lungs? Is he breathing well on low oh-two?" Kret asks, referring to the supplemental oxygen the patient is breathing. Because the patient is still a bit foggy and has some difficulty speaking, his daughter is responding to the questions. Kret begins to talk directly to her, rather than to the patient. She points over to her father to remind Kret to keep talking to him. He quickly looks back to the patient. It's natural to talk to the person responding to your questions, but Kret knows he needs to keep the patient front and center.

"The biggest obstacle to going home right now is feeding," Kret concludes. He doesn't have to remind the family that the missing speech therapist is part of that obstacle. He leaves the room to get some answers. Paging the therapist doesn't work. All he gets is a message that the pager he called is "unavailable." Kret is beginning to share the family's annoyance. He also doesn't want to see the man's recovery delayed by a day because of a missed evaluation. He finally reaches a live person in the speech therapy department. That person doesn't know what happened, but promises to call back.

Shortly the call comes back. It turns out the regular therapist is out of the hospital today and for some reason the original substitute didn't make it to this patient. But another therapist has been notified and, even though it's late, promises to come by today. Kret gets to deliver the good news to the family.

This time things work out well. A little over an hour later, Kret gets the report from the speech therapist. He checks in with the patient and family during early evening rounds. "The speech therapist says it's okay to start eating food," he tells them. "It's good news. We'll keep the feeding tube in for the time being to make sure you are getting enough nutrition; but it's progress."

"We try to model for the residents how surgeons should communicate with patients," says Brett Sheppard. "We take the time to sit with the patient, even if it seems like it's using up a lot of time. Good communication can prevent errors; and twenty-five percent of lawsuits are due to communication errors. But we do need a communication curriculum."

John Hunter agrees that residency programs don't do a good job of systematically teaching young doctors how to talk to patients and families. The residents are supposed to soak up the examples of their seniors. Gradually they take on more responsibility, perhaps go to give an update to waiting family members when the attending is absorbed in managing a crisis in the OR. The general goals of communicating with patients and families seem obvious, but the specific skills and methods of teaching them have not been scrutinized and standardized to the extent that other things surgeons need to learn have been.

One lesson residents will pick up from seeing senior surgeons engage with patients and families is that communication doesn't always mean telling them every detail.

Hunter goes into the surgery waiting area to meet with the family of a patient he just finished operating on. The report is good. "It went fine," Hunter says. Not perfectly, however. He explains that some of the sutures didn't do the job at first, but that problem was fixed. "We got a good result," Hunter wraps up.

But if the family members had been in the OR, they would have seen also that Hunter considered halting the procedure at one point due to concern about unusual heart rhythm readings. In that first debriefing immediately after the surgery, he didn't point out that in the middle of the day the procedure was put on pause. Another surgeon who handled a special part of the operation was busy with another case and couldn't get away when he was needed in Hunter's OR. For about two hours the patient was on the table and under anesthesia, unaware of the organizational bottleneck that was holding up the procedure.

Such delays are not out of the ordinary and, as Hunter told the family, the end result was good. His initial report to the family was not a stitch-by-stitch recital of the day—just the big picture.

Residents also learn that when it comes to communication, just as with surgery, each patient is unique.

"I've seen both attendings and senior residents take different tacks when laying out the options for treatment," says intern Nick Tadros. "Some patients really like it and want to know all the details. Some patients don't seem to care. And some think that when you give them options, it means you don't know what you're doing."

WHILE SURGEONS QUICKLY SENSE THAT DIFFERENT PATIENTS WANT TO hear things in somewhat different ways, their understanding of patient communications lags behind the sophisticated perspective of medical marketing experts.

"I would say, unfortunately, I think they are at opposite extremes," marketing consultant Carol M. Morgan says of physicians and marketers. Morgan has advised pharmaceutical company clients and others about how to categorize patients in various segments, in order to better craft effective marketing tactics. "Pharmaceutical companies are investing millions of dollars in this kind of research, studying their advertising to measure their effectiveness, and then spending money on their direct-to-consumer advertising versus at the other end, and while there is increasing emphasis on the doctor communicating with patients, it's still not at the level of the doctor quickly understanding what segment the patient is in."

For example, Morgan and her business partner, Doran J. Levy, Ph.D., analyzed the health and healthcare perceptions of more than 20,000 consumers, and then distinguished several broad categories of attitudes and behaviors. They gave labels to varieties of medical consumers such as "Proactives," "Faithful Patients," "Trusting Believers," and "Informed Avoiders." Morgan says that if you show a TV drug ad to a couple of people from different segments, even if they have similar health situations, they are likely to respond quite differently.

"One, the Faithful Patient, will say, 'Gee, that sounds really interesting. I'll go talk to Dr. Smith. Maybe he'll get me on this drug and that will solve my problems,'" Morgan says. "And the other person [the Informed Avoider] will say, 'Another disgusting ad! This isn't for me.' "

PART OF THE COMMUNICATION CHALLENGE IS THAT PATIENTS AND DOCTORS are in very different worlds. For a patient, surgery is a traumatic and rare event. For a surgeon, it's part of a regular workday.

"We do want to recognize the gap in where we're coming from," Tadros says. "For the patient it's a once-in-a-lifetime event, but for us it's just another surgery. Not that we aren't taking it seriously, but we couldn't handle being as emotionally involved as they are."

And yet, Tadros says, it is an honor and privilege to be a patient's doctor.

"A surgeon gets to be part of one of the biggest events of their lives, like a minister performing a wedding gets to be part of a big event, even though he may do a lot of them.

"When you step back and think about what we do, it's weird and scary and big. Sometimes we forget how different it is from what most people do. I'll be talking to a friend about what I did and he'll go, 'What! You did what?!'"

IN MEDICAL EDUCATION, FORMAL INSTRUCTION IN PATIENT COMMUNICATION has lagged behind the more obvious topics of anatomy, biochemistry, surgical skills, and so on. Part of the reason may be the belief that since everyone communicates every day, young doctors already know how to do it. But the truth is that many people, surgeons included, fumble at communicating; and they may not even realize when patients have misunderstood or misinterpreted what they were told.

Training can help. One review concluded that medical students who are specifically taught how to talk with patients do a better job of it. The researchers found that not only did students get better with practice in real clinical situations, they also performed better when they had classes in communication before ever getting to the clinic. Examples of this sort of preclinical training include role-playing with people who are hired to act like patients. Sometimes the actors give the medical students incomplete information or find ways to misinterpret what the students say, in order to demonstrate the kinds of things that can go awry when trying to communicate with real patients. The most effective teaching methods include recording student-patient interviews, critiquing the student's performance, and then having students discuss the challenges and techniques with each other.

A nurse asks intern Loïc Fabricant to go talk with a patient and his family. They want to know when the patient can go home. It's probably the most common question that patients recovering from surgery have. But Fabricant knows only the barest facts about this man and his recovery. That's because the man is not one of Fabricant's regular patients; he is on another service that Fabricant is "cross-covering." *Cross-coverage* means that Fabricant is basically pinch hitting for other doctors. So before going to the patient's room, he pages a senior resident. "I just want to get my story straight before I talk to them," Fabricant says. "I don't want to go in to see the family and just say, 'I don't know.'"

The patient hasn't been drinking enough water. He can't go home as long as he still depends on IV fluids. But as Fabricant talks with the patient and his family, there seems to be something else going on. The conversation goes around and around, repeating the same point about hydration and other things, as Fabricant probes to find out what's really going on with the family and the patient. From a strictly medical standpoint an argument could be made either way, so the personal wishes of the patient and family about whether to discharge him that day or the next are the deciding factor.

The patient wants to go home right away. And at first it seems like the family agrees with trying to go home later that day. But Fabricant senses that perhaps they are just agreeing with his first suggestion; that there's something else they aren't telling him yet. So he asks several times, in different ways, if they want to leave today. Eventually, he begins to sense that the patient's wife would rather have him stay one more night. It turns out that they live hours away and so if they left today, they'd have to somehow manage him overnight in their motel room. They would much rather wait until morning. But it took a while before they would say anything that might seem to be contradicting the authority of the doctor. A clumsy communicator could have missed the subtle clues entirely.

Despite the family's feelings, the patient wants out as soon as possible. Fabricant does need to know that he will drink enough fluids to stay hydrated without an IV. That point becomes the basis of a negotiated arrangement. Fabricant plunks a large bottle of water in front of the patient. "Here," he says. "Drink this within an hour and I'll take the IV out."

Not only does this deal help answer the question about hydration; it lets the family have another hour to think things over. Perhaps by the time Fabricant returns, they'll all be in agreement about when to leave. As with so many situations residents confront, the medical questions are often far simpler than the social dynamics.

MUCH OF THE ROUTINE COMMUNICATION WITH PATIENTS COMES WHEN the residents do rounds on the hospital floor. During rounds, one of the junior residents will typically recite the background of and treatment plan for each patient. More senior residents and attendings then pepper him or her with questions. Some of the questions are meant to learn more details about the patient, lab reports, wound healing, and so on, but much of the exchange is intended to test the junior residents' grasp of key concepts and the preferred options for tests and treatments.

"Chuck Eaton. 54. Has stage 3B non-small-cell lung cancer with possible invasion of the pleura. And a history of COPD. He's had extensive chemo-radiotherapy with minimal regression of the tumor. He's been admitted for radical and block re-section," says Meredith Grey, as she presents the basic facts about a patient in "Yesterday" (2-18).

On *Grey's Anatomy* this recitation of facts and interrogation of residents tends to take place in the patient's room.

"This is Dr. Burke's patient, Kalpana Vera," Izzie Stevens reads from the patient's chart in "Deny, Deny, Deny" (2-04). "She presents with multiple syncopal episodes and ventricular arrhythmias."

"So you've been passing out?" Bailey asks the patient.

"Yeah. And having palpitations," the woman replies.

Stevens continues presenting the case. "Past medical history of rheumatic heart disease with mitral valve stenosis."

"They had to ship me from Zambia to the States for three months of treatment when I was eight. Rheumatic fever almost killed me," the patient explains.

"Dr. Stevens. What are the primary causes of ventricular arrhythmias?" Bailey asks. But Cristina Yang appears at the door and jumps to answer first.

"Valvular disease, mitral valve prolapse, stimulants, drugs, and metabolic abnormalities."

But at OHSU surgery residents and attendings don't just spill out everything in front of patients. They usually review the cases first, in a workroom or in the hall, so they have thoroughly talked things over before bringing the patient into the conversation.

On a summer afternoon, the team gathers outside the room of a patient who had kidney surgery almost three weeks earlier but then took a turn for the worse. "We don't know what's wrong," admits one of the residents. "He was readmitted. He just didn't look well when he came in for his clinic visit."

"There has to be an infection somewhere," says the senior resident. "Enterococcus, Staphylococcus, non-Candida fungus."

"It's suspicious," the attending says.

"His white blood count was twenty, now it's twelve. I'm kind of confused," the senior resident admits.

"We also got a hepatic consult," adds the intern in the group.

By first reviewing the case out of the earshot of the patient, the surgeons can speculate, challenge each other, and freely admit confusion or uncertainty without unduly frightening the patient. They can cover the facts quickly, without worrying about explaining all the jargon and abbreviations. Then when they step into the patient's room, the attending surgeon or senior resident is prepared to give the patient the summary of the situation and plan for the next steps of testing or treatment.

However, surveys and other studies indicate that patients prefer that doctors discuss their cases at the bedside. They say that way they can get a better sense of what's going on with their care. And when the team does all of the case discussions in the patient's room, rather than first spending several minutes out in the hall, patients get a sense that the doctors are spending more time on their cases.

In one study, researchers did in-depth interviews with patients, who repeatedly said that they want physicians who care about them. Technical competence is necessary, but not enough. The researchers said patients also complained about having teams of doctors and others come into their rooms without taking time to introduce each person. On the positive side, patients usually want to support teaching efforts, so they tend to report a more positive view of their doctors when the teaching aspects of rounding are clearly pointed out to them during the team visits.

FABRICANT GETS A PAGE. HE PHONES THE NURSE, WHO TELLS HIM THAT ONE of the patients is angry. The patient wants to speak to somebody about why he's here and what they are doing with him.

"I have no idea," Fabricant admits. It's another example of Fabricant being called in because of cross-coverage duties to deal with the immediate needs of a patient he doesn't normally care for. The patient is in a halo, a device to keep his head locked in place, in order to protect a damaged spine. Fabricant doesn't know if the patient's regular doctors were planning to discharge him with the halo on or keep him in the hospital until it is no longer needed; nevertheless, he'll have to try to respond to the patient's urgent questions. "So he's pretty stressed?" he asks the nurse. "Okay, I'll come see him."

He hangs up the phone. "Oh, God, I have no idea what exactly I'm going to tell him."

Later in the day, Fabricant reports, "The angry patient in the halo called me Darth Vader."

You can't win them all.

COMMUNICATION GOES BOTH WAYS. IT'S NOT JUST A MATTER OF HOW OR what surgeons say to patients. Patients are individuals with attitudes, beliefs, and personalities that need to be taken into account. Extreme examples include patients who have not only physical problems but also severe mental health issues.

As second-year resident Katrine Lofberg, M.D., makes rounds with the wound care team, she helps change the bandages on a patient with a very large abdominal wound. She is there to learn a sophisticated technique for encouraging the healing of extensive wounds using a vacuum-sealed dressing system. The wound is challenging. Once the old dressing is removed, much of the patient's abdomen gapes open. The situation would be overwhelmingly stressful for anyone, but this man has an additional burden: paranoia that threatens to send him into a panic if he senses that things aren't going well.

As Lofberg works on cleaning his wound, she keeps encouraging the man, telling him how good things look. Although Lofberg tends to be upbeat around all her patients, she makes an extra effort to emphasize the positive with this patient, recognizing that he is frightened and fragile.

This patient is not the only one on this floor today who needs careful handling.

It's only the second day for intern Jason Jundt, M.D., on this service. He goes to the bedside of a woman who needs her dressing changed. He removes the gauze stretched across her midsection to reveal a hole in her skin bigger than his hand. He delicately lifts a flap of skin and deeper tissue around the edges of the hole in order to check for signs of infection. The patient is receiving pain medication, but she is alert and talks with Jundt almost as if everything were normal, even as he pokes around the wound that looks almost like something created by a Hollywood special-effects unit.

With the deep and broad wound exposed, the woman becomes anxious. "Look at the TV, not at the wound," Jundt advises her. "What show is this? I don't get MTV at home," he says, trying to distract the patient to head off her growing distress.

Lofberg comes in to help Jundt. She's been on this service longer and has had a chance to get to know this patient. "I like it when you are here," the patient tells Lofberg. "He wasn't very gentle." The woman nods toward Jundt. "He acts like he's in the military." He is tall, athletic, and clean-shaven with close-cropped hair. Although he may be less experienced than Lofberg, it seems that the real issue here is the patient's personal preference. She just feels a stronger rapport with Lofberg.

And so the management of this dressing change becomes more than just a matter of technical skill, it also involves communication style and other personal attributes.

IN ONE OF THE EARLY EPISODES OF *GREY'S ANATOMY,* IZZIE STEVENS RUNS into a patient who doesn't want her to care for him.

"I just need to do a brief exam," Stevens says when she comes into a patient's room in "No Man's Land" (1-04). "If you could sit up for one moment. Thanks. This might be a little bit cold, so just take a deep breath. If you could just take a deep breath," Stevens repeats as the man balks.

"You're not a doctor," he says.

"I'm Dr. Stevens, but you can call me Izzie. I'll be helping Dr. Bailey with your biopsy this morning."

"No, I don't think so, no."

"Mr. Humphrey, this will just take a moment."

He continues to resist her.

"No, get me Dr. Bailey or Dr. Victor."

"I just need to do a brief—" The patient cuts her off.

"You don't need to do anything," he says. "Is this you?" The man opens up a magazine to a photo of Stevens modeling underwear. She had worked as a model to help pay for medical school. To this patient, the image in the magazine ad is incompatible with his idea of a competent surgeon.

"Is this you? It is, isn't it? You know, get out of my room!"

In the end, Stevens retreats.

THE WOMAN ASKS FOR MORE PAIN MEDICATION. SHE'S ALREADY RECEIVED A substantial dose, but Lofberg agrees to let her have more. Her distress at seeing the wound and feeling the doctors work on it may be magnifying her sensation of pain.

Lofberg engages her in a conversation about her family. Meanwhile Jundt continues to clean and prepare the wound for a fresh dressing. The woman frets that the wound will disrupt her life. "You won't be limited long term," Lofberg reassures her. "What are your plans for the future?"

Then it's time to clean underneath the flap of skin and tissue. It's the most painful part of the dressing change.

"Are you ready for wound cleaning?" Lofberg asks.

"No," the woman says, her voice tinged with fear of the pain she knows is coming.

"Do yoga breaths," Lofberg tells her.

"Owwww!" she yelps as Jundt lifts the skin around her wound. She complains about how much a cleaning solution stings and pleads with Lofberg to let her skip it this time.

"Here are the options: we can use the stinging solution and you can heal faster or we can use plain saline and it'll take longer."

"Can we compromise, and just use the stinging stuff every other day?"

Lofberg relents. "Okay, we'll do just normal saline today. Then I'll get a definitive answer from the wound care team tomorrow."

The woman grips Lofberg's hand as Jundt pushes fresh gauze into her wound.

"Owwww!"

"I'm sorry, I'm sorry." Lofberg tries to comfort her. "Okay, that's beautiful, that's perfect."

"It's pretty good," the woman says. Now that the most painful part of the process is done, the woman is able to relax a bit. She helps them put the fresh bandage over, even giving them tips she's picked up during her long recovery, such as putting tape on the edges of the bandages to keep the stuffing from coming out, and putting small squares of gauze under the straps used to hold down the bandage, so that they don't irritate sensitive skin.

"You're done!" Lofberg announces. The patient gives a big smile in return. "Thanks, everybody," she says.

SURGERY RESIDENTS ALSO WORK WITH PATIENTS DURING CLINIC VISITS TO follow up on their recoveries from operations. It's a less intense atmosphere than in the hospital, but here, too, there is more to learn than merely the physical aspects of healing.

"In the clinic you're dealing with people after surgery and new patients and patients with chronic issues," explains intern Brian Caldwell, M.D. "They don't need the same level of attention as patients in the hospital, but there's always a clinic time crunch."

Indeed, on this clinic day the vascular surgery team is again working to dig out from under a backlog of clinic patients. A nurse comes in to the physicians workroom and asks, "Will someone see this patient?" She gestures to the schedule. "She's been waiting two and a half hours." But one of the residents just shrugs. He's not in charge, and everyone there is trying to get through the cases as fast as they can.

While doing what he can to help see the patients, Caldwell is also trying to soak up everything he can from watching how the attendings work the cases. "I listen to what the attendings say and listen to what's important to them, see how they ask questions. When I see something good, I lock that away. You learn the most from the challenging patients. I think I'm pretty good with people, but there are some I have trouble with. So I watch attendings who can just get right through everything to get to the real issue. I listen for the phrases they use to get patients to quickly give them the information they need."

Caldwell learned a key lesson from a recent experience in which he was not the doctor. He was the patient. He got a new perspective on a common medicine that causes a bit of pain when it is injected into patients. "I used to just order it for patients without thinking," Caldwell admits. "Now I think, 'Ouch, that hurts.' " His treatment also included rules on what he should eat. "I always wondered about patients who didn't eat properly, but it's different when it happens to me." Now he has a better appreciation of the situations some patients find themselves in and perhaps he may be able to more easily establish a rapport with the patients he sees in rapid succession in the clinic.

This afternoon also delivers another lesson that's not surgical, but still valuable. Caldwell goes to see a man with blood flow problems in his legs. He inspects ugly red sores on the man's legs. He checks the pulse in his feet. He asks about diabetes or other things that can affect how well the blood vessels do their job. In this case the patient's current problems appear to be related to an injury that is not healing properly.

With the information from that initial interview in hand, Caldwell returns to the workroom to consult with an attending. And that's where he learns the lesson. As he is waiting patiently for one of the surgeons to finish writing a note, a senior resident swoops in and grabs the attention of the attending.

"I was waiting to let him gather his thoughts," Caldwell says. But he was outmaneuvered and so has to wait even longer. When the surgeon returns to the workroom, Caldwell doesn't hesitate this time to jump in before someone else can steal him away again.

Follow-up clinic visits are vital to managing the recoveries of surgery patients, but they also remind many residents why they chose surgery over medicine. Caldwell admits that an afternoon in the clinic makes him want to run back to the OR. "In medicine, you are in the clinic all the time," he says. "In surgery, you get to see and do things that you never do anywhere else."

GOOD COMMUNICATION REQUIRES DEVELOPING SOME SORT OF RAPPORT with patients. But surgeons try to avoid getting too close. Certainly, they are wise to steer clear of the disastrous entanglements that are so common on *Grey's Anatomy,* as when Alex Karev got involved with the amnesiac patient he named Ava or, even more catastrophic, the obsessed relationship Izzie Stevens had with Denny Duquette.

In "Six Days: Part 1" (3-11), George O'Malley is making rounds. The patient in the room is his father.

"Good morning," Chief Webber says to O'Malley's father. Then he turns to the interns. "Who's presenting?"

"George!!" they cry.

"Harold O'Malley, sixty-three. Status: post-aortic valve replacement. Morning chest X-rays showed no atelectasis after aggressive CPT for the last two days. Scheduled for a transhiatal esophagectomy tomorrow at nine."

In the real world, Nick Tadros says that scene wouldn't happen. "My father said that if he ever needed surgery, he would want me to do it. [But] there's no way I'd ever operate on a family member," he says. "It wouldn't be possible to be objective and focus on the job."

David Cho, M.D., is making rounds on the transplant floor. As the team starts to go into a patient's room, a child in the room looks up and points as though he recognizes Cho. Cho suddenly ducks back out in the hall.

"It may be a friend of the family," Cho explains. "I may have been at his wedding.

"I don't want a personal relationship to cloud my judgment. I haven't had an issue, but the general practice is to steer clear of treating acquaintances. If the relationship is too close, you may hand off the case to someone else."

A TIP ABOUT DISCHARGING PATIENTS: DON'T GIVE THEM YOUR PERSONAL phone number.

David Cho takes a call. It's from a recently discharged patient. Cho answers the questions politely. This patient calls a lot. "He thinks I'm his personal physician," Cho says.

"When you give instructions to the patient, give them phone numbers to call up during the day and in the middle of the night," third-year resident Terah Isaacson tells a group of interns. "But be sure to tell them to ask for the service, not you. They often don't understand rotations and will call you, instead of the person who replaced you on the service."

"Never call a patient from home, they'll get your number on caller ID," warns vascular surgery fellow Aaron Partsafas. "Always call the hospital switchboard and get transferred. I called from home once and got seventeen calls from the patient."

TOO MUCH DISTANCE BETWEEN DOCTOR AND PATIENT CAN ALSO BE A problem. While the medical jargon surgeons throw around is practically a foreign language to most patients, communicating well with patients is even more challenging when they actually speak an entirely different language.

"Okay Mrs. Lu, I'm Dr. Stevens," Izzie Stevens tells a patient in the Emergency Department in "The First Cut Is the Deepest" (1-02). The woman appears to be Asian. She has a deep cut on her arm. "I'm gonna sew up your wound. And you're gonna need about six stitches. Are you allergic to any medication?"

The patient answers in Chinese.

"Oh I'm sorry, I don't, I don't um," Stevens says, flustered. "Do you speak English?"

The woman responds in Chinese.

"Uh, I'll find, uh. Does anybody here speak Chinese?" Stevens calls out. Everyone in the room just stares at her.

A bit later in the episode, Stevens asks Cristina Yang to interpret for her patient, apparently without realizing that not only is Yang of Korean, not Chinese, ancestry, but she was born and raised in Beverly Hills.

ONE OF THE PATIENTS BEING MANAGED BY INTERN JASON JUNDT IS HEALTHY enough to go home. But making the arrangements is a bit more difficult than usual, because the man doesn't speak English. Each time Jundt wants to discuss something with the patient, he calls the man's son. He has heard that interpreters are available by phone, but he hasn't tried using that system.

Jundt telephones from the nurses station. "He should be ready to go within the hour," Jundt tells the man's son. Out of the corner of his eye, he sees a nurse raise her eyebrows . . . as if to say "Oh, really?" Jundt realizes that maybe he underestimated the work that needs to be done to discharge the man from the hospital, so he quickly revises what he's telling the son. "Don't worry about rushing over. Take your time getting here." The nurse nods in agreement.

When the patient's son arrives, Jundt meets him in the man's room. He explains the situation, including what follow-up care will be needed, the plan for scheduling clinic visits, and so on. The patient just watches, waiting for his son to translate. Even though the son speaks English, the communication seems a bit strained, as if he and Jundt weren't quite on the same wavelength. The son complains that the discharge day kept changing. He doesn't understand why it took so long.

The son is also worried he won't know what to do to provide proper care for his father at home. Jundt assures him that he will get complete written instructions and will have a phone number to call if he has questions. Then Jundt mentions that the patient might have a few symptoms related to the placement of a tube, because the procedure can sometimes cause a minor injury. That gets the son's attention. He wants to know more details about this possible injury. It's clear that the son thinks it sounds more serious than Jundt intended.

AN INTRODUCTION TO MEDICAL TRANSLATION AND INTERPRETER SERVICES is part of the orientation given to all new residents at OHSU. The new doctors are told that they should not rely on family members to interpret, unless the situation is urgent or the matter is a simple one. Family members are not trained medical interpreters and may unintentionally twist the message. Also, the patient may not want to discuss his or her medical condition in front of relatives.

Federal government rules state that institutions that accept federal funds must provide "meaningful access" to health benefits. For patients who don't speak English, meaningful access includes having conversations with doctors or other providers interpreted to make sure both sides understand each other. These services must be provided at no additional cost to the patient.

Spanish speaking interpreters are available on the OHSU campus 17 hours a day. But 80 percent of the translation is done by telephone; because it's much cheaper and quicker than locating and dispatching an interpreter to the bedside or clinic. On this campus, there are five main languages other than English spoken by patients. In addition to Spanish, the most common languages here are Vietnamese, Russian, both the Mandarin and Cantonese dialects of Chinese, and Serbo-Croatian or Bosnian. But the health care providers here encounter 10 times that many languages. Interpreters were needed for 57 different languages in just one year.

Despite the availability of these services, while waiting for an interpreter, staff in the hospital often try to muddle through. In the intensive care unit on a winter's night, doctors and nurses ask each other about the Spanish words they needed to tell a patient to wiggle his fingers and toes.

He seems to be in pain, and they ask, "Dolor?" gesturing to try to get him to indicate where it hurts. Then as they get things figured out they break out in a rendition of "Feliz Navidad."

It's no wonder that multilingual doctors, nurses, and others are in heavy demand.

The challenge is more than just translating words. Personal and cultural styles of communication can skew an exchange between surgeon and patient. Using a bilingual dictionary or an online translator would be not only cumbersome but would probably fail to convey important nuances of meaning. That's why the professionals who step in to these situations are often called interpreters, instead of translators. The job is to get the meaning and intent across, as well as the bare medical facts.

"I was treating a Hmong woman," Tadros recalls. "She kept looking to her husband to answer the questions. Even when I asked her whether she was in pain, she looked at her husband." The issue was not the words; it involved the distinct social histories and expectations of surgeon and patient.

Research into how well residents are trained in providing cross-cultural care indicates there is still a lot of work to do. As one national survey found, almost all residents said it is important to address cultural issues when providing care and the overwhelming majority said they believed they have a general sense of how to provide care to diverse groups of patients. However, up to half of the residents reported they received little or no specific instruction in dealing with cultural challenges. And four out of five surgery residents told the researchers that they had received little or no evaluation of their skills at providing cross-cultural care. The researchers concluded that there is a need for significant improvement in how residents are taught to communicate with different types of patients.

Additional Reading

California Primary Care Association. *Providing Health Care to Limited English Proficient (LEP) Patients: A Manual of Promising Practices.* Sacramento: California Primary Care Association 2001. Available at: www.cpca.org/resources/research/pdf/PPGuide.pdf. Accessed August 2009.

Fletcher, K. E.; Furney, S. L.; Stern, D. T. "Patients Speak: What's Really Important About Bedside Interactions with Physician Teams." *Teaching and Learning in Medicine,* 19, no. 2 (2007): 120–127. Available at: www.ncbi.nlm.nih.gov/pubmed/17564539. Accessed August 2009.

Morgan, Carol M.; Levy, Doron J.. *Marketing to the Mindset of Boomers and Their Elders: Using Psychographics and More to Identify and Reach Your Best Targets.* St. Paul, Minn.: Attitudebase, 2002.

Morgan, Carol; Levy, Doron. "To Their Health: Rx Companies Are Trying to Figure Out the Best Method for Reaching Aging Boomers." *Brandweek,* January 19, 1998. Available at: http://findarticles.com/p/articles/mi_m0BDW/is_n3_v39/ai_20165080. Accessed August 2009.

Smith, S; Hanson, J. L.; Tewksbury, L. R.; Christy, C.; Talib, N. J.; Narris, M. A.; Beck, G. L.; Wolf, F. M. "Teaching Patient Communication Skills to Medical Students." *Evaluation and the Health Professions,* 30, no. 1 (2007): 3–21. Available at: www.ncbi.nlm.nih.gov/pubmed/17293605. Accessed August 2009.

Yedidia, Michael J.; Gillespie, Colleen C.; Kachur, Elizabeth; Schwartz, Mark D.; Ockene, Judith; Chepaitis, Amy E.; Snyder, Clint W.; Lazare, Aaron; Lipkin, Mack Jr. "Effect of Communications Training on Medical Student Performance." *Journal of the American Medical Association,* 290, no. 9 (2003): 1157–1165. Available at: http://jama.ama-assn.org/cgi/content/full/290/9/1157. Accessed August 2009.

Youdelman, Mara; Perkins, Jane, *Providing Language Interpretation Services in Health Care Settings: Examples from the Field.* New York: The Commonwealth Fund, 2002. Available at: www.commonwealthfund.org/Content/Publications/Fund-Reports/2002/May/Providing-Language-Interpretation-Services-Health-Care-Settings--Examples-from-the-Field.aspx

Weissman, J. S.; Betancourt, J.; Campbell, E. G.; Park, E. R.; Kim, M.; Clarridge, B.; Blumenthal, D.; Lee, K. C.; Maina, A. W. "Resident Physicians' Preparedness to Provide Cross-Cultural Care." *Journal of the American Medical Association,* 294 (2005): 1058–1067. Available at: http://jama.ama-assn.org/cgi/content/abstract/294/9/1058. Accessed August 2009.

CHAPTER FOURTEEN

Treating Bad People

It's a little after midnight as intern Marcus Kret is called to the room of a patient he hasn't seen before. She's had several surgeries. She came to the hospital this time because she felt pain in her abdomen after eating breakfast.

Two men sit by the window on the far side of the woman's bed. They watch as Kret quizzes the woman about her illnesses but then also glance up at the TV, which is showing a sports program with the sound off.

At first glance, it looks like the men might be friends or relatives of the patient, until you notice their uniforms. They are corrections officers. The woman isn't tied to her bed just by sickness; she is also handcuffed. She is an inmate, brought here for treatment of symptoms that are beyond the scope of the prison's health clinic. Kret continues his examination of the woman as if she were any other patient. And that is what he is supposed to do, provide treatment without regard to whether someone might judge the patient to be a "good" person or a "bad" person. She is a patient, that's all.

*   *   *

CRISTINA YANG HAS TROUBLE SEPARATING HER PERSONAL FEELINGS ABOUT A patient from her ethical responsibilities as a physician in "Enough Is Enough (No More Tears)" (2-02). She discovers that a patient awaiting a liver transplant has been beating his wife. Also it turns out that the man's uncontrolled anger probably caused a car crash that not only put him and his wife in the hospital, but killed the driver of another car.

The man's son could donate part of his liver. But when Yang presents the medical options she seems to emphasize the risks of partial liver donation, as if trying to dissuade the son from helping his father.

Preston Burke pulls Yang aside.

"Seibert is a wife beater. Her films show years of abuse," she tells him.

"I didn't know that. But still—" Burke responds.

Yang interrupts. "Multiple fractures. She has a kidney bleed from a beating she took last week. Plus, it was his road rage that caused the accident. The guy in the other car died!"

"And that means what? No heroic measures? Leave him on the table?" Burke tosses back.

"Well if it were up to me . . ."

"Think like a surgeon Dr. Yang! We have a dying patient and a liver that could save him."

"Well this is more complicated than that."

Burke answers harshly. "No. For social workers, yes! For the family. Not for you. It isn't up to you!"

KRET LISTENS AS THE INMATE WHO IS HIS PATIENT SUMMARIZES HER lengthy medical history, including surgeries on one leg, a kidney, part of her colon, gallbladder, and appendix. Some of the procedures were done here. And she praises one of the surgeons who operated on her several years ago. "He's awesome!" she says.

Some of her medical problems may be linked to her past behavior, legal and not. She points out that she no longer smokes cigarettes. They are now banned in the prison. But other surgeries were to treat the consequences of a genetic condition completely out of her control. To Kret, all that matters are the current facts of her physical condition, he doesn't appear to dwell on whether there's any blame to be assigned. And when he needs to lift her gown to continue his examination, he asks her guards to step outside the curtain in order to respect her privacy, just as he would with any other patient.

Nevertheless, Kret is not oblivious to the woman's circumstances and how it might slant her answers to medical questions.

"It's my first patient in custody here," Kret says. But when he was in medical school in Chicago, he did rounds at the famous public hospital there. "I saw lots of inmates at Cook County Hospital." That experience taught him to read between the lines of some answers. "Oh, yeah," he says. "They'll say, 'I don't feel safe going back to jail,' for instance. Of course, they don't want to go back. Or they say 'I get methadone' and then they'll make up some ridiculously high dose. I learned to always confirm what they say."

Intern Loïc Fabricant says that even though, as physicians, they work to treat inmates just as they would any other patient, as people, they do think about what their patients have done.

"I had a maximum-security prisoner for a number of days. He was shackled hands and feet, and there were two armed guards in the room at all times," Fabricant says.

It affects the mood in the hospital room.

"You know this person has done something really bad. It does create a challenge to treat them like any other patient. If you are aware of why they were incarcerated, it's kind of hard not to be biased. But we cared for the guy just like we would anyone else. I don't feel like my care was compromised by being aware that he was a criminal, but it definitely made me think about it. "

THE WORTHINESS OF PATIENTS AGAIN PLAYED A ROLE IN A SET OF EPISODES during the fifth season of *Grey's Anatomy* when the surgeons were called on to treat a serial killer who was stabbed in prison. When the death-row inmate learns that he could die without treatment, he declines surgery, hoping to cheat the executioner. In a twist on the usual dramatic story line about a doctor reluctant to treat a bad person, Derek Shepherd pushes for a way to override the prisoner's wishes and keep him alive long enough to be sent back to death row.

Shepherd explains why he wants to stray from a physician's duty to follow the wishes of the patient.

"Two guys shot my dad for his watch," he says in "Wish You Were Here" (5-11). "My mom saved up for it. Two guys came into his store and they shot him because he wouldn't give it up. That's how my dad died. We are supposed to treat everybody the same, but they are not all the same."

FABRICANT REMEMBERS A PATIENT HE HELPED TREAT WHEN HE WAS A medical student.

"He was on extended life support. He had done some really, really awful things."

Naturally, he says they wondered about all the resources being devoted to this man; but they did no less for him than they would have for any other patient. Fabricant also points out that the man's family had broken off contact, and so the end-of-life care may have gone on longer than it might have, if a family member had been there to make the decision to withdraw futile support.

Fabricant says that even as he and his colleagues wonder about the backgrounds of some of their patients, they know that their professional competence is purely in medicine.

"You never know everything about a person. We probably take care of people all the time who we think are wonderful, but who really aren't. It's definitely not the place of the health care professional to pass judgment."

THE MAN HAD COME TO THE HOSPITAL AFTER A FIGHT. HIS FACE WAS BEATEN badly. But during his hospital stay, both his medical problems and his background story got more complicated. He entered as a victim of an assault. Then signs of other injuries appeared. They seemed older. Maybe the fight that landed him in the hospital hadn't been the first.

Even though the man had been on the losing end of this round, perhaps he had somehow instigated the attack. Fragments of background information bounce around the operating room. The man is sedated, but even if he were awake, the surgeons probably wouldn't ask who started the fight. They are focusing on the injuries and will let others sort out the social circumstances that started this fight and perhaps others. It's possible their patient is a perpetrator, not just a victim. But the gossip doesn't really matter. And their attention returns to the surgery.

On another evening, a young woman waits in an Emergency Department examination room. She can't bend her elbow. The pain and swelling started a couple of weeks ago. The likely cause? The woman admits she slipped from her effort to stay sober and injected herself with drugs. She says that after the slip she went right to a detox center to get clean again.

Here's where the confidentiality promised all patients comes into play. If the woman didn't trust the doctor, she might not have revealed what she had done, thus making it harder to reach an accurate diagnosis. A pair of medical students are trailing along, watching the senior resident examine the patient's arm. What they see is a focus on the facts that are relevant to deciding how to treat the swollen arm. There is no air of judgment. It seems as if *nail* and *building a tree house* could be substituted for *needle* and *injecting drugs* without altering the tone of the discussion and the attitude in the room. The senior resident decides that the best thing to do is to cut open and drain what looks like a pocket of blood, called a hematoma, near the woman's elbow, and then clean out any infection they find.

Of course, the woman's history is not ignored, at least not where it's medically relevant. Surgeons need to predict what they are likely to find when they cut into a patient.

Once in the operating room, the surgeons discuss how to cut open the hematoma. As they expected, the problem is an abscess filled with bloody pus. The senior resident directs his junior partner as she sutures the wound. At this point, the woman's IV drug use is relevant.

"You don't want to just stick your finger in," the senior resident warns. "Especially with an IV drug user, you want to look out for foreign bodies, including broken-off needles. And assume they are infected with hepatitis. A lot of them have it."

Standard infection control practices, also known as *universal precautions,* are based on the assumption that any blood or other body fluid could be infected with a dangerous pathogen, no matter how nice the patient seems to be. Nevertheless, it's not surprising to see heightened awareness of the potential risk in this case.

Another tip: Wear a face shield when cutting open an abscess like this one, just in case the contents of the abscess suddenly geyser out.

Fabricant says interns tend to deal with a lot of needle abscesses when they are on the emergency general surgery service. Part of the reason is that while the surgical treatment is typically straightforward, managing a patient with a drug addiction can be time-consuming and frustrating.

"As the intern, you're the one who manages their other problems. Inevitably, they would get admitted, and I would spend the next week trying to deal with their withdrawal and find [them] a place to go," he says. "It was a good example to me of how much that problem taxes our whole system. I would spend more time managing that kind of patient than someone else who actually had more complicated medical issues."

WHILE THE SURGEONS ARE TREATING SOME PEOPLE YOU MIGHT NOT WANT to invite home to meet the folks, at the same time they also deal routinely with cases that seem extraordinarily unfair. Of course, disease and suffering are never welcome, but some cases stand out.

In "What Have I Done to Deserve This?" (2-19), Izzie Stevens is upset that things are looking grim for a patient she likes.

"Ah it's just . . . it's just not fair you know. It's really not fair." Stevens sighs. "We treat jerks all the time. Patch 'em up, send 'em off whether they deserve it or not."

The same episode features a young couple about to be married. The groom has an aneurysm in a heart artery. The surgery to repair it is risky.

"They seem like a really nice couple. They don't seem like they deserve this," George O'Malley says.

"They never do," Preston Burke responds.

"Really? I guess I just think I believe in karma. You know, I mean, good people deserve good things. At least that's how I thought the universe worked," O'Malley says.

Residents often see bad things happen to good people.

At 6:15 in the morning, the residents who have been on call overnight are briefing the daytime team. One of the patients who arrived during the night is a middle-aged woman with metastatic breast cancer. One of the on-call residents talks about wanting to do everything possible to help her, even though the outlook is not good.

"She's a good person," the resident says. And she notes that the woman's family has been dealt a bad hand: her son also has a life-threatening disease. "Her husband stands to lose both his wife and his son in the same year."

ON A CHARTER FLIGHT HOME FROM HARVESTING ORGANS FOR A TRANSPLANT in "Sympathy for the Devil" (5-12), Arizona Robbins is talking about Valentine's Day plans, until Alex Karev snaps. "What is wrong with you? We just took a liver and intestine from a little kid, a dead little kid, and you don't even care. You're talking about rainbows and relationships and crap. What the hell is wrong with you?"

"You don't think I know that they just pulled the plug on a kid? You don't think I get that? You don't think I know about the tiny coffin they are going to stick him in? I know about the tiny coffins. I see them all the time. In my sleep," Robbins responds. She tells him that the only way to deal with the losses is to focus on the future and the patients that can be saved. "You turn your back on the tiny coffins and you face forward."

SAJID KHAN SAYS HE FEELS THE LOSSES MORE WHEN THEY HAPPEN TO PEOPLE he identifies with. He admits that when an elderly patient dies he is sad, but he isn't old enough to have a sense of what it feels like to be at the end of a long life. On the other hand, he remembers a woman in her twenties.

She was badly injured. Khan assisted with her surgery. But then she died in the ICU.

"It was very difficult for me, because it was a girl who was not much younger than I was. And then I saw her husband, whom she had just gotten married to. Situations like that make me look at things in perspective," Khan says. "And think, this is not right that this person had to pass away like this. It was very, very sad."

He says he is also hit hard when he sees young parents grieving. "I can relate to them. I could see myself in their situation."

Additional Reading

American Medical Association. Health and Ethics Policies of the American Medical Association House of Delegates and the Code of Medical Ethics and the Current Opinions of the Council on Ethical and Judicial Affairs. Chicago: AMA, 2008. Available at: www.ama-assn.org/ad-com/polfind/Hlth-Ethics.pdf. Accessed August 2009.

CHAPTER FIFTEEN

Death

"My mother used to say that for a surgeon, a day without death is a rare gift. Every day we face death. Every day we lose life," Meredith Grey says in "Freedom: Part 1" (4-16).

Fortunately, in the real world patients rarely die during surgery. But death is part of the job. It comes in many forms. Sudden death after a car crash. Long-awaited death from cancer. Death that erases all the possibilities of youth. Death that inexorably dims the low spark of old age.

"People say there are spirits in that room," a coworker tells Renee Minjarez one night in the surgical intensive care unit. "There's no such thing," Minjarez scoffs. Spirits or no, death is close in two rooms on this hall tonight. One who is approaching death brings anguished shock. The other is the expected final chapter of a long life. Each demands professional skill; but each demands more than that, too. Surgery residents have to learn how to recognize when rescue has slipped beyond reach. At that point, the job changes.

The laughter of a child leaks through the closed door at the entrance to the ICU; but there is silence at the other end of the long hall. A woman is not doing well. She was terribly injured in a car crash several hours earlier. Her family has just arrived. Before bringing them in, Minjarez turns to the nurse. "Are you ready?" There is a delicate and intense task in front of them, but success will have little to do with either surgical skills or medical knowledge.

They turn down the lights in the patient's room. Minjarez turns to third-year resident Sajid Khan. "Were you in on her surgery?" she asks. Khan was not in the operating room when trauma surgeons tried, but failed, to undo the crash injuries, but he does fill her in on a few more details that will help Minjarez answer some of the questions she knows will soon be asked.

Because the attending surgeon is not available, Minjarez, as the chief resident on duty tonight, is the one who meets the family members. She stands close to the two young men and quietly describes the injuries. She shows them scans, pointing out the irreparable damage. A chaplain arrives to help guide the family members.

Although Minjarez was not directly involved in the examination and treatment of the woman, with the information that Khan gave her and her experience from working on many similar cases, she knows the ultimate conclusion. The brain scan images may look like abstract patterns of gray and black to the untrained eye, but to Minjarez their import is unmistakable: the trauma, swelling, and bleeding have pushed part of their mother's brain down the opening where her spine comes out of her skull. There is nothing anyone can do.

"That was a pretty sad night," Khan recalls. "The only reason she was breathing at that point was because the advances in medicine allowed her to do that. But that's not always the best thing for the patient. It's very difficult to get into those situations. You have to find the right balance and just say, 'You know what, I've done all I can do as a doctor.' You just have to let go."

As Minjarez is standing with the woman's family, Khan is called to a nearby room to check on another ICU patient.

"Can you open your eyes?" Khan asks an elderly man. The man's face is mostly covered by a mask that is pushing air into his lungs. "Wiggle your toes," Khan again tries to get a response. The man's chart says he is DNR/DNI: Do not resuscitate. Do not intubate.

*   *   *

WHEN CRISTINA YANG IS FACED WITH A PATIENT WHO HAS SIGNED DNR instructions in "No Man's Land" (1-04), she resists, taking actions that violate her duty to serve her patient. The patient is a retired nurse who used to work at Seattle Grace Hospital. They are talking when the woman falls silent and monitor alarms sound.

"Liz? Liz, stay with me. Stay with me, Liz," Yang calls out. She calls a code. A team rushes in.

"Here we go. Bag her. Push epi and atropine," one of the responders says. But then a nurse rushes in. "She's DNR. She's DNR. Do not resuscitate! Dr. Yang!" he yells. But Yang isn't listening.

"Come on, people! Push another epi! Come on!" She begins rescue breaths.

Preston Burke arrives. He is the attending for this patient. "What the hell are you two doing?" he demands of Yang. But Yang is focused only on attempting to resuscitate the woman, rather than honoring her wishes. She continues with rescue breathing. Only when Burke pulls her away does she relent. "All right," Yang finally concedes. "Let her go down. Let her go down," Burke says.

While the scene dramatically highlights the inner conflict that health care providers sometimes feel when a patient reaches the point that further intervention is pointless, acting contrary to a patient's clear instructions should never happen. When it does, the problem is typically miscommunication.

ON THE SURGICAL INTENSIVE CARE UNIT, KHAN TALKS WITH THE NURSING team and with other doctors about how much to do for the man in this room. They need to all be on the same page about what actions to take and what things they will no longer do. They know this man will not recover. Khan double-checks the instructions left by family and others close to the man to confirm his wishes.

Then they go to the controls for monitor alarms that call for attention if breathing, heart rhythm, or other vital signs veer out of balance. They turn off some alarms. There is no longer any reason to respond.

Two patients are near death. Many others require attention, too. Khan takes a moment to call the resident who will be taking his place in the morning to brief him on the ICU patients. There are so many that he jumps right to "the big story" on each. One has lost a leg. One has been in and out of the ICU for several months. Three patients are recovering from car crashes; one is improving and will likely transfer to another ward the next day. There is a woman recovering from multiple stab wounds. Several patients have complicated chronic diseases in addition to the challenges of recovering from recent surgery. They are managing respiratory distress, pancreatic masses, an aortic dissection, abdominal aortic aneurysms, a man who received a kidney transplant but the new kidney is failing, and another couple of patients who have been in the ICU for over a month.

"As I'm describing it to you, I'm realizing how sick these patients are," Khan tells his fellow resident. He hangs up the phone and goes back to the dying man's room.

One of the ICU nurses is in the room, standing uncomfortably. "It's strange not to do something," he says. "I suspect it'll be in the next couple of hours," Khan replies to him.

Two doors down, Minjarez steps out of the room where two sons are trying to absorb what has happened to their mother. There are small tears on her cheek. "Are you all right?" a coworker asks. She shakes her head.

Attending surgeon Bruce Ham, M.D., arrives to check on the patients. He has been tied up with other surgeries. He looks in first on the elderly man whom Khan has been watching. Ham inspects the mask that helps the man breathe. Then he comes over to Minjarez.

"Take the mask off," Ham tells her. As the attending surgeon, Ham has the ultimate responsibility for the treatment of the patients on this service, and that includes determining when it is time to remove the machine pushing air into this patient's lungs. "It's miserable. The skin is breaking down. We're treating ourselves, we're not treating him."

They take the mask off, talking to the man as they do it, even though he isn't able to respond. A nurse goes to get some morphine. Ham knows this patient. The man has been dealing with chronic disease for some time. A recent car crash precipitated this crisis. Ham massages the man's shoulders. He looks at the monitor, at the colored squiggly lines and the bold numbers tracking and cataloging each breath, each heartbeat. Then he reaches up and turns the monitor off.

Khan watches from the other side of the man's bed. Later, he recalls learning from Ham's example.

"Every situation is different," Khan says. "Some people bond with the patient a little bit more, some people distance themselves a little bit more from the patient. It depends on the individual. The way Dr. Ham reacted to that is not the way every attending would react to that, but it is the way some attendings would react to that.

"You have to find the right balance between doing everything you possibly can and then opening your eyes once in a while to say, 'Am I being too medically aggressive on this patient?' Doing everything possible for the patient might actually not be the best thing for the patient," Khan says. "Medical school doesn't really prepare you for that at all." This is what residency is all about, drinking in the experience, watching senior surgeons make difficult decisions. In this case, watching a surgeon, who has studied and trained and practiced for decades how to take potent action to fight disease and extend lives, make the decision that now, for this man, the best treatment is to step back.

Minjarez enters the room. "For God's sake," she says when she sees the monitor is off. A coworker takes the breathing machine out of the room. She begins to take pieces off it as she rolls it down the hall, beginning to get it ready to help someone else.

Ham leaves the man's side. He washes his hands and then walks over to the window. The window blinds are down. Ham faces the blinds and stands for a moment. Outside, a new day is just 45 minutes old. In this room, a man's life, his patient's life, has just minutes remaining.

Ham turns. He strides purposefully out of the room and quickly down the hall. Another patient is in an operating room, waiting for him.

Three minutes elapse.

Khan leans over the bed and puts a stethoscope to the man's chest. He enters a note in the chart. He moves on to the next room.

Meanwhile, two doors down, a son is facing a terrible decision. His mother's brain is damaged beyond repair, but as long as the machines are running, she appears to be still alive.

"We had to ask the son what his thoughts were on it. We were very realistic in telling him what had happened," Khan says. He adds that without instructions, they would have been obligated to keep the life support devices in place, despite knowing there was no chance the woman could recover.

"It was a very sad situation, because it was a son making a decision, without a father around or anyone else except his younger brother, making a decision about their mom. I felt really bad. I still think about it, how horrible to be in that situation," Khan recalls.

Ultimately, the son decides the machines should be turned off.

"THEY DON'T TELL YOU, WHEN YOU BECOME A DOCTOR, THAT IT'S GOING to be like this. They don't tell you that you're going to lose more patients than you save," Derek Shepherd sighs in "All by Myself" (5-10) after a young patient suddenly dies in the operating room.

The good news for surgery patients is that actually very few die in the OR.

"If that happens, I've done something really wrong, either technically or in patient selection. It does occasionally happen that someone will have a massive intraoperative heart attack and not make it off the table, but it's very, very rare," says cancer surgeon Kevin Billingsley.

Except for trauma cases and other emergencies, surgeons rarely operate on patients if there is a substantial risk of death.

"I've been doing complex surgical oncology practice for ten years and it's . . . knock vigorously on wood . . . I've never had it happen," Billingsley says.

"I'M NEVER HAPPY WHEN SOMEONE PASSES AWAY. IT NEVER REALLY FEELS good. It really feels pretty bad," Khan says. "It makes me reflect back and think about the significance of life and how valuable life is. When I saw that gentleman pass away, I started thinking about what his life was like, and how he was put into this situation." Khan says at his age it's harder for him to fully relate to the perspective of elderly patients. He simply hasn't lived long enough to be able to put himself in their positions. And he admits that when someone closer to his age dies, it hits closer to home.

In both the deaths during this ICU nightshift, the patients ceased breathing after machines were turned off. Advances in medical knowledge not only change lives, they have irrevocably altered how and when we die.

THE RESPONSIBILITY OF DECIDING WHEN AND HOW HARD TO PUSH MEDICAL interventions is illustrated when an ambulance crew delivers a man terribly injured in a car crash to the Emergency Department entrance of Seattle Grace Hospital in "Enough Is Enough" (2-02). The man's skull is fractured.

"How long has he been down?" Miranda Bailey asks the paramedic.

"We've been doing CPR for about 20 minutes. It took fire 20 minutes to get him out of the car. He's pretty much gone."

"He's not gone until we say he's gone. Keep coding," Bailey orders. She tells George O'Malley to save the man.

"But . . . he's dead," O'Malley says.

Bailey doesn't like his response. "Did you not hear me? He's not dead until we say he's dead. You know what to do; so do it."

As O'Malley glumly walks into the hospital to continue resuscitation and treatment, he mutters to himself, "He's dead."

IT'S LATE ON A FRIDAY NIGHT WHEN TRAUMA PAGERS ALERT THE TEAM TO AN incoming patient. The description of the patient is sketchy: Motor vehicle crash. Pupils fixed and dilated. Heart rate in the 90s. Possible partial amputation of an upper extremity (jargon for "arm"). Coming in by Life Flight helicopter.

The team suits up in paper gowns and face shields, prepared for a bloody scene.

When the patient arrives, they work quickly and professionally, but there is little sense of urgency in the orders for tests or interventions. The patient is not expected to survive, yet, of course, no one wants to give up too soon; so they go through the motions, working through the trauma checklist. But without any reasonable hope for a save, there is no enthusiasm evident on the faces of the senior trauma doctors.

In this case, the conclusion arrives quickly. In many, many more cases the point of futility is harder to define.

"We try to recognize when care is futile, when the quality of life has reached such a place that it's not worthwhile to continue," says Donald Trunkey, the former chair of the OHSU Department of Surgery. "Now, these are tough decisions. I try to teach the residents that they can't do it by themselves, because then they're playing God; but you've got to do it in concert with another physician, and you've got to somehow include the family. I want to emphasize that you cannot play God."

But residents do have to learn how to determine both when they've done everything that makes sense to try and how to talk to the patient or the family.

TALKING TO PATIENTS AND FAMILIES IN THE EMERGENCY DEPARTMENT IS A difficult assignment.

"You've never met them before. When it's a bad injury, you have to tell the family that the patient is probably going to die," says Laszlo Kiraly, a fifth-year resident. "It's not fair. I don't think people can rationally handle the decisions under these circumstances in emergencies. They are not prepared. You can tell them they will die, but then offer them a procedure, while saying they will probably die anyway, and most take it, even though it's most likely to lead to a lingering death in ICU. You get less enamored of [aggressive medical intervention] as you go on."

IT'S THREE O'CLOCK IN THE MORNING. OTHER THAN THE LOW SOUNDS OF ventilators and occasional monitor beeps, it's quiet in the intensive care unit. The nurses are snacking and chatting. They care diligently for their patients. They regularly help people survive terrible injuries and illnesses. But they also have other patients whose bodies they test and inject and intubate and access day and night for weeks or even months . . . only to ultimately fail.

"I want a bracelet that says, 'Take me out back,' " says one. "I don't want a tube down my throat. I don't want someone telling me, 'Wiggle your toes.' "

Another recalls a patient who pushed back against the indignities of the constant poking and prodding in the ICU. "I had a young guy getting a neuro exam. Everyone was standing around the bed and he was told by the doctor, 'Show me two fingers.' " The nurse then smiled as she recalled, "He saluted with one finger on each hand! The doctor said, 'That's unacceptable!' " The nurse imitates a deep, indignant tone of a miffed physician. "The staff was trying hard not to laugh out loud!"

Like Kiraly, many others here become less enamored of intensive care.

The trauma team gets an alert that a new patient is arriving soon from a small-town hospital. It's the second time this shift that this ambulance crew has made the nearly two-hour drive. The fragments of advance information are disheartening. The elderly woman fell. Doctors at her local hospital report that her pupils are fixed and dilated. A brain scan shows bleeding within her skull is pushing her brain to the side. The outlook is bad. Indeed, some here wonder whether there is anything that can be done.

"It must be hard to be a doctor at a small hospital," says third-year resident Terah Isaacson. "Maybe you're neighbors with the patient's family. I wonder if they don't want to tell them there's no point. Now the family has to drive all the way here. But we've accepted the patient, so we have to try."

While waiting for the ambulance to arrive at the Emergency Department, some are blunt about what looks like a futile exercise.

"Where is the patient coming from?" a resident asks. When she hears the answer, she remarks, "Oh, they don't have a neurologist there."

"They do have a morgue," another staffer says.

"It's not like they're going to take a case like this with a midline shift [in the brain] to the OR," agrees a third person. The remarks can seem harsh. But the people here want to save lives, not merely extend the process of death.

When the woman arrives, she receives the same examination and thorough assessment any other trauma case would get. Despite the gloomy advance report, the team checks everything again. But as they confirm the woman's condition, some shake their heads. Almost a dozen people cluster around a computer monitor to look at the CT scans that arrived with the patient. A neurologist goes into the trauma bay to do his own examination.

Half an hour later the woman is taken down the hall to the CT scanner. As fresh images scroll onto the control panel screen, the damage to her brain is obvious. "Ooh, it looks worse," one person says. They don't put any IV lines into the woman. They would be needed only if the neurosurgeon wanted to take her to the operating room, but further surgery seems unlikely. "There's no point in torturing this woman," someone says. "I gotta find the social worker."

INTERN NICK TADROS RECALLS BEING INTERRUPTED AS HE'S HELPING TAKE care of a stabbing victim.

"I get a page saying, 'Your patient is coding.' "

It was a woman who had been through two surgeries; but she seemed to be doing better. Tadros worked the code for over a half hour. It was just like in the advanced cardiac life support training at the start of the year.

"I called it. Twelve fifteen, that's what time it was. Twelve fifteen P.M."

Tadros wasn't the first person to give the woman's husband the bad news, but he had gotten to know him while she had been on the ward.

"The risk is that you always want to say too much. It's one of those things you can't really do anything to fix it. It's a horrible thing and really sucks. And so you can just kind of admit that and tell them you're sorry for their loss."

While he was affected by the patient's death, his main concern was whether there was anything he could have done differently.

"This one was so out of the blue. Everyone from the attendings to me, to the nurses, we were all saying, 'What happened?' That makes it easier to accept. Not like a patient who has a problem where I could've done something or should have done something.

"The most lasting effect I guess was mostly with my other patients. They always say don't practice 'last patient medicine,' but everyone kind of does. It was something that was always in the back of my mind for a little while when I was rounding with my other patients. What could we have done differently? What went wrong?"

A month later, Tadros finally received autopsy results. The most likely cause was a heart arrhythmia. The news was anticlimactic, but there was a bit of comfort for Tadros. "At least it was not something that we missed," he says.

ACCORDING TO SURVEYS, MANY MEDICAL STUDENTS AND RESIDENTS SAY they don't feel prepared to deal with patients who are dying. And senior physicians often feel unprepared to do more than just let the students and resident watch them at work. In response to one national survey, less than one in five students and residents said they had received formal education in end of life care. One study of how surgeons communicate with patients and families noted that "[s]urgeons are known for their cool detachment in moments of stress. In this situation, a family might misconstrue such attempts at maintaining a professional air as cold, unsympathetic, or evasive."

In recent years, training programs have tried to do more. Medical schools and residency programs have added lectures, readings, discussions, and role-playing sessions to teach end-of-life skills, as well as some of the other interpersonal and ethical challenges health care professionals encounter.

At OHSU, surgery skills labs are scheduled on Monday mornings, right after the weekly "grand rounds" lectures. On this Monday, while some residents are practicing laparoscopic suturing and others are learning how to use Doppler ultrasound to pinpoint vascular problems, a group of second-year surgery residents gathers around a conference table to talk about what to do when a patient may be beyond rescue and is unconscious or otherwise unable to communicate.

"The guideline is to do what the patient would have wanted," says Karen Kwong, M.D., the resident program adviser who leads these ethics skills labs. Of course, that fundamental principle can be challenging to interpret when a decision must be made about how—and how much—to treat a patient who is deathly ill. One of the residents says, "When I ask family members what the patient would want, ninety percent of the time the answer I get is, 'Well, they wouldn't want to be a vegetable,' which is just so unclear."

They have been reading case studies of advance directives and surgical patients, but these residents don't really need to study the case reports: they each have seen cases that are just as tough.

"I just had a kid who was dying, who we were forced to put a chest tube into, to prolong his death," one of the residents says. "The reason for the chest tube was that we hadn't had the discussion with the family about the end of life. The kid had been in the hospital for months with ALL [acute lymphocytic leukemia] and an infection. It was wrong."

Another resident also had a pediatric case in which it seemed that the medical interventions offered only a long, ugly decline.

"We had a kid who'd been in the hospital since he was born. He had no kidneys. He'd been through respiratory failure, tube feeding, brain problems," the resident says. "So he's been there forever. We weren't doing anything for him except changing his wound dressings every three days. Everyone who went in there felt horrible. But you'd talk to the mom, and the mom says, 'No.' The mom won't hear it. It makes you want to scream. It's horrible."

One resident points to a powerful reason that family members may resist advice to withdraw support. "A lot of times there is guilt involved. They feel like they need to say they want to have everything done."

"Nobody wants to be known as the one who 'killed' Dad," Kwong agrees.

Other residents chime in, saying it is important to make clear in such cases just how unlikely it is that further intervention will make a difference . . . and that going back into surgery or opting for other interventions can cause further damage. The surgeons say they can help families by reassuring them that, even if there are further actions that could be taken, they have done everything that is likely to help.

Kwong notes that even when patients have made clear their wishes in advance, surgeons need to check again. "At the time people make these decisions of DNR or said that they don't want to be a vegetable; when the time comes, sometimes they change their decision," she says.

They talk about how to define the line beyond which further treatment is futile. Kwong points out that the line is different for different people.

There may be instances, Kwong tells the residents, in which "the oncologists offer them chemo, with maybe a one percent difference [in survival], and people will take it, because they want that one percent." In many cases, Kwong says, the key is how the options are presented to the family.

THE ETHICS SKILLS LAB PARTICIPANTS WOULD PROBABLY HAVE CRITIQUED the way Chief Webber presented the cancer treatment options and odds to George O'Malley's father in "Six Days: Part 2" (3-12). O'Malley's father had asked for an aggressive operation. Webber agreed, despite finding evidence that the cancer had spread too far to be removed. O'Malley's father then died from the extensive surgery, instead of from the cancer.

George O'Malley sharply criticized Webber.

"He could have lived for weeks or months. We could have had months with him. My mom . . . she could have had months with him," O'Malley points out.

"He wanted a chance to fight the cancer, George. It was his choice."

"He didn't know any better! You knew better! You shouldn't have done it. You shouldn't have done it!"

ONE OF THE CASE STUDIES THE GROUP DISCUSSES IS A DISPUTE BETWEEN family members: Some want treatment to stop and others think there is a reasonable chance the patient could recover. Unfortunately, painful family discord can flare up at crucial moments.

"We had a patient who was not going to make it," former Department of Surgery Chair Donald Trunkey recalls. "It was clear that we were into the futile care area. He was slowly dying of multiple organ failure following a trauma. So I talked to the wife, who was the legal guardian, and I said, 'I think we've reached a point here that what we are doing is futile. I don't think that there's any chance that we're going to get a good result. He has too many organs failing.'"

His body was being supported by a ventilator, a kidney dialysis machine, and other devices and drugs.

"I said, 'I would recommend that we withdraw care.' She was absolutely incredible. She said, 'Oh, yes. He told me several times that he did not want to be kept on life support.' So then I went out and broke the news to the family. We're talking fourteen people. Everybody was so grateful . . . except the youngest son. He just absolutely devastated the whole family by saying, 'No, we're not going to do this. You're not going to kill my father.' It just really got ugly."

The patient's wife had full legal authority to act, but she was stymied by her son's opposition.

"I said, 'What do you want done?' She said, 'I want him to have comfort care now.' I said, 'I will do it, because you are the legal guardian. You can blame me for doing it.' That was the way we resolved it. I did not want to put a schism into the family."

The skills needed at these pivotal moments have little to do with surgery, and yet they are among the most important skills a surgeon, or any physician, must have in order to serve the needs and desires of patients and families. Trunkey says he shares his opinions with residents, but that the most powerful teaching comes from role modeling.

As one report on educating surgeons to deal with end-of-life care put it, "Most importantly, [practicing surgeons] must model the appropriate behaviors for their charges personally, whether it be in the consultation room breaking bad news compassionately or at the bedside easing the path to the next world. In these golden hours, the educated surgeon who wields new and mighty resources can be the greatest champion of the patient who is at the end of life."

After an overnight shift in which he saw two patients succumb to injuries and illness, resident Khan also emphasized the importance of witnessing the care firsthand.

"The only way you can learn is by going through residency. I remember when I was a naive medical student, [in] my first or second year of medical school, before we even did our clinical exposure, I used to tell my friends that residency doesn't need to be this long, you learn everything you need in medical school. Now that I'm actually going through residency, I realize that's not the case, residency might not even be enough time to learn everything," Khan says. "Becoming a surgeon and learning how to take care of patients is one part of it. But another part is learning about nights like that and how to deal with it emotionally."

"YOU'RE BEHAVING LIKE THE ONLY REASON SHE'S IN THIS HOSPITAL IS TO die." Cristina Yang reacted to the decision not to pursue aggressive treatment for a patient in "No Man's Land" (1-04).

Death comes to all. But sometimes we have some control over where we die. It is interesting that where we live appears to determine where we are likely to die. As one research report on the subject noted, "Where Americans die is much more influenced by what part of the country they live in than by what their preferences are for location of death." Late one night in the intensive care unit, one OHSU surgeon put the variations in end of life care more bluntly, "I'm glad we don't flog our patients here." He was referring to the fact that terminally ill patients in Oregon are far less likely to spend their final days in a hospital undergoing intensive treatment than are patients in some other parts of the country. The diseases and injuries that people face are pretty much the same everywhere, and the medical and surgical knowledge and skills are similar in different regions. And yet, the decisions health care providers, patients, and families make about medical interventions, including whether to fight to the last breath in a hospital or go home or to a hospice facility to die, are quite variable.

By using information from the Medicare program, researchers at Dartmouth University have documented stark variations in the practice of medicine between different parts of the country. Many of these variations seem to have little to do with underlying rates of disease or injury. And by several measures, compared to residents of other states Oregonians spend fewer days in the hospital during the final six months of life, are less likely to die in a hospital, and if they do die in a hospital the final stay is shorter and costs less.

TIME IN HOSPITAL DURING LAST 6 MONTHS OF LIFE	STATE	HOSPITAL DAYS PER DECEDENT DURING LAST 6 MONTHS OF LIFE (2005)
States in which patients spend most days in hospital	New York	15.45
	New Jersey	15.27
	District of Columbia	12.8
	Delaware	11.8
	Rhode Island	11.8
States in which patients spend fewest days in hospital	Washington	7.08
	Wyoming	7.06
	Oregon	*6.22*
	Idaho	5.79
	Utah	5.61
National Average		10.81

LIKELIHOOD OF DYING IN HOSPITAL	STATE	PERCENT OF MEDICARE DEATHS OCCURRING WITHIN HOSPITAL (2005)
States in which patients are most likely to die in hospital	New York	37.23
	New Jersey	35.81
	Mississippi	34.88
	South Carolina	34.36
	Hawaii	33.51

LIKELIHOOD OF DYING IN HOSPITAL	STATE	PERCENT OF MEDICARE DEATHS OCCURRING WITHIN HOSPITAL (2005)
States in which patients are least likely to die in hospital	*Oregon*	*22.58*
	Idaho	21.51
	Arizona	20.17
	Colorado	19.19
	Utah	17.25
National Average		28.64

LENGTH OF FINAL STAY IN HOSPITAL	STATE	HOSPITAL DAYS PER DECEDENT DURING HOSPITALIZATION IN WHICH DEATH OCCURRED (2005)
States in which patients had longest final hospital stay	New York	4.43
	Hawaii	3.95
	New Jersey	3.75
	District of Columbia	3.21
	South Carolina	3.14
States in which patients had shortest final hospital stay	*Oregon*	*1.38*
	Arizona	1.33
	South Dakota	1.33
	Idaho	1.24
	Colorado	1.22
	Utah	1.1
National Average		2.32

COSTS OF FINAL HOSPITAL STAY	STATE	INPATIENT HOSPITALIZATION REIMBURSEMENT PER DECEDENT DURING HOSPITALIZATION IN WHICH DEATH OCCURRED (2005)
States with highest costs for final hospital stay of patient who died in hospital	New York	$7,502.19
	District of Columbia	$6,390.75
	Hawaii	$6,143.37
	Maryland	$6,002.18
	New Jersey	$5,965.06
States with lowest cost for final hospital stay of patient who died in hospital	*Oregon*	*$3,007.53*
	Kansas	$2,638.43
	South Dakota	$2,513.10
	Idaho	$2,360.88
	Utah	$2,346.22
	North Dakota	$2,304.42
National Average		$4,065.41

Source: Data from The Dartmouth Atlas of Health Care (www.dartmouthatlas.org).

THE VARIATIONS IN HEALTHCARE PRACTICES MAKE A HUGE DIFFERENCE IN spending. For example, a recent report from the Dartmouth researchers pointed out that Medicare spends more than twice as much per person in Miami as it does in San Francisco, and yet there doesn't seem to be a real difference in the health or longevity of Medicare recipients between those cities. The Medicare bills for patients in some Oregon cities are substantially lower than the national average. The researchers point out that understanding these variations could point the way toward controlling increases in health care costs.

"I'm not sure why there are regional differences, but there are, there just are," says Trunkey. But he has a sense of different attitudes about death. "In the Pacific Northwest we have a much more open view. Washington and Oregon have these right-to-die laws. We've addressed it. And that attitude permeates into medical care. It's been very positive in regard to these right-to-die issues, because I don't see patients suffering from cancer pain anymore. Doctors are, I think, spending more time with their patients and giving them appropriate pain management, because they don't want a person to have to exercise their right to die."

As Trunkey mentions, Oregon was the first state to allow physicians to openly prescribe lethal doses of medicine for certain terminally ill patients. Voters in the state of Washington recently passed a similar law.

During the first decade, fewer than 60 terminally ill patients a year in Oregon died by using the lethal prescriptions they obtained under the rules of the Death with Dignity Act. And very few physicians have ever written a prescription for a lethal dose of medicine. There are more than 30,000 deaths in Oregon each year, so the Death with Dignity Act cannot directly explain broad patterns of how and where Oregonians die. In a sense, the act is a reflection of a cultural attitude that is more conservative about medical intervention at the end of life.

The community attitudes existed long before the Death with Dignity Act was proposed. And researchers have documented that even before the law took effect and in places where physician-assisted suicide is not sanctioned, some doctors have gone along with requests from patients for lethal doses of drugs.

Trunkey says he did it even before he returned to Oregon from California decades ago.

"In San Francisco, when it was obvious they were getting close to the time, I would give them a liter of Brompton's solution and just say. 'Take as much of this as you want, but just remember if you take that whole bottle, it will kill you.' I didn't tell them what to do, but I gave them the option."

Brompton's solution or mixture is a sedative and pain medication that typically contains several drugs, including morphine, cocaine, ethyl alcohol, and chloroform water.

But there are also other factors that are connected to the decisions that doctors, patients, and families make at the end of life.

For example, researchers say that the number of people who die in hospitals appears to be related to the number of hospital beds available. As in many aspects of medicine, the more something is available, the more it is used. In other words, if you look at two similar communities, if one of them has more MRI scanners, the people who live there will tend to get more MRI scans. The same pattern is seen with hospital beds. It makes sense that if bed space is tight, doctors will try to send people home as soon as possible; but if there are plenty of beds, then they will let people stay a bit longer on average.

Also, in places like Oregon, where hospice care is more available, there are more options for patients. And greater use of hospice means fewer patients die in hospitals.

"YOU LOST HER?" IZZIE STEVENS ASKS MEREDITH GREY IN "SUPERSTI-tion" (2-21).

"Yeah," Grey answers.

There has been a string of patient deaths, but sometimes when some-one says they lost a patient, that's exactly what they mean: The patient is missing. It's happened more than once on *Grey's Anatomy,* including when Meredith Grey's mother, Ellis, wanders away from her room a couple of times in "Deny, Deny, Deny" (2-04).

It happens in real hospitals, too.

The nurse comes into the workroom and tells an intern, "I've lost a patient. He keeps leaving. I haven't seen him in an hour."

The man had asked for his belongings, but the police have them.

"I think maybe he bolted," the nurse says.

Additional Reading

Bradley, C. T.; Brasel, K. J. "Core Competencies in Palliative Care for Surgeons: Interpersonal and Communication Skills." *American Journal of Hospice and Palliative Care,* 24, no. 6 (2007–2008): 499–507. Available at: http://ajh.sagepub .com/cgi/content/abstract/24/6/499. Accessed August 2009.

Dartmouth Atlas Working Group. The Dartmouth Atlas of Health Care. Available at: www.dartmouthatlas.org. Accessed August 2009.

Fisher, Elliott S.; Bynum, Julie P.; Skinner, Jonathan S. "Slowing the Growth of Health Care Costs—Lessons from Regional Variation." *New England Journal of Medicine,* 360 (2009): 849–852. Available at: http://content.nejm.org/cgi/ content/short/360/9/849. Accessed August 2009.

Huffman, J. L. "Educating Surgeons for the New Golden Hours: Honing the Skills of Palliative Care." *Surgical Clinics of North America,* 85, no. 2 (2005): 383–391. Available at: www.ncbi.nlm.nih.gov/pubmed/15833479. Accessed August 2009.

Klaristenfeld, D. D.; Harrington, D. T.; Miner, T. J. "Teaching Palliative Care and End-of-Life Issues: A Core Curriculum for Surgical Residents." *Annals of Surgical Oncology,* 14, no. 6 (2007): 1801–1806. Available at: www.ncbi.nlm.nih.gov/pubmed/17342567. Accessed August 2009.

Meier, Diane E.; Emmons, Carol-Ann; Wallenstein, Sylvan; Quill, Timothy; Morrison, R. Sean; Cassel, Christine K. "A National Survey of Physician-Assisted Suicide and Euthanasia in the United States." *New England Journal of Medicine,* 338, no. 17 (1998): 1193–1201. Available at: http://content.nejm.org/cgi/content/full/338/17/1193. Accessed August 2009.

Moinpour, C. M.; Polissar, L. "Factors Affecting Place of Death of Hospice and Non-Hospice Cancer Patients." *American Journal of Public Health,* 79, no. 11 (1989): 1549–1551. Available at: www.ajph.org/cgi/reprint/79/11/1549. Accessed August 2009.

State of Oregon. Death with Dignity Act. For the annual reports, see http://egov.oregon.gov/DHS/ph/pas/index.shtml. Accessed August 2009.

State of Washington. Death with Dignity Act. Initiative Measure 1000. For information, see http://wei.secstate.wa.gov/osos/en/Documents/I1000-Text%20for%20web.pdf. Accessed August 2009.

Sullivan, Amy M.; Lakoma, Matthew D.; Block, Susan D. "The Status of Medical Education in End-of-Life Care: A National Report." *Journal of General Internal Medicine,* 18, no. 9 (2003): 685–695. Available at: www.springerlink.com/content/33v117r6r4387222. Accessed August 2009.

Tolle, Susan W.; Rosenfeld, Anne G.; Tilden, Virginia P.; Park, Yon. "Oregon's Low In-Hospital Death Rates: What Determines Where People Die and Satisfaction with Decisions on Place of Death?" *Annals of Internal Medicine,* 130, no. 8 (1999): 681–685. Available at: www.annals.org/cgi/reprint/130/8/681.pdf. Accessed August 2009.

Wennberg, John E.; Thomson, Peggy Y.; Fisher, Elliott S.; Stukel, Thérèse A.; Skinner, Jonathan S.; French, John; Sharp, Sandra M.; Bronner, Kristen K. "Use of Hospitals, Physician Visits, and Hospice Care During Last Six Months of Life Among Cohorts Loyal to Highly Respected Hospitals in the United States." *BMJ,* 328 (2004): 607. Available at: www.bmj.com/cgi/content/full/328/7440/607. Accessed August 2009.

CHAPTER SIXTEEN

The Personality of Surgery

A doctor is a doctor is a doctor, right? Yes and no.

In Britain, physicians usually are called *doctor* but surgeons use the title *Mr., Miss,* or *Mrs.* As the Royal College of Surgeons of England website explains, physicians have been trained at universities since the Middle Ages, whereas until relatively recently surgeons typically served an apprenticeship and did not necessarily attend a university or medical school.

Rather than being joined with physicians, surgeons in Europe share a history with quite another craft, notes surgeon and historian Ira Rutkow, M.D.

"They were actually barbers. They were uneducated and unschooled. They traveled from town to town. They didn't operate in the sense that you and I think of it. If somebody had an abscess, they knew how to open an abscess. Of course, this was in the days before anesthesia and antiseptics," Rutkow says. "And in Europe the physician, as opposed to the 'surgeon,' was always the educated individual, meaning he had a university education, went to medical school, and actually had a medical degree, an M.D. degree."

Indeed, from the mid-sixteenth century until the mid-eighteenth century, barbers and surgeons in England were members of a united guild, the Barber-Surgeons Company. However, each group had its own colored pole. In England, red and white striped poles designated surgeons, and blue and white stripes were displayed by barbers.

Of course, today surgeons in Britain must have a degree from a medical school, just as physicians do.

Rutkow says the history in the United States was different. Rather than coming from different educational and social classes, physicians and surgeons in America were usually one and the same.

"The physician in America was sort of a jack of all trades. He did surgery. He did general practice. He did everything. He was a general practitioner," Rutkow says.

As training requirements and licensing regulations became more specific and demanding in the early part of the twentieth century, the rising standards were applied equally across medical practice. Rutkow points out that even today, there is only one type of medical license that determines whether an individual may prescribe drugs or remove a tumor or perform any other medical intervention.

"When you get your license, theoretically you could operate on somebody's heart the day you get your license. Now, you would kill them. You would get sued. And you would probably never practice medicine again. But by virtue of being given a license, you can do whatever you want within medicine," he says.

The board certifications, hospital privileges, and reimbursement standards are essential standards that in practice determine who can prescribe, operate, and get paid for treating patients, but these requirements are not laws.

And even if there is really only one legal definition of an M.D., physicians and surgeons are typically different sorts of people . . . and they have been since long before modern medical regulations took effect.

"Surgeons want to see results. You operate on somebody, they either get better or they don't. If you are an internist, you can go for eight weeks giving medicine, wondering if the patient is going to be helped or not; so there are differences in the personality types. No two ways about that," Rutkow says.

In a speech made at the end of his term, a president of the Society of University Surgeons referred to the common personality traits of surgeons.

"Surgeon personality traits and behavior are quite diverse but tend to reside somewhere between strong and brash. *Not always right, but never in doubt* or *Ready, fire, aim* are phrases not infrequently applied to surgeons. Many of these personality traits are necessary for optimal performance during such surgical situations as managing an unstable trauma patient, controlling a hemorrhage, or reconstructing a liver or kidney ex vivo, to name but a few," said Brad Warner, M.D.

But the pediatric surgeon from Cincinnati Children's Hospital Medical Center in Ohio went on to caution, "On the other hand, I think we get carried away at times in our behavior and take some of these traits a little too far."

Donald Trunkey, who was chair of OHSU's Department of Surgery from 1986 until 2001, agrees that surgery attracts people who generally share a certain type of personality.

"There's no question about it. Surgery does attract a more aggressive personality," he says.

And though he has risen to a prominent position in his profession, traveling the world to teach and lecture on surgery, Trunkey says he didn't like the surgeons he saw in medical school.

"None of my role models in medical school were surgeons. They were rigid; they were just terrible role models. Both of my role models were internists; so I decided I was going to go into internal medicine. But then I did three months as a sub-intern. The only way interns could get a vacation in those days was to find a stupid medical student to take their call for a week. So I did it for three months," Trunkey recalls. "At the end of those three months I said, 'God, I cannot do this the rest of my life!' You are dealing with old people with chronic diseases; they don't get well. They get better and then they get worse again."

He moved from Seattle to Portland to do a rotating internship.

"I had been on surgery for one month and I said, 'This is what I want to do.' I feel very comfortable making decisions and living with those decisions, right or wrong. That's what you have to be able to do."

*   *   *

"SO . . . UM . . . DR. BAILEY?" GEORGE O'MALLEY ASKED TENTATIVELY IN "I Am a Tree" (3-02).

"Surgeons don't say 'Um,' Dr. O'Malley," Bailey snapped. "You want to be a surgeon, learn to speak like one."

FREQUENTLY IN *GREY'S ANATOMY*, CRISIS STRIKES IN MID-OPERATION, requiring a sudden change of plan. And although the overwhelming majority of surgeries in real operating rooms go pretty much as expected, decisiveness, especially under stress, is still an essential characteristic for a surgeon.

Trunkey recalls that when he was on the faculty of another academic medical center, he had a resident on his team who avoided making decisions about whether or not to operate. The resident couldn't seem to come up with a game plan for a patient without leaning too heavily on the advice of his attendings. Trunkey says he and the other faculty members let the resident complete the program. But he advised the resident to always work as part of a group, so he had other surgeons to support him. Trunkey bluntly warned him not to take on any big surgeries, and he had misgivings about what kind of surgeon that resident would become.

Some years later, Trunkey says he found himself again faced with a resident who lacked that vital decisiveness.

"This one just saddens me to this day, because this guy was probably the nicest kid we had in the entire time I've been here. He was a real gentleman, a real nice guy. Same thing though, he could not make a decision," Trunkey recalls. "I chose to deal with this one differently. I sent him to a psychiatrist. The psychiatrist sent me back a letter. He said, 'You are absolutely right, but I can't do anything about this. I'm as frustrated about this as you are. I can't teach him judgment.' "

"So I did something probably very cruel in retrospect, I dropped him from the program."

The resident was in his next-to-last year. He says that ultimately the resident found a place in another program and went on to become a surgeon. To this day, Trunkey wonders whether he was wrong to cut the resident or whether it was wrong to let someone with his personality go on to practice surgery.

Trunkey says he has worked with surgeons who are indecisive, and he wonders about their choice of careers.

"Once you get as much information as you can, you've got to make a decision and live with it. And if you're not comfortable with that, you're probably in the wrong profession," he says.

"I'VE GOT A FIVE-MINUTE RULE, IF YOU DON'T SEE IT IN FIVE MINUTES, THEN open them up." Robert Martindale, M.D., is talking about laparoscopic procedures and cases for which plans change when things aren't going quite right.

Although minimally invasive procedures are increasingly popular because they usually mean faster recovery times, they also can be more difficult. Instead of directly observing and touching a patient's internal anatomy, during a laparoscopic procedure the surgeon is seeing and manipulating internal organs through small tubes punched through a patient's skin. Trocars are pointed hollow devices used to punch through the skin. Often the trocar is combined with a cannula, the technical name for the tube that provides a tunnel into the patient. A fiber optic camera peeks through one cannula, while the surgeon places blades, clamps, needles, and other tools through additional cannulae.

This afternoon Martindale is moving back and forth between supervising residents in at least two operating rooms. One patient needs to have his gallbladder removed. The plan is to perform a "lap chole" or laparoscopic cholecystectomy. Martindale leaves to check on another operation. When he returns, things aren't going as smoothly as hoped.

"Are we in?" he asks the chief resident, referring to whether she has the laparoscopic tools in place to open access to the gallbladder.

"I thought we were in," the resident replies, "but the pressure is too high." Carbon dioxide (CO_2) gas is pumped into the abdomen, inflating the area to give more room in which to see and maneuver.

The chief resident is struggling, trying to fix things. "I'll wash my hands," Martindale says. He scrubs in and eventually gets the instruments into the proper location. It turns out that they hadn't quite punched through the final inner layer of tissue before they started pumping CO_2. So instead of inflating the abdomen, they had just been pushing open a space between layers of tissue.

"Look at that gallbladder!" Martindale exclaims as the camera gets a view. The gallbladder is huge, protruding down much farther than normal. It is stiff; filled with gallstones and bile.

Though one problem is solved, this case isn't going smoothly. Although the patient had opted for a laparoscopic procedure, the potential need to change course in the OR had been discussed in advance. If the anatomy isn't clearly visible, there could be a greater risk of cutting or poking in the wrong place.

"They couldn't see things properly. I told them to go ahead and switch to an open procedure," Martindale says later.

Another surgeon comes in to talk with the residents about a case that is on the schedule for the next day. "What's going on?" she asks. "Laparoscopic cholecystectomy that went open right at the beginning of the procedure," one of the residents answers. The surgeon's reaction: "Wow. That's neat."

Of course, the turn of events is not great news for the patient. He'll face more time in the hospital and bigger scars that will take longer to heal. But for a surgeon, it's a break in the routine, something unexpected and novel, interesting and perhaps instructive.

Then the surgeons start taking out the stones. It's no wonder the patient was suffering.

"Oh, that's a big stone, holy moly."

The gallbladder is full and pink, not the normal robin's egg blue. The surgeons puncture it, being careful not to miss. They don't want to hit the pancreas or other organs. The fluid that drains out is whitish, not green.

"That means it's been about seventy-two hours [that the gallbladder has been blocked] and enzymes have had time to break down the fluid," Martindale explains.

Finally they wash the big stone out of the duct. Then the chief resident continues to use a fiber optic camera to search for more stones hidden in the duct. Martindale guides her as she aims the scope. "You're going into the pancreas, but that's okay. There's the stone, two stones," he says.

But then black spots start spreading across the video image on the OR monitors. The image from inside the patient's body reaches the camera along a bundle of flexible transparent fibers. Now that fiber optic line is failing. Someone says that another doctor had reported the scope was broken, but it wasn't fixed. As each fiber cracks, another black spot appears on the monitor. No replacement scope is available right now, so they press on.

Martindale explains how to use a balloon catheter to retrieve stones lodged in the duct. The catheter is threaded past the stone and inflated. Then the resident gently pulls back on the catheter, the balloon pushing the stone from behind.

The image on the monitor continues to darken. Everyone is hunched over the patient trying to finish a job that has turned out to be much tougher than expected. Martindale has tightened his supervision of the residents. The balloon catheter trick doesn't get the last stone out, so Martindale tells them to try a grasper.

"We're using all the tools," he says. "The grasper is the last resort. It's old-fashioned. We used to use them all the time."

Finally the last stone is extracted. Martindale backs off and lets the residents place drain tubes and close the patient. The procedure went longer than expected.

Seeing things through to the end, a need to finish a job, is also an essential trait for a surgeon. In medicine, physicians tend to see patients, send them off with prescriptions and instructions and then check them again another day. But once surgeons begin a procedure, they need to keep at it until it's done. There are circumstances in which surgery is halted—perhaps after a dangerous reaction to anesthesia or the discovery that the problem is not treatable after all—but these circumstances are quite rare. Smaller delays and surprises, however, are all too common. And the end of the day is sometimes elusive.

Martindale had promised his wife he'd be home at 5:30 P.M. It is 5:45 when he asks a resident to call home with apologies that his wife has heard many times before. He is still scrubbed in, so he can't touch the unsterilized telephone.

"She's so nice," the resident says as she hangs up the phone. "She just said no problem. You owe her," the resident admonishes him.

The gallbladder removal began about 2:30 P.M. It was supposed to be a straightforward laparoscopic procedure. But then the familiar twists and turns of surgery dictate the afternoon will take a different and longer course. At 7:00 P.M., after more than four hours, Martindale can leave the remaining details to the residents.

Throughout the long afternoon, there was one decision after another to make. They weren't the sort of life or death pivot points that are so frequent on *Grey's Anatomy;* yet even the small choices have potential consequences for the patient.

"Real lifesaving decisions happen only rarely," Martindale says. "But we commonly make judgments that affect lives."

For example, do the surgeons settle for a colostomy or do they try to preserve normal colon function for a patient? If they attempt a full repair, the odds may be against success, perhaps leading to more surgery for the patient later on. But a colostomy changes a patient's life forever.

What's more, in the OR there's little time to deliberate. Surgeons act on the information available, incomplete as it is.

"I worry for days after a case where something didn't look quite right or where there was a lingering question about a choice I made during the procedure. Every time my beeper goes off in the middle of the night to tell me about a problem with a case we'd done, I think, 'I knew it would be that patient,'" Martindale says.

And yet the next day he wades right into another series of operations and the spot decisions each case requires.

SURGEONS NEED TO BE ABLE TO MAKE FIRM DECISIONS; BUT THAT DOESN'T mean merely choosing what to cut. Sometimes the best decision is to do nothing. And while surgeons must make decisions based on incomplete information, they also need to know when there is simply too little information to justify moving ahead and which tests could be useful, without using the search for more information as an excuse to put off a decision.

Those nebulous statements are brought down to specifics with each patient that comes into the hospital. And each week, surgeons here meet to review the lessons of recent cases.

Chief resident Laszlo Kiraly flashes details of a trauma case onto the screen. He admits to his colleagues gathered for an early morning conference that the report from the field about the incoming patient had him scratching his head.

"We were confused by the story of a piece of a 'mall' breaking off and hitting the patient in his chest," Kiraly said as he clicked the computer mouse. The image switched to a photo of a shopping center.

The early report said the patient had lost a lot of blood at the scene. But he hadn't been crushed by a slab of facade. More details came in. The man was being transferred from a rural hospital.

And then a key fact made things clear. The patient had been splitting wood. He wasn't hit by a piece of a *mall,* but rather a piece of a *maul,* a long-handled hammer or mallet. Actually, it may have been the wedge in the log that had shattered on impact, but whatever the source, a splinter of metal shot into the man's chest near his shoulder. The shard was still there. Doctors at the local hospital reported that blood was collecting, a large hematoma had formed. They were worried the metal fragment had injured an artery.

From his seat in the audience, surgeon Martin Schreiber challenged the residents about what they would do in the minutes before the ambulance pulled up. "How would you prepare?"

"I'd alert vascular," says one, referring to the service that specializes in blood vessels. Schreiber adds that he would also alert interventional radiology, in case they needed to use imaging scans to guide an attempt to remove the piece of metal.

Kiraly says that when the patient arrived they noted a radial nerve deficit—that is, the man had lost some feeling in his hand. That's important because it could be a sign of damage to the brachial nerve. That nerve is wrapped around the axillary artery, the main artery that leads into the arm. If the nerve were damaged, that artery could be, too; thus checking the man's hand offered clues to a seemingly unrelated issue, the blood flow in his upper chest.

Schreiber presses one of the other chief residents at the conference. "How would you proceed?"

"I would go to the OR," the resident replies, then describes the kind of incision to use.

"Does anyone disagree profoundly?" Schreiber shoots back.

"I do," a senior member of the faculty chimes in. Clearly they think the resident would have been reaching for the scalpel too quickly.

Indeed, of all the tools surgeons employ, sound judgment is the toughest to master. As Meredith Grey says at the beginning of "Sympathy for the Devil" (5-12), "My mother used to say this about residency: It takes a year to learn how to cut. It takes a lifetime to learn not to."

Back in the trauma conference, Kiraly says that what they actually did was get a scan of blood flow in the area, an angiogram. It looked normal, though Kiraly notes that according to medical articles some patients with upper chest injuries have a blood vessel injury that doesn't show up on a vascular examination. They focused on controlling bleeding in the area. He says that it turns out the metal did go through the artery and it damaged the nerves, but didn't cut all the way through the nerves. They left the metal fragment where it was, because to remove it would have required going in from the patient's back.

"Operative skills are important, but probably more important is judgment. Judgment is the most important thing that we can teach. Almost anyone can learn how to operate, not everyone can, but most people can," Schreiber says. "The question is: When to operate, how much to operate, when to stop operating, when to quit, and when to come back and operate again. Those are all really important decisions, kind of subtle, but that's a huge part of being a surgeon."

ATTENDINGS AND RESIDENTS ARE REVIEWING A POTENTIAL VASCULAR surgery case by looking at imaging scans in the angiography reading room. The patient is an athletic woman in her 40s. She has had problems with blood clots. But attending surgeon Gregory Moneta, M.D., is skeptical about the value of operating on her.

"Is she a candidate for surgery?" Moneta asks the residents. "This scan doesn't do it for me. Ask her first about her willingness to have a surgery." He also warns them about running tests simply because they are not sure what to do. "Don't do a venogram just to satisfy your curiosity. Everything in surgery has a goal. Figure out the goal first, then think about what tests will help you make a decision."

Each day and with each patient, the surgeon must look at the scalpel and ask, "Will cutting do more good than harm?"

Moneta concludes by giving the residents some advice about dealing with patients who ask for operations they may not need.

"We don't have to do surgeries," he says. "You don't order them up like pizza. I was once told by another surgeon that if a patient asks for something you don't want to do, first say that you don't want to. Then if that doesn't work, say you don't know how to do it. Then if that doesn't work," he starts to smile, "fall on the floor and have a seizure."

IF YOU PREFER SLOW DAYS OF QUIET CONTEMPLATION, IF JUGGLING multiple activities and busy days overwhelm you, well then the life of a surgeon may not be for you.

Intern Loïc Fabricant likes to stay busy.

"Oh, yeah, definitely, absolutely. I'm not good at sitting still. When we have weeks off, the surgery-types go bonkers, because we aren't busy enough. That's definitely the case," he says. "I spend a lot of time snowboarding. I like to sail. I really enjoy being in the outdoors. I do a lot of cooking, I like good food."

At least that's what he does when he gets a rare break from the hospital.

"You don't have much time for those things, but I do as much as I can," Fabricant says.

Chief resident David Cho tells a similar tale.

"Whether it's productive or not, I have a hard time sitting still," he says and he rattles off a string of outside activities.

"I rock climb. I learned to rock climb in medical school from a friend of mine. I climb because that's a relationship between you and the mountain or the wall. It's technique and it's art and it's intense. I cook. I like to cook a lot. My fiancé and I have developed some pretty fancy dishes. I don't think it's because it's like surgery; it's just that everything I do happens to be similar." The list doesn't stop there. "I'm in a band."

And then there is the martial arts training he's been doing for 15 years.

Cho fits in well with many other surgeons who always like to be on the move. He says his original plan was to go into primary care, but then he got a glimpse of what surgery was all about.

"Pretty much two minutes after our first anatomy lecture, I said, 'I'm going to do surgery.' I'm one of the few people I know who figured that out early on and stayed with it," Cho says. "It was a foregone conclusion for me at that point. It's the ultimate example of being able to take your power and all of your decision-making ability and all of your training and things that you have done and use it to help one person. That's what I think it is. You are actually physically touching the person and you are manipulating their body and helping them through it. That was the incredible thing for me."

"THE CHIEF RESIDENT WHEN I WAS ON EGS [EMERGENCY GENERAL surgery] last year was cool, calm, and collected," says resident Sajid Khan. "I try to follow his example. When you lose your cool, that's when you have problems." Khan says that his ability to keep an even keel is one difference he has noticed in himself over the past year of residency.

"The best surgeons are cool, calm, and collected," Khan continues. "They know what the patient needs to hear. You don't make things up, but how you say it is important."

Khan points to Department Chair John Hunter as a surgeon who sets an example of cool, calm, and collected in the OR.

Hunter is directing surgery fellow Charles Kim, M.D., during a procedure to remove a damaged section of a patient's esophagus. They are working near the common bile duct. "This is high-priced real estate here," Hunter remarks. Cutting the wrong thing could have serious consequences for the patient. But there is no sense of anxious tension, just focus. Hunter describes the maneuver he wants Kim to make. During most of the procedure, Hunter has just watched and advised Kim, assisting with holding instruments, while giving the younger surgeon opportunities to gain experience. But now, for a moment, Hunter takes tighter control, putting his hand over Kim's and moving it along the right course. With that delicate move accomplished, he again relaxes, letting Kim move forward.

"Surgery is like LEGOs," Kim explains later. "Once you learn how the pieces go together, then you just look at the overall plan, not at each block. Surgery is also like jazz. You learn chords and then add your own style. Junior residents focus on how to tie knots, how to cut, how to stitch. Seniors have the basics down, so then they can focus on specific points of the procedure."

During his eighth and final year of formal training, Kim is working closely with Hunter to learn advanced techniques of minimally invasive surgery. In addition to five years of surgery residency, Kim has done two years of surgery research and now this fellowship to focus on laparoscopic surgery and similar methods, before moving on to begin practice as a full surgeon. Hunter helped pioneer many of the techniques he is now teaching the younger surgeon. But there is no air of bravado in this OR, and Hunter is not possessive with his surgical techniques. He notes that not all surgeons or institutions are as willing to share.

"Some places have had noncompete arrangements, so that trainees don't go out and compete with the surgeons who trained them," Hunter says. "But I don't believe that any surgeon deserves franchise rights to a particular procedure, even if they developed it. Former trainees will come to you for consults and will send you referrals. It hasn't cut into my volume."

During the procedure, the surgeons discuss how to adjust the music on the stereo, experiences at recent surgery meetings, and a range of other topics that have little to do with the patient on the table. It's not that they aren't paying attention, but Hunter and Kim have performed this procedure many times, so they can spare some attention for other matters. And yet there is vigilance for any surprises. And at critical moments, all the focus comes back to the surgical field.

"It's J-tube time," Hunter says. "This is the hardest part of the operation." And a moment later, he calmly, but sharply, commands an assistant. "Will you hang up the phone and get a thirty-cc syringe?"

The ability to manage focus and attention is critical. Complex procedures can last many hours, with periods of routine and peaks of intensity. Nine hours into this day, all eyes are focused on the video monitors as the surgeons' hands press a new instrument through a new hole into the patient's abdomen. From the inside, a fiber optic camera captures a view of a spike punching through the inner tissue layer into the abdominal cavity. "There it is, there it is," Hunter says.

Even though the surgeons have done this sort of operation many times before, they keep in mind all the things that could go wrong—both now and later. Hunter and Kim switch positions, with Hunter taking the lead now. "We do things to help us sleep at night," Hunter says, referring to an extra step they've taken. "We probably didn't really need to, but if we didn't, I might worry later."

CHIEF WEBBER IS GLARING AT THE WHITEBOARD THAT LISTS SCHEDULED surgeries in "It's the End of the World" (2-16). The board is nearly empty.

"Quiet board means trouble. A quiet board is death! A quiet board bodes bad news!" he mutters.

"HAVE YOU GOT THE PAGER, LASZLO?" MICHAEL ENGLEHART ASKS LASZLO Kiraly. He takes the pager as he assumes responsibility as chief resident for the night shift of the trauma service. Kiraly also hands over the list of patients. It is short.

"You know what that means, a one-pager," Englehart says. Like Chief Webber, he is worried that the current calm may be followed by a flood of patients.

Whenever things are quiet, the residents hesitate to say anything, fearing they may jinx the rest of the shift.

ALTHOUGH EVERY SURGERY IS A SERIOUS MATTER, SURGEONS ALSO NEED TO find some humor and levity when and where they can; even when it is hidden among the damage and disease all around them.

At the weekly conference of the trauma service, fifth-year resident Michael Englehart is presenting the case of a patient who was a passenger in a car that crashed and rolled. The car was destroyed. It took rescuers over an hour to extricate the driver. The patient briefly lost consciousness, but she had been buckled in and was able to get herself out of the wrecked car. She had the sort of "seat belt sign" bruise pattern trauma surgeons often see in crash survivors. It's both good and bad news. Good because it means the person was belted in, but potentially worrisome, too.

"We go home worrying about bowel injury in these patients," Englehart says to his colleagues. Especially if the lap belt crosses the belly instead of being low and tight across the hips, belts can injure internal organs. "This one handled it right. There was probably no bowel injury, but sometimes there is, and we have to always watch for it. Bad consequences are possible."

After recounting the specific treatment of this patient, Englehart reviews the medical literature on injuries related to seat belts. He projects a slide of a young driver doing a "gangster lean," slouched in the seat. Though the driver in the picture is wearing a seat belt, because he is slouched back, he could just slide right under the belt in a crash.

Then Englehart makes a surprising statement. "But the gangster lean can be acceptable." How? He flips to the next slide. It's a passenger, strapped in, but slouching back even more than the driver in the last slide. The audience breaks into laughter . . . because the passenger in this picture is a baby facing backward, snuggled and safe in an infant car seat.

A light-hearted interlude offers welcome relief.

ON THE WHITEBOARD IN A PHYSICIANS WORKROOM IS SCRAWLED: "PRAYING for Poop!"

Potty jokes are a staple of playgrounds, but they also circulate in the hospital because, let's face it, pooping properly is a basic bodily function that doesn't rank much lower than breathing.

Alex Karev confronted the vital importance of poop in "Physical Attraction . . . Chemical Reaction" (4-07).

"How is it going, Jerry?" Karev asks his patient.

"If by, 'How is it going?' you mean, have I had the pleasure yet of taking a crap, Dr. Karev, the answer is, it's not going. Nothing's moving."

"It's been five days since your bowel resection, you should be . . ."

"Crapping by now? What's the problem? Did you people botch the surgery? Is there crap leaking out into my body?"

"The surgery was a success."

"Listen, Dr. Karev. I've been divorced twice. My children won't talk to me. I've battled addictions, filed for bankruptcy, my life has basically sucked, but through it all, the one thing I had going for me was, I crapped like clockwork. It's a simple pleasure. I want it back. So get your little prescription pad and write me a prescription for something to make me crap!"

There is a serious side to the subject. After the trauma of abdominal surgery, the patient's intestines may stop the peristaltic motion that moves material along. In most cases, this ileus, as it is known, lasts only a couple of days. But if the intestines don't get moving again, that's a problem. So the first poop after surgery is a welcome milestone of recovery.

Also, the texture and other characteristics of poop, or stool, can reveal important clues about what is going on inside a patient. It's a subject every resident pays attention to, so when a resident in the physicians workroom started talking about stools, Nick Tadros listened. "We're getting some cool new stools." Cool new stools? Tadros was puzzled. He looked over at the other resident's computer screen. But the resident wasn't reviewing a patient's chart; he was looking at a furniture store website. When he said "cool new stools," he was talking about the zebra-patterned bar stools he and his wife had just purchased.

It is not the first time Tadros has experienced this kind of double-take.

"It happens. When I'm out of the hospital, I'll hear something that doesn't make sense. Then I realize they are using a word that means a different thing in the outside world."

BEHIND CLOSED DOORS, TIRED AND STRESSED RESIDENTS AND ATTENDINGS sometimes slip into humor they wouldn't want patients to hear.

As they compared notes about different attending surgeons, one resident mentioned a surgeon he thought was fun to work with. "We had good times at three A.M. He tells inappropriate jokes in the OR."

Researchers at another medical school looked into jokes about patients by gathering medical students into focus group discussions. The students said they don't intend to be mean about individuals, even as they reported that students, residents, and even senior faculty all made jokes about patients. The humor often seems to offer relief from or a defense against the pain and suffering health care professionals work with shift after long shift.

Patients who seem to be at least partially to blame for their own problems are among those most likely to be the butt of jokes, including obese patients and drug users. Difficult patients can also become targets. On the other hand, the researchers heard that dying patients are off limits.

AS MARK SLOAN ENTERS SEATTLE GRACE HOSPITAL ON A RAINY MORNING in "Six Days: Part 1" (3-11), Alex Karev greets him with a coffee.

"Bone dry cappuccino," Karev says.

But when he takes a sip, Sloan erupts, "What the hell is this, Karev? Vanilla? Are you trying to poison me? Or are you just trying to make my day a little bit worse? . . . You know if you can't handle coffee, you can't handle plastics. Maybe you ought to head back to the gynie squad where life was all pink and squishy."

THE STEREOTYPE OF THE EGO-DRIVEN SURGEON WHO ABUSES THOSE around him is an extreme. But it happens. In a report on disruptive clinician behavior, the authors referred to the case of a surgeon in California who became aggressive when nurses refused to follow his orders to skip the required sterilization of surgical equipment, so he could rush ahead with an operation. Sheriff's deputies were summoned when the surgeon became abusive. According to one report, a witness heard the surgeon shout, "I am a [expletive] doctor, and I'm going to do what I want." The surgeon lost his privileges, though later he was fully reinstated.

Although such dramatic examples are rare, the Joint Commission accreditation organization requires hospitals to have standards that address disruptive and inappropriate behavior. The Joint Commission says hospitals should have codes of conduct that define acceptable behavior and then create processes for managing "disruptive and inappropriate behaviors."

*   *   *

FOURTH-YEAR RESIDENT KARIN HARDIMAN, M.D. CUTS THROUGH THE layers of the patient's skin with a Bovie electrosurgery knife. Intern Emily Bubbers is helping pull the tissue apart as Hardiman cuts. It is the initial incision of an operation that will expose the patient's liver, where scans indicate a tumor is growing.

The attending surgeon scrubs in and then checks with the women on the team. "How ya guys doing?" asks Susan Orloff, M.D.

The anesthesiologist and anesthesiology resident are both women, as is the circulating nurse.

"Who are you?" Orloff asks the scrub tech. The circulating nurse cuts in. "He's cute. Eye candy," the nurse jokes. For a patient, surgery is no laughing matter, of course; but the light banter is a sign of confidence. These surgeons and the other professionals in the room have done this sort of procedure before and they are ready to do it again.

The nurse's offhand remark highlights another observation: In a gender-reversal of historic patterns, all the M.D.s in this OR are women.

Hardiman reaches the patient's liver and begins checking the site of the suspected tumor. "Lumpy, bumpy there," she says. "Maybe a little bit of fullness." Orloff reaches in to also check the diseased organ. As she pushes her hand into the abdominal cavity, the patient's intestines pop up. Hardiman pushes the intestines back into place.

"We're going to have to do this," Orloff says. "So we might as well do it now." She makes a cut further up in the direction of the patient's head in order to get a bigger opening to work in. Hardiman continues to cut as Orloff guides her. Bubbers helps by sealing off small blood vessels using an argon laser coagulator and adjusting the lights so the other surgeons can get a good view of the liver.

"He's so narrow," Orloff remarks. So many patients today come to surgery for treatment of diseases related to sedentary lifestyles and obesity that it is increasingly unusual to see a slim patient. The surgeons need a wider opening. Orloff digs into the bin holding all sorts of retractors to find one with the right length and width. It takes muscle to pry skin and tissue back and then tighten down the screws holding retractors in place on the rig.

Orloff moves around to the left side of the patient. She exposes the tumor. It is a big hard dome of tissue protruding from the liver. It is even larger than it looked on the scans. "Ugly," Orloff mutters. "That's the technical term."

Orloff wants a larger opening still. She pulls up on the patient's rib cage. The job requires force. She asks the scrub tech to go beyond his normal duties and help them. He steps away from the instrument trays to lend both hands and his muscles to the task. The tableau of female surgeons being assisted by a male scrub tech again highlights the changing gender ratios in medicine. Surgery may have lagged behind other specialties, but the trend is clear.

Hardiman and Orloff review the scans showing a mass in the part of the liver nearest the kidney. They work out how to extract a sliver of tissue to send to the pathology lab using a specialized biopsy tool. "Just to review, you press it to the liver, go in, and then pull out," Hardiman says to Orloff.

When they retrieve the tissue, Orloff tells the circulating nurse what she wants the pathologist to do. "Frozen core biopsies. Right lobe lesion. Rule out malignancy . . . hepatocellular carcinoma," she says.

The surgeons continue to scroll back and forth through the scans of the patient's midsection, trying to locate key liver structures so they can figure out what they want to cut out and how to remove the diseased tissue without losing something important. As Orloff and Hardiman look at the scans, Bubbers reaches in to the patient to feel the liver and tumor. There are no standard parts diagrams for people. Each patient, each organ, each tumor, is different. So the surgeons quite literally feel their way along.

Bubbers has to leave to go back to the patients in the hospital. Hardiman takes the lead for part of the procedure, stapling tissue together. "Karin, you did it. Good job," Orloff commends her when she inspects the work.

When the pathologist's report comes back, it contains no clear conclusions about the mass in the liver near the kidney. It might not be hepatocellular carcinoma, but the pathologist can't rule it out. In the face of this uncertainty, Orloff decides to remove the mass.

"Just take it. It's not a chip shot, but we can do it," she says. She reviews the pros and cons with Hardiman. They want to remove any potential cancer cells if possible, and the liver is a resilient organ, which can regenerate to a certain extent; but they also want to preserve as much of the vital organ as possible. "You take more, take more, take more and then all of a sudden, crash," Orloff cautions.

Bubbers returns from the hospital floor. She uses Orloff's digital camera to snap pictures of the tumor, of Hardiman operating, and of the patient's scans.

"Emily, were you here for the last resection?" Orloff asks her.

"No,"

"Scrub in. It'll take five minutes. I want you to see this." It's an invitation no intern is likely to decline.

The team approaches a critical stage in this procedure. They will be removing a segment of liver and then will need to staple the area closed as quickly as possible. The scrub tech lines up a row of loaded staplers. Each one can seal a few inches of tissue at a time. They plan to fire one after another in rapid succession.

As the operation enters its fifth hour, the surgeons remove the segment of liver that contains the suspicious mass, and drop it in to a pan. Suddenly, blood starts filling the cavity. They suction it away. The pace shifts into high gear. The anesthesiologist asks, "Why didn't you warn me?" "We just cut a vein and we're closing it up," Orloff replies as she works quickly. Hardiman says later that they hadn't seen a branch of a vein leading out of the liver. The patient's blood pressure drops. Orloff is able to block the bleed with her finger, but she has to release it in order to fix it. "We have to sew it up, but we can't clamp it and sew it at the same time," Orloff says. Bubbers is suctioning blood with vacuum instruments in both hands as fast as she can . . . while Orloff is stitching rapidly, her fingers flying.

"The bleeding is stopped," she announces.

Hardiman says Orloff is frugal with her patients' blood. While other surgeons doing a similar procedure might routinely lose a liter of blood, Orloff is more meticulous about locating and closing blood vessels, rather than simply cutting them and then stopping the bleeds; so this bleed was unusual for her. After the bleed is contained, the mood in the OR relaxes again, Orloff backs off to coach the younger women on this all-female surgery team as they put the finishing touches on the procedure.

*　*　*

THAT SCENE WOULD HAVE BEEN UNIMAGINABLE IN EARLIER DECADES.

"My surgery education was abusive," vascular surgeon Erica Mitchell, M.D., recalls. "The cycle of abuse by faculty has to stop. I swore that when I could, I'd make a difference."

Indeed, at OHSU things are different for women now. There are about equal numbers of men and women doing surgery residency here.

"The word on the street is there are a lot of women on the faculty. There are people who can be role models. It's not going to be a program that hazes and brutalizes people or that is sexist by its nature. It wouldn't dare!" Surgery Residency Program Director Karen Deveney says with a chuckle. She recalls how she fought to get into the residency program at the University of California San Francisco at a time when she says it was common knowledge that the faculty would accept one, only one, woman each year.

A decade later, she was on the UCSF surgery faculty, but she was the only woman and she found that attitudes hadn't completely changed. One day when the surgeons were meeting to review residency applicants, a colleague told her what another surgeon had said, out of her earshot: "Doesn't it just piss you off to see all these women and foreigners applying in surgery? Whatever happened to the good old all-American boys we used to get?"

Now the chair of the UCSF Department of Surgery is a woman. Deveney says it is not so much that surgery has changed, but that society in general has changed. However, Deveney says she still sees gender bias. For instance, she says when projections indicate coming shortages of surgeons, some observers blame the rising proportion of surgeons who are female.

"That they won't be working as many hours as men and so on. I think that there are some built-in untruths and biases. It irritates me, to tell you the truth; because I don't think it has anything to do with gender, it's generational," Deveney says. She says there are also claims that women are more likely to drop out of surgery residency, but she hasn't seen it. "There has been absolutely no difference in attrition between men and women in our residency."

Progress for women in surgery has not been equal everywhere. While many surgery residency programs in the western United States have similar numbers of men and women, sometimes more women than men, nationally only about one of four surgery residents is a woman. And Deveney says she tells women to not bother applying for programs in some parts of the country.

When intern Ashley Stewart was visiting residency programs, she was startled to hear a faculty member turn to the group of applicants and say "I'm addressing the women now." The surgeon then told a story about a woman who was a surgeon in Russia. When her ability to practice was challenged by a priest, the surgeon said the woman beat up the priest. "That's the kind of women we want," the surgeon announced. That's not the kind of program Stewart was looking for.

"If programs in different parts of the country are doing something to discourage women from applying or seeking to train there, that's their loss. They are losing out on fifty percent of the good people," Deveney says.

MAN OR WOMAN, THE JOB OF A SURGEON IS TO GO INTO A PATIENT'S BODY and try to fix things. Whether the thing needing fixing is a clogged heart artery or a cancerous tumor, it might seem that one kind of surgery is much like any other. But actually, there can be fundamental distinctions between the kinds of people who do well in different surgical subspecialties, as *Grey's Anatomy* illustrated in "Wishin' and Hopin' " (3-14).

Cristina Yang is examining Meredith Grey's mother when Ellis Grey starts prodding Cristina for information about her daughter.

"You and Meredith are good friends? I can tell; because you're afraid to look at me, as if I might ask you some personal question about her and you'll accidentally slip. But you don't do anything accidentally, do you?" Ellis Grey says. "Has Meredith chosen a specialty?"

"That's a personal question," Yang responds.

"For surgeons, the most personal question you can ask. It tells you who they are," Ellis Grey agrees.

Yang asks Ellis Grey's opinion about the specialty she dreams of. "If I chose cardiothoracics, what would that say about me?"

"Heart surgeons are the know-it-alls. They're the most ambitious, the most driven. They want it all and they want it now. And they don't want anything getting in their way," Ellis Grey says.

In some ways, residency is a long courtship, each rotation an extended date with a specialty. Well, more than a date, really. The residents move in with a service for weeks at a time. The attendings and residents size each other up for compatibility. Technical skill is not the only issue. No, at the heart of the matter is personality.

All services are busy in a major hospital. And each one has challenges. But some services beat to a faster tempo; while others tend to involve more planning. Trauma cases often must be solved quickly; and trauma surgeons frequently don't know what they will be doing next until their pagers blare. A cancer may have been slowly growing for years or even decades before it is recognized; typically there are at least days and perhaps weeks or months for doctors and patients to deliberate before heading into the OR.

CRISTINA YANG STUMBLES UPON A DERMATOLOGY WAITING ROOM IN "Brave New World" (5-04). To her it is an alien land. She gets Meredith Grey and Izzie Stevens to join her there. The show portrays a warm and fuzzy environment, a landscape marked with very different milestones than the ones they are used to.

"We could transfer, maybe we'd be happier," Stevens says.

"We'd die of boredom," Yang retorts.

"We'd die with great skin," says Grey.

"I had the biggest derm emergency that exists today and I was fine for about a minute, because the woman almost died," Yang tells them. "But then we saved her. And all she needed was a stupid biopsy."

Stevens and Grey tell Yang what marked their day.

"I tore a guy's face off," Stevens says.

"I reattached a coronary artery," Grey adds.

The depiction of dermatology practice may be warm and fuzzy, but it's clearly not a match for Yang and the others.

"I hate you both. We are not happy, glowy people," Yang observes.

"Yeah," Grey says.

"We gotta get outta here," Yang says.

"Yeah," the others agree.

*   *   *

FOURTH-YEAR RESIDENT KHAN SAYS HE SEEMS TO BE GRAVITATING toward cancer surgery.

"The procedures are long and technically demanding, but they are planned," he says. "There is basic science and preparation for each procedure. It's not like trauma, which involves more emergencies."

"IN GENERAL, PEOPLE CAN BE CATEGORIZED IN ONE OF TWO WAYS: THOSE who love surprises, and those who don't," Meredith Grey says in "Into You Like a Train" (2-06). "I've never met a surgeon that enjoys a surprise, because, as surgeons, we like to be in the know. We have to be in the know. Because when we aren't, people die and lawsuits happen."

Actually, while no one likes bad surprises—and all good surgeons are meticulous about plotting out the potential twists and turns of an operation—some surgeons, including trauma surgeons, tend to lean toward anticipating what challenges may roll in the emergency department with little warning, while other surgeons prefer to construct their operative plan with time for thorough deliberation.

THE CHIEF OF THE DIVISION OF SURGICAL ONCOLOGY, KEVIN Billingsley, confirms Khan's depiction of cancer surgery as belonging in the latter category.

"Trauma surgeons are a very different breed. They can be sitting around the hospital doing nothing, it's the middle of the night, and the next thing they know they are operating on someone who's been shot and is bleeding out and is half dead. That's not me. I don't like that. That takes a very different set of skills. It takes being able to make very rapid decisions that are life and death, often with very little information," Billingsley says. "That doesn't mean that there aren't some very tense moments in a number of the cases that I do, but often I know it's going to be difficult. I expect it."

*   *   *

THE TUMOR DISTENDS THE WOMAN'S BELLY. NOT ONLY IS HER SKIN STRETCHED, but all of the organs in her abdomen have been pushed far to the right. The tumor grew out of the adrenal gland on top of her left kidney. Now that kidney is near the midline of her body. The pancreas, which should be near the back of her abdomen, is squished up under her skin. Next to it is the spleen, pushed so far out of place that it will likely have to be removed. Indeed, the plan for the operation includes possibly removing several organs that may be infiltrated by cancer or too damaged to save.

Billingsley met the patient a couple of weeks before this operation. As he planned the procedure, one of his chief concerns was avoiding damage to the nearby mesenteric artery. "Injuring it could be catastrophic, because of all the organs it supplies with blood," he says. Many adrenal gland tumors are removed laparoscopically, leaving only tiny wounds. But clearly this case is different.

Billingsley marks a long incision line. Then Melanie Morris, M.D., who is serving her two-month rotation as chief resident on this service, begins to cut through skin and tissue to expose the tumor. There is some concern about whether the tumor will push organs up out of the abdomen when they cut open the taut skin, but the initial incision goes smoothly.

"I need the shears. The big ones," Billingsley tells the scrub nurse. He takes the tool, which looks like something for pruning tree branches, and snips through a rib, exposing the tumor.

"Wow, this thing is huge," exclaims the scrub nurse.

"Yes, it is," Morris says.

"It's about what I expected," Billingsley adds.

The tumor and abdominal organs had been scanned in detail before the operation, so Billingsley could see precisely how big it was and the dislocations of organs and major blood vessels. But scans are flat. They are painted in shades of gray. Directly seeing the tumor is different. The size of a small bowling ball, it is mottled red, pink, and whitish. The surface, also like a bowling ball, is hard and smooth, crisscrossed with red filaments.

They lift the bright red spleen off the tumor and place it gently on the woman's skin. Billingsley reaches both arms deep into the woman's abdomen, puts his hands under the tumor and lifts firmly, testing to see how and where the growth is attached. Morris cuts around the tumor. Then they lift it again.

"It feels like it's right there," Billingsley says. "Rock back," he tells Morris. She reaches under the tumor and pulls it toward her. "Oh, there you go."

The tumor lifts, but it is not quite free. "I want to weigh this thing when we get it out," Billingsley says. "Whew." Trying to pull the tumor loose is hard, physical work. They locate and tie off blood vessels. They steadily work to cut through the tissue holding the tumor in place.

Almost two hours into the procedure, they cut the final connections and lift the tumor out, leaving a gaping hole. They rest the tumor on the woman's belly and inspect her organs.

"I think Mr. Spleen is still well perfused," Billingsley says, smiling.

"Yay, spleen made it!" Morris exclaims. The pancreas seems to have survived as well. It's good news. There are no obvious signs that tumor cells invaded either organ.

"I'm sampling some lymph nodes," Billingsley says. The lymph nodes will be sent to the pathology lab to check for tumor cells. "Then we'll put Humpty Dumpty back together again."

They weigh the tumor on the kind of hospital scale often used to weigh newborns.

"Ten-point-one pounds."

"Is that all?" Billingsley remarks.

"That thing felt really heavy," Morris adds.

Billingsley has removed tumors that weigh almost three times as much as this one. It's no record, but its removal will make a dramatic difference to the patient. Billingsley snaps pictures of the tumor on the scale, before placing it in a large plastic tub.

Morris and a medical student inventory the woman's organs. Her heart is beating strongly. Her lungs show black spots, apparently from years of smoking.

"Does everything look happy in there?" Billingsley asks.

"It does. We just took a little tour around," Morris replies.

Now that the invader is gone, they place the organs back into a more normal arrangement. They close the diaphragm. Billingsley says the tumor was adhering to the diaphragm more extensively than he expected, but otherwise the procedure went much as he expected when he planned it.

"The large tumors are not necessarily the most technically difficult," Billingsley says. "For example, some pancreatic tumors can invade blood vessels. That's tougher."

As they screw a metal plate onto the woman's rib to reconnect it, Billingsley asks the medical student, "Do you know what you want to do?"

"No," the student admits. "Things keep changing."

"Surgeons are the best!" Morris advises.

After the procedure, Morris says that one of the good things about cancer surgery is the way the procedures are usually well planned in advance.

"But the bad side is the clinic," she says. "It can be so depressing. Cancer all day, every day."

AFTER THE SURGERY WAS DONE—SURPRISE, THE TUMOR WASN'T A TUMOR after all. It was a giant hematoma, a collection of clotted blood. From the outside, and even in scans, the two abnormalities can look alike. It was good news for the patient. Now she needn't worry about undetected cancer metastases.

EACH SERVICE IS INDIVIDUAL IN WAYS THAT ARE BOTH IMPORTANT AND trivial.

"When you're on the vascular service, the intern's only job is to know where the patients are," a senior resident says. "You need to lead the team on rounds and the attendings don't like to double back."

Stewart confirms the story. "The job of the intern is to find all the patients and put them in order from top floor down. They hate to backtrack."

But a rule that is sacred on one service may be blasphemy on the next.

"This is the way to do it, we're told. It's presented as dogma. Then you go on to the next service and they say, 'What are you doing?!' " Stewart says.

MARK SLOAN BERATES ALEX KAREV FOR VIOLATING HIS PREFERENCES IN "Six Days: Part 1" (3-11).

"Karev, how did I tell you I like my charts? I like to round on pre-op before post-op. Do you like wasting my time? Is it fun for you?"

"No, sir."

"Then get it right."

BECAUSE EACH SERVICE HAS ITS IDIOSYNCRASIES, TIPS FROM AN INTERN wrapping a rotation can be lifesavers.

Just before the interns switch services, Bubbers joins intern Jason Susong, M.D., and fourth-year resident Karin Hardiman in the cafeteria to get tips on the liver transplant service.

"The thing about liver is that you are the only one on the floor. The chief resident is in the OR or the clinic," Susong says.

"They have a lot of meds," Bubbers notes.

"They are very complicated patients," Hardiman confirms.

"On Thursday, start your rounds earlier or you'll be behind all day," Susong advises Bubbers.

Then he warns Bubbers about a staffer who can be trouble. "Tell her, 'You're awesome.' And don't get on her bad side." But Susong says that a surgeon who has a reputation for striking fear into residents isn't really as scary as everyone thinks.

They run down the current patients on the ward, including a man who has been in the hospital more than he's been home over the past year.

"Call me any time," Hardiman tells Bubbers.

"How about at three A.M.?"

"Anytime. The most uncomfortable thing is not knowing."

MIDWAY THROUGH HER INTERN YEAR, LAURA MATSEN IS FINALLY GETTING to work on the orthopedics service. "Ortho" residents start off rotating through a variety of services along with the general surgery residents, but then they branch off into their specialized training. So far, Matsen says her experiences on the orthopedics service reinforce her choice of specialties. She says she likes that fact that most orthopedics diagnoses and outcomes are clear-cut.

During a skills lab one day, the instructor projected an image of an angiogram. The class was all about blood vessels, but Matsen zeroed in on the shadow of a bone in the image. "That's so pretty!" she said.

"We look at their x-rays from before and after surgery. And it's so clear that something was done. It doesn't always work, but it's pretty clear why it didn't work. It's very mechanical. Generally, if you follow logical thought, then the patient gets better. Whereas I feel in general surgery, sometimes people get stuck with an ileus [a disruption of intestinal function that is common after abdominal surgery] for weeks and weeks, and you don't know why and you can't figure out anything to do. I like how visual and mechanical and structured orthopedics is."

And she likes the sometimes physical nature of the work, including popping dislocated joints back into place, like the two hips she recently relocated.

"That was fun. It was a lot of pulling; and I got nervous that I wouldn't be strong enough to do it."

TRAUMA SURGEONS AND HEART SURGEONS, FOR EXAMPLE, OFTEN SEE the results of their efforts very quickly. Either the procedure works . . . or it doesn't. Things are different for cancer surgeons. Even when a procedure to remove a cancerous tumor accomplishes what the team set out to do, it may take a long time before they and the patient know whether it changed the course of the disease. Cancers are often slow-growing, and they may return months or years later, even when the surgery appeared to remove all detectable signs of disease.

"I think oncologists have a bit more of a sense of humility than some of our surgical counterparts. If you want to be the conquering hero every day, oncology is probably not the right field, because you are dealing with a disease process that you're often not going to cure. And you are not sure if you have fixed the problem or not for a couple of years. And some of the good outcome has to do with your operation and some of it may have to do with the disease biology," cancer surgeon Billingsley says.

So when looking at a resident who is considering surgical oncology as a career, like Khan is, what are some of qualities Billingsley looks for?

"If they like talking to patients, they are often well-suited to oncology," he says. "Because in oncology we spend a lot of time answering questions and talking about issues that are uncomfortable. 'Am I going to die?' 'What if the operation doesn't work?' 'How long am I going to live?' 'The cancer is back now! Oh my God!' If you don't like that, you're not going to do well in oncology; whereas in many surgical fields, you actually don't need to spend that much time talking to patients."

While surgeons in many specialties chose their path in part because they could spend more time taking action than talking, in contrast to their colleagues in medicine; Billingsley says that talking to patients, getting to know them and not just their diseases, is one of the things that drew him to oncology.

"Often I have a relationship with people for an extended period of time. You become quite close to the patients. They are intense interactions. The relationships are very meaningful," he says. "The other thing that I like, frankly, is that most oncologic surgery is scheduled and planned. It's a field that attracts people who like to plan a complex undertaking. They know when they are going to do it. They've mapped out all the potential pitfalls and avenues of surprise and retreat."

Khan also likes the planning and relative predictability of cancer surgery. He says he doesn't mind the length of some of the big, technically demanding procedures, which can last all day, like the Whipple procedure that Cristina Yang tried to get in on in "No Man's Land" (1-04).

YANG BURST INTO THE PATIENT'S ROOM BEFORE DAWN TO CHECK ON A NEW patient.

"You have an abdominal mass consistent with pancreatic cancer," Yang says as she reviews the patient's chart.

"Oh, and you are hoping they're gonna give me a Whipple, a pancreatic duodenectomy. This hospital sees those maybe once every six months. That's why you got here at four thirty, huh?" the patient guesses. She was a nurse and has figured out what Yang is after.

*   *   *

ACTUALLY, WHIPPLE PROCEDURES AND SIMILAR OPERATIONS AREN'T QUITE that rare. But they are long and complex.

Just after eight o'clock in the morning, surgeon Brett Sheppard is outside an OR, where one of the chief residents and some medical students are preparing for a Whipple procedure. This one begins as a laparoscopic procedure.

"Lights, camera, action," says chief resident Minhao Zhou, M.D., as he begins to thread a fiber optic camera into the abdomen of a patient with pancreatic cancer. This patient's symptoms began with pain due to pancreatitis, an inflammation of the pancreas. Further investigation revealed cancer. Pancreatic cancer is often discovered too late to be treated effectively. But in this case there might be a chance to remove the tumor before cancer cells spread.

The powerful light coming from the tip of the fiber optic device makes the patient's belly glow red, like the cheeks of children on a campout who have wrapped their lips around a flashlight.

"That's a pissed off pancreas there," Sheppard says when he sees a hard nodular area on the monitor. "Okay, let's go ahead and open him up."

Sheppard leaves the OR to scrub in. Zhou pulls the fiber optic camera back out. Then he marks a large chevron across the patient's belly pointed toward his head. With Sheppard back in the room, Zhou begins to cut as Sheppard assists by holding the patient's skin and organs so Zhou can work his way toward the diseased pancreas.

They take a biopsy, a small slice, of abnormal-looking liver and send it along to pathology for a quick check. If cancer cells have reached the liver, there may not be any point to continuing with the operation. Zhou, in his fifth year of residency, is learning by doing; meanwhile, a pair of medical students assist in small ways, using forceps to pull up on a flap of skin or setting up a rig to hold retractors in place.

The students are connecting the anatomy they have been learning in classes and labs to the view they now have of a living patient. There are no labels or color keys here. At first glance, the intertwined tissues and organs are a confusing jumble. It takes time and experience to make sense of the scene.

Sheppard explains the technique they are using to separate the duo-denum (part of the small intestine) from the retroperitoneum (the back of the abdominal cavity). "What's behind the duodenum and underneath the liver?" he asks one of the students. Then he points to a large blood vessel. "What's that?" he asks the other student. "IVC?" she guesses, hoping she's correctly identified the large vein, the inferior vena cava, that carries blood from the lower body up to the heart. "Yes."

Sheppard keeps up a steady stream of anatomy quiz questions for the medical students. He explains what to cut and how to cut in order to open up the correct area as well as what not to cut, of course. It's obvious that he enjoys introducing them to his world.

The Whipple procedure (generically know as a pancreatoduodenec-tomy, or pancreatic duodenectomy) involves removing the head of the pancreas (the organ that makes insulin), most of the duodenum (part of the small intestine), and perhaps also sections of bile duct, the gallbladder, and a bit of the stomach. Then after all this internal plumbing is taken out, new connections are made so that the patient can still eat and digest food.

"When was the first Whipple? And what happened to the first patient" Sheppard asks. The answers: 1935 and he died. Although revised versions of the procedure named after Allen O. Whipple have become the most common operation for pancreatic cancer, when it comes to pioneering surgeries, it's often better to be the surgeon than the patient. As Sheppard tells the students, the death rate among patients undergoing a Whipple procedure was about 60 percent in the early days. By the 1960s things had improved; 60 percent of the patients lived, but the risks were still enormous. Sheppard says that now the mortality rate of this extensive surgery is below 5 percent, perhaps only 1 to 2 percent in some programs. He asks the students to explain the dramatic improvement. The answer: partly better surgery but also safer anesthesia and improved technology.

The phone in the OR rings. It's the pathologist. Over the speakerphone, he tells Sheppard that the liver biopsy contained only fibrosis, no malignancy. "Sweet. Thanks," Sheppard replies as he returns to teaching while doing. Signs the cancer had spread might have dashed hopes for a good outcome. There might have been little point in continuing the surgery.

"I try to be a classic 'Whipple-ist,' " he tells the medical students, "but the gallbladder was in the way, so we'll take it out. Why did we start laparoscopically?"

"To see if there was obvious spread of cancer," answers a student.

"What percent of procedures end there?"

"Ten percent?" the student guesses.

"Or less," Sheppard says. "It used to be higher. What's changed?"

"Better imaging?"

"Yes, better imaging."

"There is the gallbladder," Sheppard announces. The circulating nurse comes over with a small jar to collect it; but the gallbladder is hugely enlarged. "Oh! It's not going to fit in that," she says.

While attention is focused on this patient, there are others also being cared for by this service. Intern Ryan Gertz comes into the OR to "run the list," review the patients, with Zhou. But Gertz is not here just to talk about patients on the floor. He's hungry for time in the OR. Although medical students on surgery rotations get to watch and participate in procedure after procedure, interns have to squeeze OR time into schedules dominated by monitoring and managing patient care before and after surgery.

Since he isn't scrubbed in, Gertz goes around by the patient's head, to stand next to the anesthesiologist. He peers over the drape pinned up to posts that protects the sterile area below the patient's neck. "It's nice to be tall," Gertz quips.

"Oh man, I should get in on this." Gertz yearns to scrub in and take part in this Whipple procedure. "It's complex. You're changing so many things in the anatomy. And you can fix people. It's not always just palliative." In other words, it can get rid of the cancer, if the tumor is confined to the section of pancreas being removed; so it offers to do more than just alleviate, or palliate, the symptoms or slow the progression.

But Gertz can't lay aside his primary responsibility to patients on the hospital floor. He managed to break away temporarily only because he had some downtime while waiting for some lab reports. Sure enough, his pager soon demands attention, and he has to abandon his viewpoint to go to the phone.

Sheppard and Zhou continue to work their way through the convoluted anatomy around the patient's pancreas. "I used to be a pro at

Twister," Sheppard remarks as he twists and turns to get the right angle. "Let's get around this artery and bulldog it," he says as he identifies a key blood vessel. Zhou then puts a bulldog clamp on it. "You really did that nicely," Sheppard compliments his resident.

Then he continues the anatomy lessons for the medical students.

"This is the right hepatic [artery] here. Does it go on top of or under the bile duct?"

"On top?"

"No, beneath. So if this is the right hepatic, what's this?"

"Left gastric [artery]?"

"No."

Even after pouring over anatomy illustrations and models, it takes direct experience to become comfortable distinguishing the arteries, veins, ducts and other tissues and organs inside the human body. At first, so many things look the same, but cutting or tying off the wrong piece could have disastrous consequences for the patient.

Sheppard directs Zhou: "Leave this alone. Use this as your demarcation and come across here." Though Zhou has his hands on the instruments, it is Sheppard's experience that is leading the way. "Got to get rid of this. Whatever this is doesn't belong here anymore. That clears up your duct. Remember the relationship to the veins. When you're in this field, Minhao, you've got to get underneath the pancreas. Come up against the duct," Sheppard advises Zhou.

They get tape ready so they can hold things in the proper position. "Here the right hepatic goes under the duct, okay let's divide the duct," Sheppard says. They pull out a clogged plastic stent that had been inserted in an earlier operation to hold open the bile duct.

Done with his phone call, Gertz is once again perched by the patient's head. This is the fun part of the job. "Yeah, better than chasing radiology results," Gertz says. And while the medical students have sometimes struggled to identify things, Gertz says he's able to make sense of the view of the patient's internal organs. "On this type of procedure you really can appreciate the anatomy. I've never seen one before."

But the patients on the floor need attention. "Anything you need?" Gertz asks the team before, reluctantly, leaving the OR.

"Go outside and enjoy the sun for us," Sheppard replies. "Somebody should." Surgeons rarely get to loll in the sun.

As Gertz exits the OR his eyes are alive, energized by the opportunity to watch experienced hands performing a Whipple procedure. "It's completely different than gross anatomy classes and labs. In those labs you lose the color and everything is matted and dry. I'd much rather see this. It has a different feel." And he talks about earlier experiences assisting with abdominal surgeries. "You have to be careful working around the spleen, etc. When you put your hands in, you definitely get the attending's attention."

Gertz admits that before he joined the "Blue" surgery service (the name of the service at OHSU that focuses on the stomach, esophagus, liver, and other organs), he was intimidated by what he had heard from other interns. "But it's been great," Gertz says. "Dr. Sheppard really likes to teach."

As the complex surgery is in its third hour, Sheppard and Zhou complete their work in the upper part of the abdomen. But there is much more to do. Sheppard occasionally stamps his feet, just to get some movement in his legs. He's been standing for hours and there are many more to go. Nurses, anesthesiologists, and other staffers take breaks and hand off duties at shift changes. But surgeons usually don't stop until the work is done.

Sheppard turns to one of the medical students. "Are you hungry? Go ahead and take a break, if you feel the need. It won't be considered a sign of weakness." After a pause he adds jokingly, "You won't pass, but it won't be considered a sign of weakness. Ha-ha!" Sheppard may have had a smile behind his mask. But the student doesn't take a break, even though at times her eyelids droop with fatigue. Appearances are important.

They use ultrasonic scalpels to open access to the top of the pancreas. "It's a woody, hard pancreas. Abnormal. The tumor is harder," Sheppard says as he sees the target of the operation. And he repeats a variation of a common saying among surgeons: "Eat when you can. Sleep when you can. And don't [mess] with the pancreas." Actually he used a much stronger word than *mess*. The point being that the pancreas is easily damaged, so it is approached with caution and only by surgeons with experience or under very close supervision.

The Whipple procedure lasts many hours not only because it involves rearranging so many organs but because all this intricate work takes place in a very delicate area, or field, as surgeons term it. "In this field you can't push as hard as you normally can because the vessels are very, very fragile," Sheppard says.

Another pathology report brings good news. The section of bile duct they removed also shows no signs of cancer.

Then as Sheppard is using a Bovie knife, which uses an arc of electric current to cut tissue, he nicks his finger. Though the cut must hurt, he pauses just to get a fresh set of gloves. When he takes the old pair off, his hands are gray and damp with sweat. They've been sealed in the tight gloves for hours. He has to work at getting his fingers into the new set.

A medical student gets to add to her experience by tying a knot. Sheppard and Zhou remove the pancreatic duct and send a specimen along to pathology.

Then the steady, workmanlike mood in the OR suddenly changes. "Bleeding," Sheppard says. He doesn't yell, but the tone of his voice is sharper. The call to attention is clear. In a moment, the bleed is halted. But that moment is a reminder that no surgery is routine and that instant reactions and decisions can make the difference between a passing flash of concern and more serious consequences.

Another good pathology report is called in. The pancreatic duct is negative for cancer.

But then there's another bleed. Work stops. "Here's a big hole in the vein," Sheppard says with urgency. This bleed, too, is soon contained.

Six hours into the procedure, there is still much to do. Sheppard and Zhou plug away at the intricate work; no rest, no meal, not even a drink of water. Like a stork, one of the medical students lifts one foot at a time to rest it. The floor is smooth and hard. The surface is designed to be easy to sanitize and for rolling heavy equipment across. It is not designed for comfort.

Imagine standing in a chilly garage with a concrete floor for seven or eight hours. Don't drink too much coffee to fight the fatigue; surgeons rarely take bathroom breaks. And when you are scrubbed in, you can't even scratch an itch on your face. Observing a long case is an endurance test for medical students and residents. Can they handle the long hours of standing without a break?

*   *   *

IN "GRANDMA GOT RUN OVER BY A REINDEER" (2-12), MIRANDA BAILEY is well into her pregnancy. During an operation, she suddenly looks woozy.

"Dr. Bailey, are you all right?" a nurse says. Meredith Grey starts to ask her if she needs anything.

"I just need a minute, Grey," Bailey tells her. "When you operate, the rest of the world goes away. Hunger, thirst, pain. You don't feel it in the OR."

IN SOME WAYS IT IS HARDER FOR OBSERVERS. SURGEONS SAY THAT WHEN they are involved in a procedure, they barely notice the clock.

Midway through the afternoon, Sheppard announces, "Call vascular and tell them we won't need them." Fellow surgeons who specialize in blood vessels had been alerted that they might be needed to handle the tricky connections that ensure the rearranged organs get good blood supply. Despite a couple of brief bleeds, this procedure has gone according to plan. "Nice job," Sheppard tells Zhou. "Now let's put him back together."

After ninety minutes more of surgery to craft a digestive system that will work despite the missing sections of pancreas and intestine, Sheppard leaves the final closing to his assistants. Finally, about eight hours after the patient arrived in the OR, Zhou folds a large flap of skin back into place. Seeing the belly button in the middle of the chevron incision suddenly makes the patient look more like a human being, rather than just an intertwined mass of organs and tissue. Surgeons have to keep both concepts in mind: the anatomical details, the ducts and blood vessels and organs and connective tissues, but also the whole person.

"If it all goes well, the attending doesn't really have to correct you at all. You're just doing all the steps and it's like a dance, where you and the attending are moving back and forth in choreography. Then all of a sudden, boom, the last stitch is thrown, the skin is closed, and you feel, 'Wow, I can do this!' It's a cool feeling," David Cho says.

"People in medicine joke all the time about the stereotypes, but it's surprising how true they can be. Definitely certain types of people gravitate toward certain types of medicine. I think that's part of what makes medicine so cool, there's a niche for everybody," Fabricant says.

"Great surgeons aren't made; they're born. It takes gestation, incubation, sacrifice, a lot of sacrifice. But after all the blood and guts and gooey stuff is washed away, that surgeon you become . . . totally worth it," Meredith Grey says in "Piece of My Heart" (4-13).

Additional Reading

Ibery, N.; Patel, P. M.; Robb, P. J. "Do Surgeons Wish to Become Doctors?" *Journal of the Royal Society of Medicine,* 99 no. 4 (2006): 197–199. Available at: www .pubmedcentral.nih.gov/articlerender.fcgi?artid=1420777. Accessed August 2009.

Mayo Clinic. "Pancreatic Cancer: Whipple Procedure." Available at: www.mayoclinic .org/pancreatic-cancer/whippleprocedure.html. Accessed August 2009.

Oregon Health & Science University. "Pancreatic Cancer: Information and Treatment Options." Available at: www.ohsu.edu/health/health-topics/getContent-ById.cfm?ContentTypeId=85&ContentId=P00415. Accessed August 2009.

O'Sullivan, Adrian. "Whipple Pancreaticoduodenectomy: A Historical Comment." Grand Rounds, 7 (2007): L1–L2. Available at: www.grandrounds-e-med.com/ articles/gr07L0001.pdf. Accessed August 2009.

Porto, Grena; Lauve, Richard. "Disruptive Clinician Behavior: A Persistent Threat to Patient Safety." *Patient Safety and Quality Healthcare* (2006). Available at: www.psqh.com/julaug06/disruptive.html. Accessed August 2009.

Royal College of Surgeons of England. "Questions about Surgeons." Available at: www.rcseng.ac.uk/patient_information/faqs/surgeons.html. Accessed August 2009.

Rutkow, Ira M. *History of Surgery in the United States, 1775–1900: Textbooks, Monographs, and Treatises.* Norman Bibliography Series 2. Novato, Calif.: Jeremy Norman, 1988.

Rutkow, Ira M. *Surgery: An Illustrated History.* St. Louis: Mosby-Year Book, 1993.

Warner, Brad W. "Society of University Surgeons Presidential Address: Professionalism and Surgery—Kindness and Putting Patients First." Surgery, 136, no. 2 (2004): 105–115. Available at: www.surgjournal.com/ article/S0039-6060(04)00174-6/abstract. Accessed August 2009.

Wear, Delese; Aultman, Julie M.; Varley, Joseph D.; Zarconi, Joseph. "Making Fun of Patients: Medical Students' Perceptions and Use of Derogatory and Cynical Humor in Clinical Settings." Academic Medicine, 81 no. 5 (2006): 454–462. Available at: www.academicmedicine.org/pt/re/acmed/abstract.00001888-200605000-00009.htm. Accessed August 2009.

Whipple, Allen O.; Parsons, William Barclay; Mullins, Clinton R. "Treatment of Carcinoma of the Ampulla of Vater." *Annals of Surgery,* 102, no. 4 (1935): 763–779. Available at: www.pubmedcentral.nih.gov/articlerender.fcgi?tool=pubmed &pubmedid=17856666. Accessed August 2009.

CHAPTER SEVENTEEN

Institutions Have Personalities, Too

Chief Webber hides in a dark room after a pediatric surgeon, Dr. Jordan Kenley, suddenly dies from a heart attack. At first, his friends assume he is distraught about the death of a colleague or worried about his own mortality. But then he tells Derek Shepherd what is really bothering him.

"I'm worried about my hospital dying. I made some calls to replace Kenley. No one wants to come here. I can't keep a cardiac surgeon on staff; Burke quit, Hahn quit, Dixon's autistic. My OR roof collapsed, the whole place flooded. The interns are literally chopping each other into little pieces. No wonder we are number 12 . . . 12!" Webber complains during "Wish You Were Here" (5-11).

Number 12 refers to a ranking that Seattle Grace Hospital was given, apparently by a national magazine, at the beginning of the fifth season. The hospital had been demoted from number 2, and Chief Webber wasn't happy at all. "This is not a number 12 teaching hospital! I do not run the number 12 surgical program in the country!" he fumed.

Although administrators snort at the rankings of hospitals and medical schools by magazines and others, calling them unreliable popularity contests, reputations and perceptions do have effects. For medical students, reputation plays a critical role in choosing which residency programs to apply to.

Like many medical students, Nick Tadros looked at dozens of surgery residency programs. He considered the information he could gather about the quality of surgery training at each one. And in the beginning, he put the programs with the greatest national prestige at the top of his list. But then he made a more personal calculation.

"I think when you are faced with this idea of actually having to be somewhere for five or ten years, you really want to be in a place where you are happy. So I think that's why the idea of fitting in with the residents and faculty really was important to me," Tadros says. "You have to be careful with academic programs because there are some that seem really good, but end up being very malignant; you don't get good training and you're not happy there."

Tadros says he looked at some programs that touted the high test scores of their residents, but he wondered if what that really meant was that residents lived in constant fear of failing a test or perhaps that the program would cut a resident who might spoil the school's average. Some surgery residents do drop out of OHSU, but residents and faculty emphasize the ways they try to support those who may be struggling, rather than simply cutting them loose.

Tadros knew what he was getting into at OHSU, because this is where he spent four years getting through medical school. On the other hand, Karen Zink went to a different medical school. She was looking for a change.

"Where I went to medical school, they didn't figure out that you can be nice to somebody and teach them surgery at the same time; those two things were completely independent. People were mean. People screamed at each other all the time. It was less fun, less collegial," Zink says.

So how did OHSU end up on her short list?

"My adviser asked me what I wanted to look for in a program. My answer was, 'Mountains or water or both,' " Zink recalls. "I also said, 'Well, I want a good program that's going to teach me to be a really good surgeon, that I'm going to be able to go into whatever field that I want to, that I could get a good fellowship if I'd like to, and I'm gonna be trained well and do a lot of cases. And I want a program that's friendly and I want this and that, but I really want mountains or water or both.' "

From the OHSU campus you can see Mount Hood, Mount St. Helens, and other snowcapped volcanic peaks, and the waters of the Willamette and Columbia Rivers. Pacific Ocean beaches are less than a two-hour drive to the west. So the location satisfied Zink's geographical criteria, while the surgery residency program itself met her professional standards.

"The program is a great program. They train you to be a really strong surgeon. You can get any fellowship you want, but the day you graduate you're comfortable operating on your own." She notes that residents here get a variety of experiences. In addition to operating in the university hospital, they also walk across sky bridges to do rotations in the Portland VA Medical Center and Doernbecher Children's Hospital and work at several community hospitals in the Portland area. If they choose, there is a rural hospital rotation, too.

But coming back to Zink's "gotta have" criteria, she must have been pleased by the attitudes of the department leaders. Intern Ashley Stewart remembers Surgery Department Chief John Hunter asking her and other applicants about their outdoor activities. "If you don't have any, you probably won't fit in. At other programs, you just get questions about the cases you've done," she says.

Indeed, right after an overview of the training opportunities, the first page of the General Surgery Residency Program website points out:

Portland is the largest city in Oregon and provides quick access to the Pacific Ocean, Mt. Hood and the Willamette Valley. In their off hours, our residents enjoy hiking, mountain biking, skiing, surfing, rock climbing, and fishing. Oregon is an ecologically-minded state that values conservation and encourages a "green" outlook on life. Many residents bike to work.

ONE EARLY MORNING IN THE HOSPITAL, SAJID KHAN FINDS TIME TO SWING by the cafeteria between prerounding (checking his patients on his own) and his team's group rounds. "It's the first time I've been able to sit and eat before rounds. It's because of the light census," he says.

Khan transferred to OHSU from a residency program in New York City. Human anatomy and surgical techniques may be the same all over, but the variations in how surgery is taught are immense.

"In New York, you have to be on your toes or you'll get walked over," he remembers. "New Yorkers like to brag. Here they are more modest about things and let [their] reputation speak for itself."

Khan was introduced to OHSU by a mentor who knew some of the surgery faculty.

"I interviewed here and they were very friendly. They took care of making all the arrangements for my hotel and so on. I don't know if you'd get that same hospitable treatment in New York City. I had originally planned to go home and think things over before making the move out to the West Coast, but I was so impressed with OHSU that I ended up signing a contract during my short visit here."

Khan says he had other opportunities at prestigious programs in New York City and Boston, but he says he's very happy he came here.

"I wondered why I had never heard of OHSU. The leadership is good. Every service has leaders that are at the top of their fields. It's a top institution, but the Portland attitude is to not brag, just let the work speak for itself."

Khan says he likes that attitude, but he also recognizes not every surgery resident would fit in here.

"I feel like they wouldn't let you in unless they felt like you were a good match."

The leaders at some other programs may see efforts to make residency nicer as a sign of weakness or low standards.

"Definitely some of the older surgeons in some of the programs have that culture, and have for decades, they have that attitude that there must be something wrong or that you can't teach somebody unless you put enough fear into them that they force themselves to learn it. I have heard that. I think it's decreasing with time. The current generation of surgery programs across the country has less of that attitude, but Portland is definitely different than a lot of the rest of the country," says Zink, who is a fourth-year resident.

The director of OHSU's Resident Wellness Program, Mary Moffit, Ph.D., R.N., says most of the faculty here would agree with that assessment. She recalls one surgeon telling her that where he did his residency training there was no wellness program and very little social support. He called it a toxic program, where residents were expected to sink or swim. Even if they had a sick child at home or another problem, they were expected to just tough it out.

What's more, Moffit says the leadership here tells residents not to let surgeons from earlier generations get away with claims that things are too easy now. In earlier days, hospital patients weren't as sick. The patients on a regular floor today would have been in the ICU in earlier decades, and today's ICU patients would have died. Today's patients require much more intense care. Even if residents spent longer hours in the hospital, they probably had more down time, even time to take naps. Also, the spouses of married residents in earlier generations probably were at home and took care of things that today's residents, in dual-career marriages, have to help with.

Trauma surgeon Martin Schreiber says he saw firsthand how surgery was taught in a program that was much more aggressive. He says the program here is trying to create more well-rounded professionals.

"We want people who can operate. We want people who are smart. We want people with good decision skills. We want people who can get along with other people, get along with the nurses, get along with their colleagues, get along with consultants. A good surgeon does all of that, not just operate, but good decision making, good leadership skills, good abilities to get along with other people. That's a great surgeon, if you can do all those things," he says.

THE QUEST TO RECRUIT RESIDENTS WHO FIT IN WITH A PROGRAM CAN HAVE a dark side, however. If almost all the faculty and senior residents of a program are white men, as was the rule in earlier years and still the case in some places, then a tendency to select people who fit in can create barriers to women and minorities.

The OHSU surgery residency program is directed by a woman, and there are many women on the faculty. However, the program has not made as much progress in developing racial diversity. Part of the issue is that Portland, Oregon, has been one of the least diverse cities in the country.

LIANJUN XU, M.D., HAS AN UNUSUAL PERSPECTIVE ON THE SURGERY residency program. It's his second time through one . . . and the first time was on a different continent.

Xu went to medical school and then did his surgery residency in China. Rather than going into practice, he moved to Seattle to pursue research into esophageal cancer. But after five years of research, he kept hearing the call of surgery.

"I decided I really wanted to be a surgeon; so I went back to residency," Xu says. Despite his years of training in China, the rules of medicine here required that he start over. "I don't think I can take any shortcuts, even though I already did residency once. The techniques and surgical skills I know, but I have to learn the paperwork and how the health care system works."

He has noticed some differences in the problems that bring people to the hospital for surgery.

"There is very little diverticulitis [a type of inflammation in the intestines] in China, but there is lots in the U.S. Liver is the number one cancer surgery in China. Breast cancer, prostate cancer, and lung cancer are tops here."

But overall, Xu says surgery and surgery residency are very similar.

"Residency life has similarities. There are long hours for residents in both countries, though in China we have 'pre-call,' which means you get a break before pulling the night shift. Surgery is similar in both places. It's the same science, the same literature, the same knowledge base."

Indeed, Xu says the differences he sees are not so much international as micro-level variations.

"The differences are as big between different attendings as they are between different countries. The variation between countries is really not that different than variations between institutions or even individual attendings," Xu says.

Additional Reading

O'Connell, Virginia Adams. *Getting Cut: Failing to Survive Surgical Residency Training*. Lanham, MD, University Press of America, 2007.

CHAPTER EIGHTEEN

Extracurricular Activities

"Especially here at OHSU, there are well-adjusted surgery residents. They are great role models to see that people are playing music, they are still rock climbing, they are still biking, they are still involved in their church or their friends and families, they are having kids. We're not a program that prides itself on its divorce rate, like some programs do," notes intern Nick Tadros.

On *Grey's Anatomy* the outside activities of surgery residents appear to consist mostly of meeting at the Emerald City Bar. Well, Derek Shepherd did take a reluctant Mark Sloan on a hike in "Lay Your Hands on Me" (4-11). Sloan didn't seem to enjoy the outing. As it turned out, the hike was not just for enjoyment of the outdoors, but really so that Shepherd could show Sloan the land he had bought to build his dream home.

By contrast, the surgery residents at OHSU seem driven to not only pursue their careers but to fill their scarce hours outside the hospital with activity, hiking included, of course, but much more as well.

DURING SURGERY AN ATTENDING AND A RESIDENT COLLABORATE ON maneuvers, one leading and the other assisting. Together they cut, hold, suture. The interplay of two surgeons during an operation is often called the dance of surgery.

Surgeons can also dance, just dance. On a Friday evening at the Ash Street Saloon, two attendings lead the way, cutting loose to the beat of 80s pop music. If you ever needed emergency surgery while bar-hopping, this would be the place. It is standing room only in a space packed with attendings, residents of all classes, nurses, and others. They are here because of the band. Surgeons not only dance, some of them also play. Members Only, an 80s cover band, features surgery resident David Cho on keyboards and vocals; internal medicine attending Madison Macht, M.D., on guitar, bass, and vocals; neurosurgery resident Zachary Litvack, M.D., on guitar and bass; and surgery intern Tim Lee, M.D., on drums.

During the sound check earlier in the evening, the band played part of "I Melt with You" by Modern English. The dance floor was empty, except for one guy doing track stands and other stunts on a fixed-gear bicycle. Soon surgeons and others started filtering in.

While residents do gather socially outside of the hospital, this band performance is one of the few times during the year when attendings and others are part of the fun.

"There were nurses there. Everybody was there. I can't think of anything else where that has happened. That's why it was so fun. Oh, my gosh, it was so awesome. I had so much fun, for many reasons, but it was just so much fun to see everybody out. And the band was so good," says intern Ashley Stewart.

They look different without the uniform blue scrubs and caps and masks they wear in the OR or the business attire suitable for seeing patients on the wards. Dressed in their interpretation of 80s band garb, the band members are the most different of all. Cho sports an off-the-shoulder *Flashdance*-type sweater and a bandana. The bass player dons a Devo hat. A wig and wild striped stretch pants decorate the lead guitarist.

"A neurosurgery resident and I and one of the internal medicine residents started the band intern year, just as a release," Cho says. It was a way to put years of lessons to work. "I took twelve years of classical piano growing up."

It was the last year before the 80-hour workweek limit took effect.

"One rainy Sunday, I think in September, we were sitting around after a post-call brunch at Zach's house, drifting in and out of food coma, watching the rain come down hard outside. Madison happened to notice the guitar sitting in the corner, and, much in the way of two dogs sniffing their way around each other to see if they got along, he sort of introduced the subject with a 'Soooo, you don't happen to play, do you?' " Cho recalls.

They played, they performed at some parties, and then they drew a crowd when they opened for a local band that included a urology resident. And the band played on.

"This show, we had about four hundred people. They had to stop letting people in for a while, and I'm told there was a twenty-minute wait to get in."

Cho says he plans to use his cut of the gate receipts to throw a birthday party for his wife. No doubt, anyone married to a surgery resident deserves a good party.

After attendings Martin Schreiber and Susan Orloff get the dancing going, others join in. And while it seems the usual hierarchy has been given the night off, a scan of the crowd reveals that, for the most part, attendings and senior residents populate the front rows, while their juniors tend to hang back a bit. Maybe it's not entirely different from conferences and grand rounds, after all. Yet the social bonds of the group are clear. Surgery is more than just a job.

"Surrounded by good people, by your people, almost anything is bearable. It makes the unfun fun, or at least bearable, and bumps and cracks are definitely smoothed out by the company of friends," Cho says.

IN ADDITION TO DOING THINGS WITH FELLOW SURGEONS OUTSIDE OF THE hospital, there is also something to be said for taking a break from other doctors.

"I think it's really valuable to have a really close group of friends in medicine and a really close group of friends not in medicine. It's nice to have the friends in medicine that you can talk to if something bad goes wrong with the patient or something is really frustrating, who have been there and completely understand. But it's also really, really nice to just be able to get away from it," says Karen Zink. "I love the chance to just get away and not think about the hospital and all and just think about other topics and talk about real people and normal subjects in the real world."

Zink is not only a fourth-year surgery resident, she's also a juggler and a unicycle instructor. Portland boasts active communities around both activities.

"I'm not saying it was a deciding factor in choosing to do residency here, but it definitely was a factor," she says. Zink's affection for unicycles is well known in the hospital. One day the local newspaper featured one-wheeled riders. "I was doing surgery and an attending burst into the operating room with the newspaper. He said, 'Zink! How many people do you know in this picture?!' I took a look and said, 'Uh, all of them.'"

Every Wednesday night, well, when she's not on call, Zink heads over to a college campus across town. A basketball court is littered with balls and batons, bicycles and unicycles, hoops and ropes. About 70 people juggle and chat to a rhythmic techno beat; another dozen warm up outside. This is not your typical health care crowd. Some hair is bright purple or blue. A juggler with a Mohawk haircut also sports multiple lip rings. But then there are also plenty of others who wouldn't stand out in a corporate cubicle farm or at a PTA meeting.

"It gets me totally away from surgeons," Zink says. "When residents get together they talk about work in the hospital. With these jugglers, we will go out to get a beer after practice, and the conversation will be about politics, the environment, anything. They are engineers, lawyers, professional jugglers, waiters; it's all types."

And yet, just as Zink is known in the hospital as the unicyclist, here she is the doctor. It can come in handy. One day, she took care of a gash in a woman's arm. Another time, a woman fell and fractured her wrist. Zink figured out what was wrong on the spot.

"I told her to go get an X-ray," Zink recalls. Then she predicted how the clinic would handle her case. "That they would tell her it wasn't broken, but in the morning they would call her back and say the day radiologist had looked at the film and discovered it was fractured. She didn't really get what I was talking about, but the next day she called me and said, 'You were right. That's exactly what happened.' They never see those fractures the first time they look at the film."

Zink is also helping plan an upcoming juggling festival. It's not easy for residents to follow through on commitments outside of work.

"Intern year I was so frustrated, I had worked a couple of extra shifts so I could have time off for the festival, but then I ended up working from six A.M. to about three thirty P.M. on both days," she remembers. "Then the next year, I was on call, so I had to leave a couple of times. This year I took vacation, so I have the whole week off."

Cho also took vacation the week of his band gig. It is the only way to be almost certain that a beeping pager won't suddenly pull you back into the hospital.

Even in outside activities, the surgeon's personality comes through. This evening Zink is trying to master a sky-high unicycle. The seat comes up to her eyebrows. A chain links the pedals to the wheel far below. A regular unicycle is more than enough challenge for most people; but mounting this high-altitude model seems an impossible challenge. Surgeons love challenges.

Zink steps on the wheel to get up to the pedal and then launch herself up to the seat. She falls. Again she tries. And falls. Again and again. The 7th try almost succeeds. On the lucky 13th try she gets up onto the seat for a moment before crashing down. The 15th try, her feet rock the pedals for a moment; then she falls. The 17th try, she is up, feet on the pedals, a few cranks . . . and then a fall. The 19th crash is a hard one. After 22 attempts, Zink moves on.

As the jugglers and unicyclists head home, the brightly lit OHSU hospital campus dominates the view of the hills across the river.

AT AN INTERN CONFERENCE EARLY ON A MONDAY MORNING, THE residents compare notes on new movie releases. Somehow, 80 hours in the hospital isn't enough to completely exhaust them. "You can sleep when you die," says Emily Bubbers.

*   *   *

EVEN IN THIS FAST CROWD, LAURA MATSEN STANDS OUT . . . OR RATHER, runs ahead. Rock climbing, marathons, and triathlons are on the calendar. Because long hospital shifts threaten to leave her too tired to work out in the evenings, she often fits in a run before work. "Before work" translates to 3:30 A.M.

"One morning when I was running, I was suddenly struck in the back of my head," she says. "I thought it was a branch falling on me, but it was actually an owl attacking my ponytail."

While working at a community hospital several miles from home, she either bicycled or ran each way every day for a month.

Her calendar includes mountain bike camping in Utah during one upcoming break. Before that, she plans to dash out on Friday afternoon for a quick weekend drive covering some 600 miles to squeeze in a day of rock climbing in eastern Washington, before getting back to the hospital for the start of her shift very early on Sunday morning.

The plans sound exhausting, but they invigorate her. "Looking forward to these little things keeps you going," she says.

Matsen ran the 26.2 miles of the Portland Marathon in 3 hours, 12 minutes and 30 seconds, finishing 26th out of more than 4,000 women in the race. "I felt really good," she says. She ran for part of the route with other residents. "The toughest part was the climb up to the St. Johns Bridge. That's where Nick Spoerke dropped me."

But the marathon was just a milepost along Matsen's training schedule for a triathlon in the summer.

OF COURSE, RESIDENTS ARE NOT SUPERHUMAN.

"I have fallen asleep in bars," admits Mitch Sally. He laughs as he says that his wife will never let him forget the incident because they were out with friends of hers. "It was a dimly lit bar. I was post-call [coming off about thirty hours in the hospital] and had one or two drinks. It was after dinner and about nine o'clock, and I just settled into a comfortable chair. She nudged me later and said it's time to go. It's a little embarrassing."

CHAPTER NINETEEN

Family

Miranda Bailey is walking down the hall of Seattle Grace Hospital with her new baby in "Band-Aid Covers the Bullet Hole" (2-20) when Chief Webber comes up to them.

"You brought your baby to work?" Webber asks.

"Yes, Chief."

"You're not going to take him into surgery with you?"

"I don't have anything scheduled for today."

"Yet."

"Okay, I can't solve a problem until there's a problem to solve. Are you saying there's a problem?" Bailey asks him.

Then Addison Montgomery chimes in. "Yeah, is there a problem, Richard?"

"No," huffs the Chief as he turns and walks away.

SAJID KHAN COMES INTO A PHYSICIANS WORKROOM WITH A VISITOR, a young visitor. It's the son of transplant surgeon Susan Orloff. He came with his mother to the hospital after a meeting with his kindergarten teacher. He clowns with the residents and feasts on fruit sherbet cups they bring him from the staff break room.

Orloff then arrives with the liver transplant residents. She finishes up their review of the patients on their list, and turns her attention to the kidney transplant residents. She and the residents head out to round on the kidney transplant patients . . . accompanied by her son. One of the residents points out the boy's photo pinned up on a hallway bulletin board alongside the pictures of staff and patients. He is no stranger here.

Rounds proceed as usual, except that one resident stays out in the hall with Orloff's son when the rest of the team goes into the patient rooms. And as one of the residents reads through a long list of lab test results for one of their patients, Orloff interrupts him for a moment to take a call from her son's nanny. In fluent Spanish, Orloff rattles off directions from the parking garage to the transplant floor.

Soon the nanny arrives, collects her charge, and leaves Orloff and the residents to carry on without their smiling, young sidekick. No one remarks that having a kindergartner come along on rounds is at all out of the ordinary. It doesn't happen every day, but surgery and residency are becoming less incompatible with a somewhat normal family life.

"I would never have thought for a second about having a child during residency. There was no way. You couldn't take care of them," says trauma surgeon Martin Schreiber. Now he sees that things are changing for residents. "They are getting married or they are married. They have families. They're having children during residency. They're going skiing on their day off. They are actually living a life. Whereas in the past your work was your life; that's pretty much all you did, was work. These guys have a life. It's really quite impressive."

Intern Nick Tadros agrees that residents are no longer expected to be consumed by their work.

"I think it's a little bit different now. People have lives and families. I'd like to start a family eventually. People do it in residency all the time now," he says.

That's not to say it's easy. During his rotation as a chief resident on the trauma service, Michael Englehart worked a month on the night shift. On the one day each week that he was not working in the hospital, he wanted to spend time with his family. But if he suddenly switched to a daytime schedule, he would throw his body clock off track, causing a case of jet lag without ever leaving the ground.

"The family is asleep on my day off," he says. "I try to sleep in after the last night shift. So I get up at around five P.M. on Wednesday afternoon. The family goes to bed at eight or ten in the evening, but I'm up until three A.M. or so. Then I'll sleep through much of Thursday before going back into work on Thursday night."

Because residents in surgery and medicine share many of the same pressures, they have banded together to form a Resident Family Network. The Welcome Brunch event at a member's home features a crowd of young children. An important component of the group is support for the spouses of residents, who are often left to fend for themselves. In addition to a few large group events like the brunch, there are book club meetings, bicycling and running groups, and other special-interest gatherings. One recent newsletter promoted a 10K run as being "*All* downhill! You'll amaze yourself at how fast you are! Ha! And, free spaghetti and beer at the finish line . . . if that's your bag." The newsletter also features simple recipes and other survival tips. Regular play groups allow the "junior residents" to occupy each other, while the parents can get in a bit of adult socializing.

Sharing the challenges of trying to raise a family while one parent—or even both—work through residency doesn't make the difficulties disappear; but it does help fight isolation that can make the task sometimes seem insurmountable.

Of course, for most residents marriage comes before children. Intern Jason Susong got married just a few months into his first year of residency. He met his wife during medical school. Early in the year, he bounced back and forth across the country to help at least some with arrangements before the wedding and then moving his bride afterward. She is continuing her own medical school education in her new home. Even though residents are able to have more of an outside life now than in previous decades, it's still a challenge to manage a wedding and start a marriage while still keeping up with the demands of residency. Susong says he's become labeled as "the intern who got married." Despite the hurdles, he says, "It's been great."

Shortly before her wedding, resident Karin Hardiman talked about squeezing the event into her work schedule. It was her research year. She had two presentations accepted at medical meetings and the timing was tight. "I'm actually going to fly from a meeting in Boston to go get married," Hardiman said with a chuckle.

Before marriage comes dating. And dating takes time, the most precious commodity in a resident's life.

While practicing the techniques for sewing together blood vessel grafts, Emily Bubbers vents to Loïc Fabricant about the difficulty of having a social life. She recently bought an outdoor grill, but now she wonders if it was a mistake. "Will I get to use it enough?"

"You'll be glad you bought the grill," Fabricant reassures her. "We need more social outings."

"I'm in need of a date," she says.

"I know some nice single men."

"You didn't introduce me to any at the party."

But a few months later, things have changed.

"I started dating someone this year," Bubbers says. With time outside the hospital so scarce, how did they meet? In the hospital. "He's an intern."

"Someone asked me if I was doing it because it's convenient. I said, 'That's the last thing two people working eighty hours a week could say.' " And the schedule ahead looks rougher. "We aren't going to be in the same hospital for the rest of this year. It's actually going to be less convenient."

Bubbers says one benefit of dating another intern is that you don't have to explain how tough your day, or day and night, has been. "That's the nice part. If someone says, 'I'm tired and I'm not moving,' there is no if, ands, or buts. It's just, 'Okay.' "

Karen Zink praises her fiancé's ability to accept what it means to be involved with a resident.

"He's a lot more patient than I would be, thank goodness. There is no way that I could ever date a surgery resident: the uncertainty, having someone promise they're going to be home for dinner and then not be. It would drive me nuts. But he's really patient, really good at dealing with it, really good at just going with the flow at any moment," she says.

Zink's fiancé is not in medicine. But they were introduced by another resident. By contrast, Hardiman wanted to find someone completely outside the world of medicine. She did it through online dating. It's an increasingly popular way of making dating more "efficient."

"Three people in my class have gotten engaged through online relationships," Hardiman says. She says she and her friends tried the bar scene, but it was a waste of time. And time is something residents can't stand to waste.

"It's hard to figure out what environment, other than [in] the hospital, where you're going to be spending enough time to really get to know someone. In the online forum, it's a little easier, because you get a description of their likes and dislikes, and what they are looking for and what they are not, and what they are like, their political views. All these things that would rule people out or in for you. And it's all right there," she says.

EMILY BUBBERS, M.D.

Status: Intern

Where from: Chicago. Medical school at Rosalind Franklin University of Medicine and Science, The Chicago Medical School.

Why did you want to become a surgeon?
"I had a chance to go watch an open heart surgery case. So I went to the hospital, put on some scrubs, stood at the head of the bed while this guy did a quadruple bypass. And I thought, cool, that's awesome!"

Bubbers says she also took a class on animal surgery in college. Thoughts of medical school were already in her mind, and she wanted to go into work that would be hands on. Surgery fit the bill on all counts.

"There never was really much of another option. It was just a matter of picking the type of surgery I wanted to do."

What's the biggest difference between what you thought it would be like and the reality?
"I don't think I ever knew what to expect. That's the problem. Everyone tells you it's hard, but I never really thought about what it was really going to be like. I knew I'd be sleep deprived. And actually sometimes I feel like I have more free time than I thought I would. So in that respect I'm pleasantly surprised, but definitely at times I feel more exhausted than I ever thought I would."

Bubbers says she has found time to go skiing a number of times during her intern year. She says it helped that ski season coincided with her anesthesiology rotation, which has more regular hours than some other services.

She doubts any warnings or advice could have really communicated to her what surgery residency is like.

"There are no words that can prepare you for what's going to happen," she says. "The hours, the fatigue, the patients, the work, the expectations; all of it. I think the reality of what we're getting ourselves into is finally sinking in. And the excitement is over. It's still fun, but we're realizing that we are in this for the long haul. When you first come in, it's fun and it's new. It's still fun, and I still like what I do, and I enjoyed the learning, but the reality is settling in."

There are still hard months ahead during the rest of her intern year and then at least four more years of residency.

"It's not the years; it's the amount of energy that's going to be expended." Bubbers says the energy is not just physical or mental, but also emotional.

What do you want patients to know about what you do?
Like many women in medicine, Bubbers says that every day she meets patients who assume she is a nurse.

She says she's been learning some important things about patients.

"They trust you. They actually really trust what you say. And all of a sudden you're being held responsible for what you say. I don't think I really thought about, as a medical student, what I was getting into."

The interns are supported by senior residents and attending surgeons as well as experienced nurses, pharmacists, and other health care professionals. Nevertheless, as Bubbers points out, they have stepped into a world in which their words and their decisions can have serious consequences.

What specialty are you most interested in?
Bubbers says she is still a long way from deciding just what flavor of surgery suits her best. Based on the rotations she has done so far, she says general surgery in a community hospital is one possibility, as is pediatric surgery. She says that for now she has crossed off vascular surgery (too tedious, she says, and the patients are so, so sick) and transplant or liver surgery.

Midway through a month on a burn unit, she says this rotation is going very well.

"I really like burns, actually," Bubbers says.

Burns are terrible injuries. She points to one child she is treating who has burns over more than half his body. She has also helped treat a patient with necrotizing fasciitis, the so-called flesh-eating bacteria. Several surgeries were needed to contain the infection and then, similar to some burn treatment, graft skin back over the damaged areas. The wounds can be horrific, but the technical challenges of treating burns and related injuries from trauma or diseases can present exciting challenges. And sophisticated burn care has an amazing ability to save lives and heal people who seemed beyond rescue.

"I'm loving this rotation, much more than I ever thought I would. It's pretty awesome. But the cases are not happy surgery all the time."

CHAPTER TWENTY

Hospital Romance

The introduction to this book highlighted some of the contrasts between fiction and reality, including the prominence of sex and romance in Seattle Grace Hospital. Surgery residents in the real world certainly devote far more of their time than their *Grey's Anatomy* counterparts to taking care of patients and less to sex and romantic intrigue, yet every now and then real events bear an uncanny resemblance to scenes from the show.

In the very first episode, Meredith Grey and Derek Shepherd meet in a bar, spend the night together, and only then discover they will be working together at the hospital. It seems an unlikely scenario, but one resident says something like it happened to a friend. He went with other residents to a bar, met a woman, one thing led to another, and only later did he learn she worked in one of the wards at the hospital.

Sometimes there is emotional trauma and strained relationships that might suit a *Grey's Anatomy* plot line. Two residents who were just friends became something more than that, but they didn't announce themselves as a couple. There was also a third resident who was interested in one of them, unaware of the shifting relationships. A fourth resident learned about the couple and, despite an expectation of confidentiality, let the news get out. The result included some angry words, hurt feelings, and lingering tension between the residents involved.

Another resident had a pattern of dating nurses on the wards where he worked. At the end of his rotation, he would move on to another service and another group of nurses. But as the rotations continued, he would find himself back where he had dated and departed before. Some discomfort ensued.

Older surgeons will sometimes reveal that *Grey's Anatomy* more closely resembles hospital life and surgery residency of their youth than it does today's reality. An objective measure of that history is the percentage of senior attendings who married nurses. But the world has changed; particularly attitudes about, and corporate policies regarding, romantic entanglements in the workplace, any workplace. Nevertheless, approaches are made and sometimes lead to connections.

The beginning of the new residency year each summer seems to bring a peak of activity. "Fresh meat" is how more than one resident puts it. More than one male intern tells of feeling overtures from female nurses, residents, and sometimes attendings. As one put it, "She was trying to eat me with her eyes." A married intern says he's been asked out by nurses, though he points out that he doesn't wear his wedding ring in the hospital.

Given that residents spend most of their waking hours in the hospital—far more hours than most people spend at their jobs—and that they share intense, stressful experiences with a small cohort of residents and other co-workers; it's really not surprising that strong emotional attachments develop. But it may be happening less now than before the 80-hour workweek limit was established. There is simply more time to meet people outside the hospital. Even when co-workers date, now they have more time to pursue romantic activities outside the building.

That point brings us to the call rooms (and other covert meeting spots) that see so much action on TV. Yes, residents say, shenanigans do take place in call rooms, but not nearly as often these days because even when residents are on call overnight, they are often taking calls from home, handling most questions by telephone or computer, and coming into the hospital only when necessary.

Still, more than one married resident admits at least thinking about conducting spousal relations in a call room. One resident, whose wife is also a resident (though not in surgery), says despite the 80-hour workweek limit, they can go six or seven days or even longer without seeing each other at home. He says they try to coordinate their call schedules, both so that their time off matches and so they can visit during quiet times in the hospital. He remembers one night when they were both working, they stole away together with the intention of taking full advantage of a call room. He remembers getting into the bed with his wife—his very attractive wife, he emphasizes—and then . . . he fell asleep. On *Grey's Anatomy*, he says, they have a lot of fun; but sometimes sleep is better than sex.

Well, that's been true on *Grey's Anatomy*, too. In "Kung Fu Fighting" (4-06), Izzie Stevens and George O'Malley are planning a night of "hot, perfect sex." But then when the moment arrives, and the couple is in bed, Stevens is just too tired after a grueling shift. O'Malley says he understands. "Do you want to maybe, uh, go to sleep?" he asks. "Yeah. Oh, thanks," Stevens replies with relief.

CHAPTER TWENTY-ONE

Hierarchy

"I can't speak for all of the schools on the West Coast, but I think that there is a noticeable dichotomy between East Coast schools and West Coast schools. Doing medical school on the East Coast and interviewing at different programs on the East Coast, it seemed that it was a lot more regimented on the East Coast," one senior resident says. "The attending talks to the chief, who talks to the junior resident, who talks to the intern. The chain of command should not be broken; interns should not speak to attendings. That's a little bit of hyperbole, but that's how it works; it's a little more militaristic than out here where I see interns just talking to attendings."

One night in the Emergency Department CT scanning control room, a senior resident looks at the patient's information and remarks, "She's just two days older than I am."

To which a junior resident retorts, "You look older."

An attending surgeon rolls his eyes. It seems like a small thing, but the joking illustrates that the residents here are willing to make light-hearted jabs at their seniors without too much fear of retribution.

"We need to break down the silos," says surgeon Brett Sheppard. "That's why I go on a first-name basis with nurses."

Indeed, this program is more casual than some others, and yet there is still a clear hierarchy. And there's good reason for residency to have a pecking order: It really does take years to learn the ropes.

"There's a transformation. It's amazing," says a fifth-year resident. "You don't even realize it's happening, and then you look at interns and realize where you've come from." She says one milestone is when a resident changes from being a ducker to a non-ducker in the OR. "When there's a sudden arterial bleed during surgery and blood shoots up out of the patient, the naive duck. At some point you learn to keep your eyes on the bleed, and you put your finger on it to stop it. You don't duck."

The hierarchy does its job when it means that residents are managing the things they know how to do and then getting help with the things that are beyond their skill. But hierarchy can feed on itself.

In the second episode of *Grey's Anatomy,* "The First Cut Is the Deepest" (1-02), Miranda Bailey snaps at her new interns.

"Stop talking. Every intern wants to perform their first surgery. That's not your job. Do you know what your job is? To make your resident happy. Do I look happy? No. Why? Because my interns are whining." As she walks off, Bailey takes a parting shot. "No one holds a scalpel until I'm so happy that I'm Mary-freaking-Poppins!"

Intern Ashley Stewart says that in medical school she realized that she was learning things other than how to diagnose and treat patients.

"A surgeon asked me about why I decided to go into surgery. I told him I had the skill to tell in five minutes what someone wants from me. He knew what I meant. He said it took years for him to learn to take care of himself, do what he wanted. He'd just learned to please others."

General Surgery residency lasts five years, not counting research years and fellowships. Each year has its own flavor and purpose.

Interns may be at the bottom of the pecking order, but at an intern conference early in the year, trauma surgeon Jennifer Watters points out that they have their own unique place in the structure of care. She is lecturing about sepsis, an infection that can rapidly escalate to a lethal threat.

"You really have the potential to make a difference. You may be the first person to see it. And what the first person sees can make the difference.

It's simple, and yet we screw it up all the time," Watters says as she urges the interns to take their sentinel role seriously.

Interns often complain about how little time they get to spend in the OR. Most of their days are spent seeing patients and then checking and updating information in patient records, all while trying to learn the intricacies of hospital operations.

In clinic one afternoon, intern Daniel Wieking, M.D., is explaining some options to a patient who has come in with pain in her side around where they had done an operation.

"I suspect there's fluid collecting, but I don't think it's infected," Wieking says. "A CT scan is precise and good at seeing what's going on. Ultrasound is also good for seeing fluid, and it has less radiation." The patient chooses to get a CT scan because it may be more likely to provide a definitive answer. Then Wieking heads back to the workroom to ask his more experienced colleagues a basic question: "How do you schedule a CT?"

"I'm not sure what to do," is something interns frequently admit.

Being on the front lines of care on the patient floors means interns have the most opportunities to get to know patients and their families. Intern Nick Tadros recalls the kind words from a man whose wife had just died.

"He was really nice to me. He said to the others there, 'This is a great guy. I really appreciate all the care.' And I thought, 'Wow. That was really nice of him to say, even in all his distress.' Granted, I'm just an intern, but when patients are on the ward, especially in neurosurgery, the interns are the ones who take care of the patients," he says.

SECOND-YEAR SURGERY RESIDENTS GET TO SPEND MORE TIME IN THE OR. They also get an introduction to the intensive care unit, where patients face serious challenges, and missteps could have dire consequences.

Chief Resident Michael Englehart is supervising Arun Raman, M.D., as the second-year resident works on placing a central line catheter into an ICU patient. They use a portable ultrasound device to search for the correct blood vessel.

"Which one is the carotid? Is vein or artery more lateral?" Englehart asks. "No, you are confusing the carotid pulse with changes in the vein from inspiration." He warns Raman not to mistake movement caused by breathing with pulsations due to blood flow in the artery.

"Take a steeper angle," Englehart advises as Raman inserts a needle. "Yes. Back up a little bit. Aim a little more lateral, sorry, medial. There, right there. Should be lots of resistance in just a little bit."

"There," Raman says as he feels the needle pierce the blood vessel wall.

Englehart starts giving some more instructions when pagers start going off. There's a trauma patient on the way. Raman is left on his own to finish up and then move on to the next urgent matter facing one of the 31 patients in the ICU today.

Raman is reminded to get a consultation from another service for a patient scheduled for surgery. He handles questions about the availability of beds. He cleans up the debris from the catheter placement procedure. As the demands continue through the evening, it takes him hours to eat his dinner, a bite here, then another bite later. "It was the coldest fish. I gagged on it," he complains.

He gets called to deal with a patient who is trying to leave the hospital against the advice of the doctors. Then he briefs the night shift chief resident, Laszlo Kiraly.

"I cleared the spine of this guy," Raman says, referring to the patient who is trying to leave. "Clearing the spine" of a trauma patient means confirming that there's no apparent risk to the spinal cord if the patient moves.

"You can't clear the spine." Kiraly reminds Raman of the limits of his authority.

"Well, actually, he cleared his own spine. He took the collar off by himself without permission."

As each year goes by, the residents get more time and more responsibility in the OR. But the moves of midlevel residents are still tentative. It is the fifth year, the chief year, that marks a major step.

"Chief year is when you start to actually become a surgeon," notes David Cho. "Juniors can do stuff, but the attending surgeon exposes things and makes the plans. With chiefs, the attendings stand back and just offer advice on refining techniques."

Trauma surgeon Martin Schreiber remembers his chief resident year. "I was operating so much I was rubbing the skin off my hands from scrubbing in," he says. "You really hone your skills at that point in time. Toward the end of that year you start saying, 'Okay, I can do this; I'm a surgeon.' Until then, you're always wondering if you will ever get to master the skills."

Cho says even near the end of residency, there seems to be so much yet to learn.

"A lot of my friends who have already graduated tell me that once you have finished residency, it still takes you a while to really refer to yourself as a surgeon. The words 'I am a surgeon' have a certain meaning to them. It seems almost inappropriate saying them until you've mastered a certain skill set and knowledge base and intuition."

Donn Spight, M.D., says even after all the years of residency, the final step looks daunting.

"Everybody in the history of residency training has felt that way. I've only been out for three years, and every class of residents, you get to that April, May, June period, and you feel, 'I'm not going to be ready to practice!' And the reality is, they will."

"MY MOTHER CALLED IT THE GREATEST AND MOST TERRIFYING MOMENT in her life: standing at the head of the surgical table, knowing that the patient's life depends on you and you alone. It's what we all dream about, because the first person who gets to fly solo in the O.R. . . . kind of a bad-ass," Meredith Grey says in "All by Myself" (5-10).

IN DECADES PAST, SENIOR RESIDENTS OPERATED WITHOUT AN ATTENDING surgeon being in the room. Residents do get procedures started and sometimes attendings leave them to close up. But flying solo through an entire operation doesn't happen anymore. Tighter scrutiny of medicine, insurance plan rules that authorize payment only for surgeons who actually took part in the procedure, and other factors mean that residents are monitored more closely.

"In my day there were no attendings around," recalls Robert Martindale. "The residents just did surgeries with no close supervision. Of course, the attendings would come if they were needed, but then they made you feel bad. They belittled you."

Even though Martindale and other attendings are physically in the OR, even when chief residents are part of the team, he says he tries not to do too much himself.

"We need to stand back and let them learn how to operate, so that when they leave here we can feel confident that they could operate on me or my family." He concedes that it doesn't always work out, that some surgeons finish residency even though they still need help in tough spots.

Looking again at the episode "All by Myself" (5-10), when Alex Karev gets to perform what's called solo surgery, he isn't actually flying solo. He didn't make the decision about whether an operation was the right treatment for the patient. The specific surgery had been already determined. He was holding the scalpel, but he wasn't yet acting as a full surgeon.

Observation doesn't go just one direction. Residents also keep an eye on attendings.

"Attendings have to be treated like a combination of cats and a small child," says one senior resident. "They have very short attention spans. They are easy to confuse, and then they won't do what you want them to do."

And some attendings may do things the way they've been doing them for years, while residents learn the latest methods, without having to forget old habits.

In "Save Me" (1-08), a patient refused to let surgeons use a pig heart valve to replace her faulty one because it violated her religious beliefs. Intern Alex Karev told her that some surgeons were starting to use cow heart valves for patients with valve problems like hers. Just then, attending surgeon Preston Burke enters the patient's room.

"Dr. Burke, why wasn't this mentioned before?" the patient's mother asks.

"Dr. Karev . . ." Burke gives a sharp look to Karev.

"The bovine valve has only been an option the last few years," Karev explains.

Later, in the hallway, Burke comes down hard on Karev.

"What incredibly small fraction of your brain were you using in there?"

"What?" Karev is taken aback.

"Correct me if I'm wrong, but did you not present an alternative procedure without consulting your attending first?"

"I thought you'd be . . ."

"What, impressed? That's just stupid."

WHEN THE HIERARCHY FUNCTIONS WELL, ATTENDINGS REMAIN IN CHARGE, while residents get to test their wings.

Near the end of an extensive abdominal surgery, Chief Resident Kiraly suggests a different kind of wound covering. He says he learned it while working at a military hospital in Germany. Attending John Mayberry, M.D., gives him the go ahead and watches the new technique with interest.

The former chair of the Department of Surgery, Donald Trunkey, says he is glad to see the end of the days when residents just blindly followed the practices of elder surgeons.

"I don't think you're going to be able to do that in the future. I think that residents are going to be able to question things. I would hope that the attendings would question things. You're not going to be able to be as rigid as surgeons have been commonly associated with being. I think it will be good. To challenge some of our principles is very, very healthy," Trunkey says.

EVEN AS THE HIERARCHY LIMITS THE AUTHORITY OF YOUNGER RESIDENTS, it puts the onus on senior residents to teach.

Intern Ashley Stewart grabs a bit of time to go meet fourth-year resident Karen Zink. Zink has offered to teach Stewart one-handed knot tying, a skill that was frowned on at the medical school Stewart attended. They sit side by side in a quiet research lab, tying and untying the strings around the waists of their scrubs. The wide fabric is a good material to practice with. Then they move on to tie real suture thread around drawer handles on the research bench, practicing how to make a slipknot so it goes down tight and then can be snapped into a square knot to secure the suture. And so the skills are passed down the line.

CHAPTER TWENTY-TWO

Taking Care of Yourself

Midway through his intern year, Loïc Fabricant says things are going well, and he is more certain than ever that he made the right career choice . . . and yet the demands are heavy indeed.

"More than anything it's just coming home from the hospital, where you've given so much, you've been on and present so much, that it's really hard to want to continue to be emotionally available. At least for me, I would really just like to shut down and not talk to anyone," he says. He adds that he isn't alone; he sees signs of similar strains all around him.

"We often hear, 'I should've come here months ago,' " says Mary Moffit. Moffit is the director of the Resident Wellness Program at OHSU. She is making her pitch to new interns during their orientation.

The program's website asks these questions:

- Are you worried all the time?

- Are you feeling down, on edge, or overwhelmed?

- Are you frequently negative or irritable?

- Do you feel isolated, alone, or cut off from others?

- Do you feel like an impostor at times?

- Are your relationships with others suffering?

- Are you experiencing high levels of stress?

The website goes on to say, "Up to 70 percent of residents experience professional burnout at some point in their training."

Anyone who makes it through medical school is already accustomed to pushing through barriers that would stymie the average person. By the time these young doctors begin residency, they have repeatedly survived daunting examinations; seemingly overwhelming study assignments; days, weeks, and months without enough sleep or relaxation or even time to do daily chores. And perhaps most important, they have seen fellow students drop from the program or fail to make the cut.

Surgeons may be more likely to encounter difficult stress and high expectations. Even as more women become surgeons, the field still has a legacy of macho attitudes. A survey comparing residents in a variety of programs found that surgery residents tended to get less sleep, less exercise, and less time with family than residents in other programs.

ONE AFTERNOON ON THE TRANSPLANT FLOOR, A SENIOR SURGERY RESIDENT remarks to his fellows, "I called the urology fellow; I woke her up at seven A.M., seven A.M.! Oh, to be a medicine fellow." Rather than just waking, at 7:00 A.M. most surgery residents have been at work for an hour . . . or longer.

THERE'S NO DOUBT THAT SURGERY RESIDENTS DON'T LIKE TO ADMIT weakness, even though they have a multitude of reasons to feel stressed and exhausted. Lack of time; lack of sleep; heavy workload and little control; subservience to seniors; difficult situations with colleagues or patients; and witnessing severe trauma, illness, and death are some of the challenges identified by the Resident Wellness Program.

Intern Ashley Stewart says she turned to the program after the unexpected death of a patient that affected her more deeply than most. First she talked to her mother and to her closest friends among the residents. She said that going over the medical facts of the case with an attending surgeon helped.

But still she had trouble sleeping, and her mind kept returning to memories of frantic and failing efforts to stop the blood pouring from the patient and then being left alone to clean the body. She says one of the counselors suggested that she speak with Karen Deveney, who is in charge of the surgery residency program. Stewart says Deveney understood why this death affected her so much more than others.

"That helped me a lot to know that somebody like her, who has seen everything, was recognizing that this was a really hard thing and extraordinarily difficult, above and beyond the normal stuff that we deal with; that made me feel better. I felt like, okay, I'm not crazy, I'm not a wimp," Stewart says. "I felt stronger after going through it, but at the same time I felt like somebody had knocked the wind out of me."

Moffit says they have met with hundreds of residents since the program was established five years ago. They average 80 to 90 visits per month with residents from all programs. To encourage residents to come, the sessions are free. And perhaps even more important, outside of the program's office there is no record that a visit even took place; nothing in the resident's school files, no reports to supervisors. Of course, like at other mental health programs, the Resident Wellness Program staff are required to break confidentiality if a resident is at imminent risk of harming himself or herself or others, or if it isn't safe to allow the resident to treat patients because of substance abuse or mental illness.

Along with her colleagues, psychiatrist Mark Kinzie, M.D., Ph.D., and psychologist Sydney Ey, Ph.D., Moffit spoke of how they are trying to boost the resilience of residents in the face of seemingly overpowering demands. Ey noted that a big challenge is reducing the barriers to asking for help. Residents are tremendously concerned about what others will think if word gets out they have spoken with a counselor. It's more than simply a concern about reputation among co-workers, residents also worry about whether anything might be reported to licensing agencies, malpractice insurers, or others who have the power to strip them of their hospital privileges or even their ability to practice medicine at all.

Moffit is so concerned about keeping the trust of residents that she won't allow tape recording of even general comments about the program.

Ey says some residents are thrown off track by negative evaluations. She says they are perfectionists. Even if they get 50 great evaluations, they can't handle the one negative report. In those situations, the wellness counselors may try to teach the residents how to strive for excellence, not perfection. They reinforce the message that residents are still students, after all. They are not expected to be perfect, and the structure of residency is designed to provide support and backup so that the mistakes residents inevitably make won't harm patients.

Ey says that along with other treatment approaches, they often use a form of cognitive behavioral therapy, which generally focuses on how our own thoughts can shape our feelings and behaviors with the idea that we can change our reactions to events and circumstances. That approach makes sense, because even with duty-hour limits and other efforts to make life a little less harsh, surgery residency will always be very difficult. This approach is also designed to be short term, with the goal of achieving rapid improvement, so that the residents can get back to doing their jobs. If residents need or want more or different services, the counselors will refer them to other resources, all without anything going into their residency program files.

The fact that the wellness program counselors are not evaluating the surgical and medical skills of the residents means that the visits offer a respite from the constant evaluations and critiques the residents face in the hospital. Moffit points out they have no other role at OHSU, they are not also trying to manage any of the residency programs, so the counselors have no conflict of interest . . . as could happen with a program director who has responsibilities larger than just the success or well-being of an individual resident.

Moffit says the number one barrier that residents say prevents them from coming in for counseling is simple, but difficult to overcome: time. Residents, especially surgery residents, live in a culture that often doesn't even recognize the importance of taking time to eat or drink. Some residents say they make a point not to drink anything during their shifts, because they are afraid of needing to go to the bathroom, which might mean missing a surgery or needing a break during a procedure, something surgeons rarely do.

They don't want to let the team down, Ey notes. Residents are incredibly dedicated. They don't want to look like wimps to their peers.

The program surveyed residents and faculty to find out more about the challenges of being a resident and the barriers to asking for help. A question about taking breaks identified a disconnect between the groups. Most residents said they could not take a break for an hour without giving a specific justification or they weren't sure whether they could take a break without getting prior approval, which would undermine the confidentiality of the counseling program. On the other hand, at least half the program directors said residents could absolutely take a one-hour break without explaining exactly where they were going.

But that result doesn't mean the residents are necessarily wrong to have doubts about taking breaks. Even if the official policy says yes you can, the subtle, but strong, cues from co-workers and supervisors can send a discouraging message. The wellness counselors say they sometimes have to work to convince supervisors to back off a bit, learn to trust their residents more, and accept that they may not always need to know exactly where a resident is going or why.

The survey found that some residents may not seek counseling because they have doubts it would really help them. Moffit says that sometimes residents get so overwhelmed that they stop believing anything could improve their situations. But she says that residents are increasingly referring their fellow residents to the program, telling them that the staff can indeed help and assuring them it is a safe place to speak freely. Another indication of the value of the program is that faculty members asked for similar support. The Faculty Wellness Program opened in 2008. Kinzie adds that medical students have also asked for access to the program.

Residents in all specialties face long hours, hard work, tough scrutiny, and other pressures. They can all sometimes feel that the all-encompassing commitment to residency means they are missing out on other vital parts of their lives. And while by some measures circumstances can be tougher for surgery residents, they also may have a special something that helps them survive. Ey notes surgery residents really do love to perform surgery, and that makes them special in a way. The intense moments of joy and accomplishment surgery residents feel when they take part in a successful operation can help wash away the fatigue and frustration of long days and nights in the clinic and on the hospital floor.

But sometimes residents realize surgery isn't for them. Kinzie says sometimes residents go into surgery thinking it was going to be something else. Then when they realize the specialty isn't a good fit, these residents really suffer.

Of course, even undying love of surgery isn't bulletproof protection against burnout during residency. The wellness program staff says that's where their counseling and referrals come in, with the goals of helping both residents and their spouses or partners manage stress, be more productive, get along better at work and at home, and simply enjoy life more.

Meredith Grey referred to the fact that surgeons, who are trained to provide care, may put themselves last in "Into You Like a Train" (2-06).

"As surgeons, there are so many things we have to know. We have to know we have what it takes. We have to know how to take care of our patients. And how to take care of each other. Eventually we even have to figure out . . . how to take care of ourselves."

TAKING CARE OF YOURSELF INVOLVES STRESS MANAGEMENT, EMOTIONAL maturity, coping skills, and more, but it's also good to gather practical tips that help residents get through 80-hour weeks, plus all the stuff of outside life.

In the vascular service workroom, fourth-year resident Karen Zink grabs a minute before the start of rounds to offer a bit of practical advice to intern Ashley Stewart.

"Put all your utilities and other bills on auto pay. Some interns have had their utilities shut off because they never checked their mail," Zink says.

"I've moved so much, the post office isn't forwarding my mail anymore.

I have to go in, in person, to my local post office. But it's only open nine to five, Monday through Friday," Stewart says. She doesn't have to point out that having time to run errands during what most people consider normal business hours is just a pipe dream for her and other residents.

Zink says she learned a lesson from the utility bill snarls that hit two of her classmates.

"This has been very important; as there are many times I would have missed bills. I have missed other important deadlines and such many times. I almost never RSVP to anything on time, including my best friend's wedding, in which I was the maid of honor. I tell all new interns to put everything on auto pay. Basically, as a resident, you have to have nothing in your life that requires direct interaction from you at any given set schedule," Zink says.

A month's worth of underwear also comes in handy, when there is simply no time for laundry.

Intern Laura Matsen has become almost obsessed with squeezing double- or even triple-duty out of every minute of the day and night. Among her strategies:

- Brush hair and teeth on the way to work.

- Read surgical journals while waiting for incoming trauma cases or when eating or brushing teeth (presumably not while on the way to work).

- Squeeze in exercise time by always taking the stairs (at a run) in the hospital.

- If there isn't enough time to exercise after work, go for a run at 3:00 A.M. before heading to work.

- Better yet, run or bicycle to work (presumably not while brushing your teeth).

"Remember that a little something is better than nothing: you'll get blood flowing, burn off a few French fries, feel better about yourself, see other people outside the hospital, and so on. One hour of exercise is often better than one hour of sleep," Matsen says. Not all residents share her devotion to exercise.

Fourth-year resident Sajid Khan doesn't claim to go running at 3:00 A.M., but he does try to get to the gym one to three times each week. "I usually go to the gym directly after work, so I don't have a chance to sit in my apartment and be lazy about going," Khan says. He also subscribes to the advice about putting bills on auto pay, though he admits he has still fallen behind on payments.

Each resident has an allowance that covers cafeteria meals in the hospital. But that still means trying to find time to actually get to a cafeteria and then chew the food. Too often a hot meal grows old and cold next to a workroom computer after a page cuts short a break.

Not every meal is taken inside the hospital.

"When I do have free time, I make large batches of spaghetti sauce, pesto, soup, or other foods, and freeze it in single servings, so when I get home without any time or energy to cook, I just need to thaw one of those," Zink says. "Also, I am ashamed to admit it, but I eat ramen noodles fairly regularly, since they cook in just three minutes. Cheese is another mainstay of my diet. Additionally, even though I am a senior resident, I still frequently do the med student thing of always keeping a granola bar in my pocket in case of emergency. And, sad as it may be, I have gone extended times where the majority of my diet is peanut butter and graham crackers from the wards (every ward in every hospital has them), eaten quickly while walking from one task to another. At times like those, I am too tired when I get home to eat much else."

Intern Emily Bubbers also has a few favorite recipes that are fast or will last.

"The most survival friendly food: Quesadilla—tortilla, cheese, and salsa—quick and easy. If I have a couple of extra minutes, I'll add black beans and/or chicken. Or it's a pound of pasta with meat sauce to last the week. Nothing fancy," she says. "I know most people just throw together a sandwich for dinner or just substitute beer for dinner." She smiles.

Khan admits to falling back on fast food, despite the irony of a doctor resorting to the kind of meals that contribute to so many of the chronic disease cases that consume all the time he otherwise could be using to prepare a healthy repast.

"I am a big fan of Taco Bell. I do not cook often and find myself going there after a hard day of work more than I'd like," Khan says. Breakfast often isn't any more epicurean, "Going to a gas station and grabbing breakfast cereal and coffee on the drive to work."

And then everyone from students to senior attendings knows and repeats this mantra: "Eat when you can. Sleep when you can. And don't mess with the pancreas."

"Every med student, intern, etc. knows those rules throughout the country. It is amazing how true each of those three rules are, and how remembering those three rules when things get crazy will save you a lot of trouble," Zink says.

Of course, while grabbing a quick nap is a good idea, slumber in the hospital is often interrupted. Matsen advises, "If you have problems waking up to your pager, put it on vibrate and ace bandage wrap it to your temple."

Still, the residents know there is more to survival than meeting basic bodily needs.

"The most useful information I got was that no matter what, you will always be tired, so go do things, like going out for dinner, drinks, hiking, to the gym, etc., anyway," Bubbers says.

And to help make sure there's still someone to go do those things with, Matsen says, "Call your significant other when you start [your on-call shift] to tell them that you miss them, because you might not think about them again till after their bedtime."

EVEN WHEN RESIDENTS TRY TO EAT AND SLEEP AND DO EVERYTHING else, they still get sick sometimes, just like anybody else. Funny thing is, many of their patients seem surprised by the fact that, yes, doctors get sniffles . . . and more.

"I'm fighting allergies," says intern Nick Tadros on a summer day. "It seems to happen when I'm stressed and tired. It's rough going on rounds with watery eyes, while sneezing and sniffling. I have to assure patients that I'm not contagious."

As second-year resident Arun Raman dashes to the cafeteria to get a drink to wash down his cough medicine, he points out, "Doctors get sick, too; though some patients seem confused by that."

When regular people get sick, they go to the doctor. But wait . . . getting a doctor's appointment usually means finding time during normal business hours. "Doctor's appointments are a distant fantasy, including the ophthalmologist and the dentist," Bubbers says.

Additional Reading

Perry, Michelle Y.; Osborne, William E. "Health and Wellness in Residents Who Matriculate into Physician Training Programs." *American Journal of Obstetrics and Gynecology,* 189, no. 3 (2003): 679–683. Available at: www.ajog.org/article/S0002-9378(03)00889-5/abstract. Accessed August 2009.
Spiro; Howard M.; Mandell, Harvey N. "When Doctors Get Sick." *Annals of Internal Medicine,* 128, no. 2 (1998): 152–154. Available at: www.annals.org/cgi/content/full/128/2/152. Accessed August 2009.

CHAPTER TWENTY-THREE

Transplant

One of the most remarkable surgeries is transplantation. An organ donated when someone dies (or by a living donor in some kidney and partial liver transplants) can have an astonishing effect on the health of the recipient.

Chief resident David Cho leads the team into the room of a young man who received both a kidney and a pancreas.

"Your sugar is down to eighty. You're making a ton of urine. You're doing great," Cho tells the man. Assuming the organs continue to function well, the patient will be free from the kidney dialysis, the insulin, and the other treatments for diabetes and kidney failure that have dominated his life. "It's absolutely a miracle," a family member says.

Indeed, while most patients with serious chronic diseases typically face a continued heavy burden of treatment, even after successful surgery, organ recipients can enjoy dramatic improvements in their health. However, they do usually need to take powerful anti-rejection drugs that may leave them more susceptible to infections and other problems. Also, their future may be threatened by failure of the transplanted organ or progression of the underlying disease.

Later in the day, surgeon Stephen Rayhill stops in to see the patient during afternoon rounds. He is also pleased with the urine output, which indicates the transplanted kidney is functioning well.

"Anything we can do for you?" Rayhill asks.

"Haven't you already done it?" a family member responds with a big smile. "It's a miracle. It's changed his life."

The previous Saturday had started with normal rounds at 7:00 A.M. But in the afternoon it all changed when Cho got a call to come procure a liver, a pancreas, and two kidneys from someone who had died. He went into the operating room at 4:00 P.M., working through the night without sleep and only a couple of breaks to write notes about the series of operations. He wrapped up his part in the surgeries at 2:00 P.M. Sunday afternoon, 22 hours after the transplant operations had begun.

While transplant teams are always ready to go to work when an organ donor dies, many kidney transplants, as well as transplants of liver segments, come from living donors who literally give a piece of themselves.

Cho is assisting John Barry, M.D., with transplanting a kidney from a living donor. The recipient is being prepared when a nurse walks into the operating room carrying an ice-filled plastic bucket. "Are you looking for a kidney?" the nurse asks. Then another item arrives from the donor's operating room: a camera. The donor wants pictures of the kidney going into its new home.

Barry led the OHSU Division of Urology and Renal Transplantation for 29 years. He's done more kidney transplants than all but a few surgeons. His surgeries are carefully scripted and methodical. The nurse pulls the bag containing the kidney out of the ice and unties it, so that Cho can reach in with his sterile gloves to pull out an inner bag. That bag in turn holds a screw top jar with yet another bag that holds the prized kidney.

Cho places the kidney into a tray on a bed of icy slush. It is a dull gray. "Get over here," Barry calls to Cho. "Kidney in the pan, kidney in the pan," he tells the scrub nurse. After laying the pan on the recipient's abdomen, Barry and Cho go to work, trimming away fat and preparing the blood vessels and ureter.

"This is the cool part," Cho says half an hour later. Barry poses with the kidney as a nurse takes pictures for the donor. They place the kidney into the recipient's body, check how it fits, then remove it. Repeating this process, it takes about an hour to make all the connections between the kidney and the recipient.

Then they announce, "Clamps are off." The gray kidney pinks up as blood flows in to be filtered.

"It's still miracle stuff after all these years," Barry says as they close.

"It is pretty. All pink," agrees a nurse.

There would be more transplants if more people left instructions to have their organs donated after their deaths. But if transplant procurement were handled the way it has been shown on *Grey's Anatomy,* there would probably be even fewer organs available.

The new heart surgeon, Virginia Dixon, is socially inept. When she asks a family to donate the organs of a young girl killed in a car crash in "All by Myself" (5-10), she instead infuriates them.

The girl's sister is sitting by the bed, stroking the girl's arm.

"Can she hear me? She can come out of it, right? The coma? People can do that?" she asks.

Dixon blurts out, "No, she can't. I'm very sorry for your loss, but tests confirm that although your sister's bodily functions are fine, her brain is dead. She has no thoughts, no emotions, no senses. I'm Dr. Dixon. I will be harvesting your sister's organs, if your parents agree."

"Please, she's our baby. We need more time," the father pleads.

"I'm very sorry for your loss, but her organs are young and vital. They could save many lives," Dixon insists. She continues to press the family for a decision until the sister finally explodes in grief and anger. "Get out! You cannot have her! You cannot take her!" the sister screams.

Then in "Stairway to Heaven" (5-13), Chief Webber sends George O'Malley to comb the hospital for patients who are on life support or "brain dead," in a search for organs for a dying boy.

"O'Malley, be sensitive to the families," the chief instructs. "We need organs for this boy, but we can only ask, we can't pressure, we can't coerce. Understood?"

The behavior of the surgeons in both of these scenes would be not only counterproductive but also in violation of the rules governing organ donation in the United States. Indeed, after "Stairway to Heaven" aired, organ donation advocates said they met with *Grey's Anatomy* staff to ask for more accurate depictions of transplant procedures. The advocates pointed out that doctors who care for patients should not and do not ask that families approve organ donation. Their job is to care for their patient and only their patient, not a potential organ recipient. One of the advocates said *Grey's Anatomy* executives wanted to hear about any perceived inaccuracies, so she drafted a letter outlining some of the concerns:

> If the public perceives a conflict [of interest] they will not trust the system. Distrust in the system is a key reason why people do not register as donors.

> The Chief is the head of a transplant center and it would be illegal for him, or any other member of a transplant team, to approach a family about donation.

> Transplant teams are not aware of potential donors in the hospital and can not seek out donors from the ICU as the Chief asked George to do.

LATE ONE NIGHT IN THE SURGICAL INTENSIVE CARE UNIT AT OHSU, the chief resident comes out of the room of a woman whose brain was irreparably damaged in a car crash. "This is the bad part," she says as she steps away. She knows that the woman cannot be saved, but she is not involved in the discussion with family members about organ donation. That delicate task is assigned to transplant specialists who are not connected to the care of either potential donors or recipients.

The resident is glad she is not part of the emotional discussion. "I've got to take care of my patient," she points out. "I don't want to get in between my patient and another patient who might benefit. So when we have a possible donor, we alert administrators. They bring in specialists who know how to approach the family."

Additional Reading

Donate Life Hollywood. For more information, see www.onelegacy.org/prod/
components/community. Accessed August 2009.

Morgan, Susan E. "The Effect of Entertainment Media on Public Willingness to
Donate Organs." Purdue University, Department of Communication, West
Lafayette, Ind. 2007. Available at: www.jrifilms.org/downloads/Effect_of_
Entertainment_Media_on_Public_Willingness_to_Donate_Organs.pdf.
Accessed August 2009.

Pacific Northwest Transplant Bank. The federally designated organ procurement
organization serving Oregon, southern Washington, and western Idaho. For
more information, see www.pntb.org. Accessed August 2009.

CHAPTER TWENTY-FOUR

Memento

In 2000, a unique movie hit the theaters. *Memento* tells the story of a man trying to investigate his wife's death, but he has a form of amnesia that makes it almost impossible for him to store new memories. To draw the audience into his world, the film has a mind-boggling twist: Most of the scenes are in reverse order, so you see a snippet of action, but don't know what came before.

Intern Jason Susong says in a way a surgeon is like the character in *Memento*. "Surgeons come in in the middle of the story. We rarely see patients beforehand or after. There is little or no context."

Of course, some surgeons do see patients more than once over the course of their lives, although the moments of direct contact may be separated by years. And surgery patients are followed for a brief time in the hospital and then perhaps a few times in clinic visits. But once the main surgical issue is dealt with, the responsibility for ongoing care usually reverts to the patient's primary care physician or another specialist.

So a surgeon will see a wound and stitch it up, perhaps without ever getting a full explanation of what happened. A surgeon will transplant a liver, while knowing only the basic facts about why the patient's liver failed, and when an organ arrives from someone who died at another hospital, the surgeon will likely receive only enough information to judge the suitability of the organ—nothing about the life of the person whose liver is now in his or her hands.

IT'S EARLY IN THE MORNING. MICHAEL ENGLEHART IS APPROACHING THE end of his night shift as the trauma team's chief resident. He just got word that the covering on a patient's abdominal wound is failing. He heads back to the OR.

As they roll the patient into the room, the attending surgeon, John Mayberry, says he didn't expect to see this woman again so soon. Just 12 hours earlier, Mayberry had placed a sophisticated and expensive covering over the patient's open abdomen. The wound vac system uses special foam pads and a plastic covering that is vacuum sealed over the open wound. It's designed for just this sort of a situation, but apparently the patient coughed so hard during the night that the covering started to fail.

Englehart wasn't involved in the last two operations this woman went through. What he knows about this case comes mostly from Mayberry and Laszlo Kiraly (Englehart's dayside counterpart) and their entries in the case notes. He talks about how the patient had been complaining about pain near her spine a few days earlier, which led them to discover an abscess near her spleen.

The team removes the failing wound covering and replaces it with a more traditional mesh that is sutured to the fascia, the tough connective tissue beneath the skin. With the major work done, Mayberry leaves the final closing to Englehart and a pair of medical students. They seal up the woman's abdomen, hoping this covering will hold longer.

ONE O'CLOCK IN THE MORNING. ENGLEHART SITS WITH JUNIOR TRAUMA resident Terah Isaacson in the nurses station on the trauma floor. "The *Memento* analogy is very true," Englehart says. "We try to piece together what happened. We see the results, but don't always know everything about what led to it, initially."

Isaacson points out that they see patients only after something bad has already happened to them. "You don't know the baseline for patients."

And it's not uncommon for the background stories told by friends or family or even the patient to change over time. They know their patient was beaten, but the sequence of events is murky. It's not even clear whether the problems they are treating now are the direct result of the most recent incident. It's possible they were caused by something that happened earlier. Maybe an earlier injury developed into a more serious problem or the injuries simply weren't examined until the woman was brought to the hospital after a second incident.

It's late afternoon the day before. Mayberry and Kiraly are exploring and cleaning the abdomen of the patient they had first operated on two days earlier. They had removed a diseased spleen in that operation and sealed in her abdominal organs with a temporary covering.

They replace the wound covering. First they place oval foam pads into the opening. Two medical students help push on the woman's sides as the surgeons tightly wrap adhesive sheets of plastic over the foam pads. They see a bit of fluid leaking. "Once you get fluid underneath, it starts to lose the seal," Mayberry cautions. Once everything is in place, a vacuum pump sucks the closure tight.

Jump back two days. Kiraly is heading to an OR. It appears that a patient has perforated something in her abdomen, but the situation isn't clear. Attending surgeon Mayberry checks in at the central surgery desk. "It looks like there's an abscess in her spleen. It's unusual. I've seen this kind of thing before, but it's unusual."

In the OR, they prepare to open up the woman's abdomen to find out just what is wrong. "We tried all morning to manage the patient's problems medically." Then they considered using X-ray scans (interventional radiology) to guide the placement of a drain tube into the abscess. The woman had come to the hospital with facial fractures from an assault. "She probably had the abscess when she arrived," Mayberry guesses.

Another trauma surgeon is watching the procedure. Jennifer Watters had been on call the night before, watching over this woman and other patients. "This patient was totally asymptomatic last night," she says, somewhat puzzled by her sudden turn for the worse. "She had complained of chest pains, but her belly was soft." Watters second-guesses her management of this patient's case. "Now I'm worried all my patients are ticking time bombs."

This woman brought many questions with her to the hospital. She may have had older untreated injuries that the surgeons didn't know about. And even when her complaints of pain led to a CT scan that revealed something in or near her spleen, the exact nature of her problem wasn't clear.

Once they open the abdomen, Kiraly suctions out excess fluid.

"I think it's been going on for more than several hours," Mayberry says. "The CT scan was done at one A.M., but on the scan it looked better than it really was. Her husband said she'd been sick for weeks." As they dig deeper toward the site of the abscess, the surgeons speculate about how a hidden infection deep in her abdomen might have affected her thinking and maybe played some role in the assault that injured her face and thus brought her to the hospital.

They'll probably never really know exactly what chain of events stretches back in this woman's history. What they do know is that she is on their operating table and there is something seriously wrong with her spleen. They decide that trying to clean out the abscess won't be enough . . . the spleen needs to come out.

As Kiraly irrigates and suctions the woman's abdomen, Mayberry steps over to a side table to examine the spleen he just removed. "Still not sure what to make of it," he says as he turns the spleen over in his hands. "I can't tell whether it's a ruptured spleen that got infected or an abscess that then ruptured the spleen. An injured spleen usually points to trauma." But if so, it seems likely that the injury would have occurred earlier than the blows to the patient's face.

It's a mystery that Mayberry puts aside with the spleen as he returns to the matter at hand: helping the woman heal. They decide not to completely close her abdomen, because postoperative swelling could squeeze and damage the patient's kidneys. Instead they place a vacuum-sealed covering to hold everything in place. The plan is to return in a couple days to see how her organs are mending.

Thus surgeons work with fragments of information and scenes without full context, often never getting a broad sense of a patient's story.

JASON SUSONG, M.D.

Status: Intern

Where from: Chattanooga, Tennessee. Medical school at the University of Tennessee in Memphis.

Why did you want to become a surgeon?
Susong's father was a dermatologist. He remembers assisting with a mole removal at age 11 or 12.

"I helped him retract and do some things. He did a little skin graft to close it. I was just blown away that my dad could do that." Then he worked as a surgical assistant while he was in college. "There was pretty much no other way [to go]. I kept looking at all the other specialties, but surgery always drew me back."

What's the biggest difference between what you thought it would be like and the reality?
Susong says he likes the way surgeons tackle problems.

"I like the finality of it and the definitive solutions. I'm just looking forward to not being a resident and being a real surgeon."

But he's learned that dealing with health problems is more complex than he expected.

"I thought most of the difficulties in solving patient problems would be due to a lack of knowledge or the capabilities of an institution, but I've found most of the problems are actually systems based."

In other words, successful surgery can't solve the underlying causes of health problems. He's seen cancer patients fail to follow through with chemotherapy and people endure surgery meant to help them lose weight, who then fail to stick to their diets.

"There needs to be a broader system to really fix the problems, rather than just the surgery. That's something I'm learning more about. It's not just, 'Can you cure the pneumonia,' it's, 'Can you make them stop smoking, so they don't get pneumonia.' " Susong says the disconnect between what we know and what we do is a problem for everyone, even doctors. "I knew people who started smoking in medical school. They knew better."

Looking back to the beginning of his intern year, Susong says, "I feel like a different person." He says the experience of residency must be something like going to war; you have expectations, but there is no way to be fully prepared for the actual experience. "You look back and you go, 'Wow, I had no idea what I was getting into.' Not in a bad sense though."

What specialty are you most interested in?

Like most interns, Susong hasn't settled on a specialty. The decision is not entirely his. He joined the U.S. Air Force, which has helped pay for his education. In return, he owes the USAF at least four years after residency.

"I'd really like to do minimally invasive surgery, but the Air Force may put me to work as a general surgeon. I need to find out more about what my post-graduation career plans are with them before I decide to specialize."

He says he enjoys working in the military health care system, in part because everyone is covered, so no worries about insurance payments, and patients have to comply with doctor's orders or else.

CHAPTER TWENTY-FIVE

Strange Memories

The double episode that opened the fifth season of *Grey's Anatomy*, "Dream a Little Dream of Me: Parts 1 and 2" (5-01 and 5-02), featured a pair of car crashes that sent three close friends and their husbands to the hospital. One of the injured women keeps asking about her husband. She quiets when she is given an answer, but then she asks again. After a while it becomes clear that her memory is vanishing after about 30 seconds.

A blow to the head often causes some memory loss. Many people who have been in car crashes or suffered other trauma report that they don't recall what happened shortly before the impact, which means the problem isn't just from a blackout after a crash.

In most cases, as the patient recovers from the trauma, memories stick as they did before. But the kind of memory flush displayed by the *Grey's Anatomy* patient is not unheard of. Indeed, the man with the most famous case of a memory that kept resetting died in December 2008 at the age of 82.

H.M, as he was called in medical research articles about his case, underwent brain surgery in the early 1950s. The surgeon, William Scoville, M.D., removed small sections of his brain to treat debilitating seizures. At the time, most neuroscientists believed that the entire brain was involved in making memories. But after the surgery, H.M. had lost the ability to make new long-term memories.

In a speech recapping highlights of his career, brain surgeon Wilder Penfield, M.D., wrote about the observations he and his colleague Brenda Milner, Ph.D., D.Sc., made of H.M.

"Bilateral removal of the hippocampus and hippocampal gyrus in man," we concluded, "produces loss of recent memory. As soon as he has turned his attention to something else, the patient is unable to remember what was happening a moment earlier. It is as though he had made no record of present experience." Or, one might add, having made the record as usual, he had lost the mechanism that enabled him to reactivate the record by voluntary initiative."

In other words, people who have this specific kind of brain damage show the kind of loop of learning and then almost immediate forgetting that is displayed by the patient on *Grey's Anatomy*. In general, these people retain older memories; they just have trouble cementing new ones.

The damage to the hippocampus, a structure near the base of the forebrain, seemed to disrupt only long-term memory.

"Such patients showed no loss of intelligence or previously acquired knowledge and skill and they could attend normally to ongoing events. Yet they appeared to be able to add little new information to their long-term store, demonstrating a continuous anterograde amnesia for postoperative events," Milner wrote.

The observations led to new ideas about how our brains work.

After H.M.'s death, MIT Behavioral Neuroscience Professor Suzanne Corkin, Ph.D., one of the researchers who had studied Henry Molaison (his full name) played a short recording of one of their conversations for National Public Radio.

CORKIN: "Do you know what you did yesterday?"
MOLAISON: "No, I don't."
CORKIN: "How about this morning?"

MOLAISON: "I don't even remember that."
CORKIN: "Could you tell me what you had for lunch today?"
MOLAISON: "I don't know, to tell you the truth."

Corkin told the NPR reporter that even though she met Molaison in 1962 and saw him frequently over the ensuing years, he did not remember her name or who she was. However, he did seem to know that they had met before and said he thought they had been in high school together. Also, as the recording demonstrates, he could carry on conversations. He could also repeat back strings of numbers or other things immediately. But after about 20 or 30 seconds, the memories disappeared.

Another odd phenomenon sometimes seen during brain surgery was shown in "The Other Side of This Life: Part 2" (3-23). During certain procedures patients are awake, in part to help surgeons avoid damaging critical brain structures. As Derek Shepherd operates on a patient with amnesia (who is also known as Ava or Rebecca Pope), Alex Karev holds up pictures and quizzes her.

"Ava, can you name this object?" Karev asks her.

"Flowers, pink and blue," she responds correctly.

Derek Shepherd moves to another area of her brain. "Avoiding area 11. Moving superiorly. This will be area 12." Shepherd says.

"Una cara con los ojos azules y el pelo rubio," Ava says.

"Was that Spanish?" Alex asks.

As Shepherd stimulates different areas of the patient's brain, she spurts out sentences in French and German, too. Brain surgery can trigger specific memories, not only languages but remembered sounds or other sensations. Milner, one of the researchers who studied H.M., recalled some of the examples that occurred during operations performed by her partner, Penfield:

A patient might hear the voice of his cousin in Africa, or he might hear a well known march from Aida and be able to keep time to the music. The sounds would unroll at the rate of normal experience and yet the patient would not be deceived by them; he would remain aware at the same time of being in the operating room at the MNI, replying to

Penfield; it was as though there were a momentary and bizarre doubling of conscious experience.

Additional Reading

Carey, Benedict. "H. M., an Unforgettable Amnesiac, Dies at 82." *New York Times,* December 4, 2008. Available at: www.nytimes.com/2008/12/05/us/05hm.html? partner=permalink&exprod=permalink. Accessed August 2009.

Milner, Brenda. "Memory Mechanisms." *Canadian Medical Association Journal,* 18, no. 12 (1977): 1374–1376. Available at: www.pubmedcentral.nih.gov/picrender .fcgi?artid=1879317&blobtype=pdf. Accessed August 2009.

Milner, B.; Corkin, S.; Teuber, H-L. "Further Analysis of the Hippocampal Amnesic Syndrome: 14-Year Follow-Up Study of H.M." *Neuropsychologia,* 6 (1968): 215–234. Available at: http://web.mit.edu/bnl/pdf/HippocampalAmnesic.pdf. Accessed August 2009.

Penfield, W. "Engrams in the Human Brain. Mechanisms of Memory." *Proceedings of the Royal Society of Medicine,* 61, no. 8 (1968): 831-840. Available at: www .pubmedcentral.nih.gov/picrender.fcgi?artid=1902435&blobtype=pdf. Accessed August 2009.

CHAPTER TWENTY-SIX

Evidence

The crash caused a "clothesline" injury across the man's midsection, leaving severe abdominal damage. The trauma team opted to quickly deal with the worst bleeding and other damage, and then return later to do more comprehensive repairs when the patient was stronger. They removed the destroyed sections of bowel, leaving the ends disconnected for now. The patient would not be eating or drinking soon.

How soon? That was one question Robert Martindale went over as he stood outside the patient's intensive care room with nutrition nurses. How well would his bowel function after the final surgical repairs are done? They puzzled over inconsistent notes in the patient's chart about just how much of his digestive tract had been removed, each centimeter of lost bowel tilting the odds he would be able to eventually resume eating normally.

Residents call him "Dr. Smartindale." He rattles off highlights of research articles like a human encyclopedia.

During trauma clinic one afternoon, an intern begins to brief him on a waiting patient. "Sounds like a sports hernia." Martindale launches into teaching mode. "The classic case is a soccer player. The abductor muscle pulls off the pubis bone. There's a good review about sports hernia from SSAT [Society for Surgery of the Alimentary Tract]. I've got a copy, I'll give it to you."

On morning rounds through the intensive care unit, he pops a question to the residents: "What are the top causes of stress ulcers in the ICU?" When he doesn't get a quick response, he answers himself. "Ventilation and coagulopathy." That is, the mechanical ventilators that help patients breathe and then disorders that disrupt blood coagulation. Martindale gives a rapid-fire summary of recent research, pointing the residents toward journal articles that come from Project IMPACT, a massive data collection effort to track what is done to patients in intensive care and what happens to those patients. Martindale's eyes light up as he extols the database that allows researchers to crunch numbers and link actions with outcomes.

When a patient needs a tracheostomy (a hole cut in the neck to bypass a blocked airway), how does performing the procedure right at the bedside compare with taking the patient to the OR? What happens to patients who receive different types of treatments meant to prevent dangerous blood clots? And a favorite subject of Martindale's: When should patients start getting fed through a tube into the stomach (enteral nutrition), rather than relying on IV fluids? For many years, seriously ill patients typically received nutrients directly into their bloodstream through an IV; in part because patients could be given a lot of calories even when their stomachs or intestines were not functioning properly. In recent years, evidence has mounted that it's often better for patients to put their guts back to work, even if they aren't able to chew food or swallow liquids.

"Data show enteral feeding cuts mortality by twenty percent. That's from multiple studies," Martindale says. "But old habits die hard. We thought we could match what the body can do, but we can't."

He proclaims the evidence for medical students, residents, and colleagues, cheering progress toward improving clinical practice, while muttering frustration about backsliding. "TPNs [patients on total parenteral nutrition, the technical term for IV feeding] went down, but then they've been creeping back up," he tells a nutritionist rounding with him in the ICU.

"Maybe it's the new residents," she replies.

Martindale knows that science needs champions in hospitals, that without them, people revert to old habits. He tells of a dietician at the Medical College of Georgia who was a ceaseless advocate for moving patients from TPN IVs to tube feeding to get their bodies back on the road to normal digestion. She was making progress. The reliance on TPN declined and stayed down. But then she went on leave. "TPN went right back up," Martindale says. "When she returned, she started pulling those rates back down."

The struggle between habits and medical evidence is eternal. One reason is that the evidence changes. When the trauma team operating on the crash victim with the clothesline injury decided to deal with just the most threatening injuries and stop major bleeding in the first operation—putting off comprehensive repairs—they were following recommendations that were surgical heresy a generation ago. That turning point in trauma practice was highlighted when senior residents presented the case during the weekly trauma conference.

"It's oh seven hundred. Trauma conference will begin," states a senior trauma resident, facing the lecture hall audience of residents, faculty, and others. Some have been in the hospital for hours doing rounds or finishing up overnight call. Others are making their first stop as the workday begins. All are gathered to hear lessons gleaned from recent trauma cases. The residents explain that this crash victim came from another hospital. There was concern about a possible life-threatening tear in the patient's aorta. Fortunately, when they took the man into surgery, they found his aorta was intact. But he had severe abdominal injuries and heavy bleeding.

"In the 1970s and 1980s, the traditional approach was to attempt a comprehensive repair during the first procedure," says the resident making the case presentation. In part, the thinking was that with a severely injured patient, surgeons had one shot to make major repairs, even in the face of internal bleeding that sometimes was impossible to control. But then some surgeons tried a different approach. The resident refers to a journal article from 1983.

"One of the most frustrating situations ever encountered by the operating surgeon is an open wound in a patient whose blood will not clot and cannot be made to clot," the article begins. "The coagulopathy [clotting disorder] can seldom be reversed satisfactorily. Thus, the usual outcome is continued bleeding and thereby death through exsanguination [blood loss]."

The article goes on to recount the experience with using standard procedures to stop bleeding while completing all the details in the operative procedure. Of 14 patients whose blood would not clot normally, bleeding was controlled in just two, and only one patient survived. Then they tried a different approach: Deal with bleeding and the most vital repairs, pack the abdomen to put pressure on the wounds and close up, returning the patient to the OR for follow-up surgery after the bleeding had been stopped. Of 17 patients treated this new way, 11 survived. It signaled a dramatic shift in trauma treatment.

This trauma conference presentation was not simply a dry review of a quarter-century-old medical journal article. The third author on the paper, Richard Mullins, who was a young surgery fellow working for H. Harlan Stone, M.D., at Grady Memorial Hospital in Atlanta in 1983, now sits along the center aisle of the lecture hall, ready to critique the performance of the next generation of surgeons.

"Harlan Stone was a complex fellow," Mullins recalls. "He had a lot to do with the modern treatment of trauma." Mullins says Stone had insights other trauma surgeons didn't have. He was engaged in patient care, and in an era when senior physicians often left hospitals in the hands of residents, Stone was there, days, nights, and weekends. And when the standard procedures didn't work, he was willing to try new things, confident in his ability to find a better way. So when he failed time and again to save trauma patients whose blood wouldn't clot during surgery, instead of just accepting that they were just too badly injured to survive, Stone made a major course correction by packing the wounds and suspending surgery. As his 1983 journal article reported, his instinct was correct. Damage control, followed by more surgeries after major bleeding has been stopped, is now the accepted course for such trauma cases.

But Stone wasn't always right, Mullins says; for instance, in advocating bandaging burns and leaving them heavily bandaged. And, Mullins says, he sometimes rushed ahead of his times, recommending radical surgery to remove stones from the common bile duct, for example. Although the procedure worked, it took a heavy toll on patients, too much for other surgeons to accept. Today, minimally invasive laparoscopic techniques allow surgeons to treat such cases without doing as much harm, so ultimately Stone's basic idea took hold, but only because less traumatic techniques were developed to achieve the goal.

And like many surgeons in earlier decades, Stone embarked on trials of new techniques with little oversight. Mullins says that although his tests of key trauma practices led to important advances, the methods he used to test his ideas probably wouldn't pass muster with institutional review boards and other bodies that now monitor medical experiments.

"IN THE PRACTICE OF MEDICINE, CHANGE IS INEVITABLE. NEW SURGICAL techniques are created, procedures are updated, levels of expertise increase. Innovation is everything. Nothing remains the same for long. We either adapt to change . . . or we get left behind," Meredith Grey says in "A Change Is Gonna Come" (4-01).

Additional Reading

Society for Surgery of the Alimentary Tract. "SSAT Patient Care Guidelines: Surgical Repair of Groin Hernias." Available at: www.ssat.com/cgi-bin/ hernia6.cgi. Accessed August 2009.

Stone, H. H.; Strom, P. R.; Mullins, R. J. "Management of the Major Coagulopathy with Onset During Laparotomy." *Annals of Surgery,* 197, no. 5 (1983): 532–535. Available at: www.pubmedcentral.nih.gov/articlerender.fcgi?tool=pubmed &pubmedid=6847272. Accessed August 2009.

CHAPTER TWENTY-SEVEN

Research

In a grand rounds lecture to the Department of Surgery, Chair John Hunter extols research.

"Most clinical care is built on an inadequate evidence base," he says. He urges the residents to pursue research, telling them there are huge opportunities to weave research into the fabric of surgical care and education. "Collect something," he tells them. "Count something." Because that's how surgery will make progress.

DEREK SHEPHERD AND MEREDITH GREY MOUNT A CLINICAL TRIAL OF a virus designed to attack brain tumors in "Piece of My Heart" (4-13).

"Tell me about the clinical trial," Addison Montgomery asks Shepherd.

"Well, if it doesn't go well, I'm killing people for sport," he jokes. "When I walk in an O.R., I'm an expert. I can stop a bleed. I can remove a clot. I'm the expert. But in a clinical trial, I'm experimenting, groping around in the dark hoping to do the right thing."

* * *

ACTUALLY, WELL-DONE EXPERIMENTS CAN REVEAL THAT WHAT EXPERTS think they are doing right is not really the best method after all.

Although the five years of surgery residency might seem quite long enough, residents routinely add a year or two of research. David Cho spent two years doing research after his third year of clinical residency. He worked with trauma surgeon Martin Schreiber, studying resuscitation and blood coagulation, fluids and blood products, and other trauma topics. And he worked on the largest study yet to compare open versus laparoscopic appendectomy in children.

Surgery research presents some special challenges. Drug trials often use placebo controls and blinding of the researchers to help protect against bias and wishful thinking. But performing placebo, or sham, surgery on a patient is quite different from giving a volunteer a sugar pill instead of the active ingredient being tested. And unlike drug research, in which coded pill bottles make it simple to prevent doctors from knowing too soon whether they are giving a patient the active or placebo pills, there's no way to "blind" a surgeon.

Because of these and other ethical and practical hurdles, the kind of randomized, controlled trials that are common in drug research are relatively rare in the world of surgery. Nevertheless, surgeons say surgery research has made progress. Cho notes that relying on expert opinion to evaluate new techniques, basically the anecdotal experience of prominent surgeons, is less common than it used to be.

"If you look at a surgery journal, even as recent as the 1980s, the methodology seems pretty weak by today's standards. It's often some senior guy saying, 'I did a hundred of these,' " Cho notes.

Sham surgeries have been used in a few clinical trials, for example to test whether fetal tissue implants help people with Parkinson disease. But there are strong ethical reservations about the risks of putting someone under anesthesia, even briefly, and then cutting and suturing the skin, so that the patient can't tell whether or not the full surgery was done. Then the patients can be evaluated by doctors who aren't told whether a particular patient got the real or sham procedure, so that their opinions aren't affected by unconscious bias.

Cho and his colleagues are comparing two types of appendectomy procedures, so he wasn't trying to craft some sort of placebo control but coming up with an ethical and yet scientifically robust trial design was still a challenge.

"It's actually a multicenter randomized controlled trial. It's been very hard to do. It's taken me three years to get this off the ground. The protocol is very complicated, and there are a lot of things to keep in mind," Cho says. But despite the hurdles, the trial is under way. Cho sees it as an example of how surgeons are trying to raise the standards of research. Nevertheless, surgery and surgery research will always be different.

"In a way, it's almost like cooking. There's an established technique. We know it works. We know if you deviate from it, it doesn't work. You can take it and be creative," says Cho. But some of it can't be spelled out like a drug prescription, it has to be seen and practiced. "You can write down: Soufflé this. But what does that mean? That part you have to learn by just being around it."

Then there is the matter of a surgeon's skill.

"Trial results can be hard to translate to regular practice," cautions trauma surgeon Richard Mullins. "Some things in life require a Tiger Woods. If I golfed, the result wouldn't be the same."

One example is research on a type of surgery meant to reduce stroke risk. The surgery involves opening the carotid artery to clean out plaque. Some large clinical trials indicated that certain patients did better after surgery than similar patients who received drug treatment. However, when surgeons across the country began using the surgery more, it turned out that often the benefits were smaller and the surgical risks were higher than had been seen in the trials.

"It turns out typical surgeons couldn't match the skill of the surgeons involved in the trials," Mullins notes.

During the question and answer session of Hunter's grand rounds presentation, Mullins asked him about the pioneering research he did in the 1980s that advanced the use of laparoscopic, minimally invasive, techniques.

"How did you hit a home run in pioneering laparoscopic cholecystectomy? Give the residents some tips."

"If you are right, you will get rocks thrown at you," Hunter reflects. "Something new that is disruptive is not going to be welcomed by all. I did have support, but it was not easy. The evidence was so clear though."

Hunter says he saw some presentations in the 1980s by surgeons trying the then-new laparoscopic tools to operate on patients through small punctures rather than opening them up with large incisions. There were no large controlled trials of the type used to test drugs before selling them . . . just pioneering surgeons trying something new and then training others.

"I was a student at one course and then a teacher at the next," Hunter says. Before operating on patients, he says training on animals was essential. "It's like performing at Carnegie Hall. The first time you've never done it before, but you have practiced for a long time."

With cholecystectomy, removal of a gallbladder, usually because of gallstones, comparing the new method to standard open surgery wasn't difficult, Hunter says, because other than the technique for getting to the gallbladder, the result of the surgery is the same.

"They were able to go home the next day, while patients who had open procedures can't even get out of bed the next day, much less even think about going home. And if the patient is fine in a week, then they are fine for the long term."

One challenge that faces researchers in both medicine and surgery is that patients are not all the same. Different people react to drugs differently. When it comes to surgery, each patient's anatomy is as unique as his or her face. Of course, a gallbladder is a gallbladder; but patients are fat and skinny, tall and short, mostly old, but sometimes young. Blood vessels aren't in exactly the same places and don't always connect in the same ways in different people. The physical variations mean that even as residents learn the best practices, they also have to adapt to the person on the operating room table.

David Cho says he is constantly amazed by what experienced surgeons can see when they look into the bodies of their patients.

"Even in a normal case, where the anatomy is straightforward and everything looks like it does in a textbook," he says, the attending will see things that are invisible to residents. "You get someone in the operating room who has an inflamed bed of tissue or something abnormal, the ability of experienced surgeons to be able to tease out what is and what isn't normal, and where you should and shouldn't go, is almost like magic."

Additional Reading

Albin, R. "Sham Surgery Controls: Intracerebral Grafting of Fetal Tissue for Parkinson's Disease and Proposed Criteria for Use of Sham Surgery Controls." *Journal of Medical Ethics,* 28, no. 5 (2002): 322–325. Available at: www.pubmedcentral .nih.gov/articlerender.fcgi?artid=1733639. Accessed August 2009.

Feasby, Thomas E.; Kennedy, James; Quan, Hude; Girard, Louis; Ghali, William A. "Real-World Replication of Randomized Controlled Trial Results for Carotid Endarterectomy." *Archives of Neurology,* 64, no. 10 (2007): 1496–1500. Available at: http://archneur.ama-assn.org/cgi/content/full/64/10/1496. Accessed August 2009.

Wennberg, David E.; Lucas, F. L.; Birkmeyer, John D.; Bredenberg, Carl E.; Fisher, Elliott S. "Variation in Carotid Endarterectomy Mortality in the Medicare Population. Trial Hospitals, Volume, and Patient Characteristics." *Journal of the American Medical Association,* 279 (1998): 1278–1281.

CHAPTER TWENTY-EIGHT

Generations

The *Grey's Anatomy* interns began to hang out in the room of a patient they just called "really old guy." The man had been in the hospital, sedated and mostly unconscious, for almost a year. Then in "Let the Truth Sting" (4-03), he wakes up. He tells the interns that his name is Charlie and he asks that they stop any further treatment. Izzie Stevens resists his request. She doesn't understand his perspective.

"A man can only hang on for so long, Blondie. After a while, it's just not worth it," Charlie says.

"Don't you have any friends, family, anyone?" Stevens asks.

"They're all dead or on their way to dead. You'll understand someday when you're older, less naive."

THE SCENE IN THE HOSPITAL ROOM IS A STUDY IN CONTRASTS, A DOCTOR AT the beginning of his career working to decipher the needs of a patient several times his senior. Clean shaven and fresh-faced, Marcus Kret looks young even among his fellow interns. His patient is wrinkled with time. He has not yet started a family. She has no surviving relatives.

Kret knows very little about the woman in the bed. She is in her 90s. The notes say she fell at her nursing home. So much blood had come out of a cut on her forehead that it took a nurse 20 minutes to clean her face. Her eyelids are purplish black and appear to be swollen shut. She is agitated. To prevent another fall, soft restraints crisscross her chest. In a slurred whisper she repeats, "Please let me go."

"Are you in pain?" Kret asks.

"Yes."

"Where?"

"My back," she says. But it is not clear exactly what is causing the pain. Her answers are indistinct.

Kret searches through the records for any mention of pain medication, for clues to her mental status, for some sense of who she is and what she needs. How aware is she of what has happened? Does she know where she is? How can Kret determine what she wants and what her best interests are? Until he knows what medications she has already received, what pain relief should he offer her? She keeps asking him to please let her get up, to please let her go home, but until he can predict what will happen, is it safe to release her? What if she injured herself further?

And then there is the vast chasm of time. She has lived four times as long as he. He was born in a world of computers and space flight. She saw horse-drawn buggies give way to automobiles and learned to read as newspapers featured dispatches from the trenches of World War I.

It is the physician's duty to act on behalf of the patient. Sounds simple. But in order to carry out the patient's wishes, the doctor must first understand him or her and, if possible, communicate with the patient about how those wishes match up against the medical realities. When doctor and patient stand at opposite ends of life's spectrum, the exchange of medical knowledge and personal values must reach across a misty span of generations.

Kret searches again through the patient's chart for more clues. A nurse points out the POLST form. "POLST? What's that?" he asks.

POLST stands for Physician Orders for Life-Sustaining Treatment. The form is meant to help make sure a patient's wishes are known and followed, especially when the patient is unable to communicate. Even when people have filled out legal forms, known as advance directives, indicating what kind of treatment they want during a health crisis, these instructions aren't always carried out. Researchers say that sometimes it isn't clear when advance directives apply, sometimes the instructions aren't clear enough to be useful to healthcare workers, and sometimes the directives just aren't found when they are needed.

It happened in "Break on Through" (2-15):

"Oh good, somebody's in here. How's she doing?" Meredith Grey says to visitors as she enters a patient's room.

"You intubated her?" one of them asks, as though shocked.

"She was struggling to breathe. Her sats were in the 80s. She was in her room all alone," Grey explains. "What?"

Grey is bewildered to see the patient's visitors outraged that she had acted to save the patient's life. Then one of them finally explains.

"Mrs. Bickham was diagnosed with end-stage C.O.P.D. She's on hospice."

"End of life care?" Grey begins to understand. One of the visitors shows her the patients chart.

"D.N.R.: Do not resuscitate."

One of the visitors is angry enough to slap Grey with her purse and curses Grey for not letting the woman die as she wanted.

"I'm sorry," Grey says.

To deal with these miscommunication problems, a group of health care professionals in Oregon created a task force in 1991 that ultimately developed a simple form with a checklist of key health care instructions listed all on one piece of paper. And they made the form bright pink, so it would stand out in the piles of medical paperwork that follow patients with serious illnesses. The form is not only for these paperwork folders; patients who live alone at home are advised to post it on their refrigerator, where emergency responders will know to look for it.

KRET LOOKS OVER THE POLST FORM IN HIS PATIENT'S FILE. "NOW THAT I see the POLST form, it looks familiar," he says. And he mentions a recent hospital conference that reviewed cases of medical interventions that went against the patients' wishes, in part because health care workers had not clearly understood what the patients wanted.

He reviews his patient's POLST form. It says she is supposed to receive comfort care only. But there's a hitch; the form is not signed. It may be accurate, but again, Kret must muddle through uncertainty, trying to get into the head of an anxious, injured, and apparently disoriented woman old enough to be his great- or even great-great-grandmother. What are the right medications to ease her pain, without simply drugging her into silence? How best to answer her repeated plea to "please let me go home"? How to calm her so she doesn't fall out of the bed?

After doing what he can here, Kret heads for the cafeteria to try to grab a bite to eat. As soon as he sits down, his pager announces a new trauma case will be arriving in the Emergency Department within 15 minutes. Two trauma cases and a couple of hours later, he returns to check on his elderly patient.

Things are better. Morphine seems to be easing her pain. And the nurse has helped her eat some applesauce. She is calmer.

GENERATIONAL DIFFERENCES AFFECT MUCH MORE THAN JUST THE COM-munication of a doctor and a patient separated by the better part of a century. Faculty and residents face the generation gap every day.

"They dress inappropriately," says one medical school faculty member.

"Some arrive in the OR unprepared," comments another.

"Some of them think it's okay to arrive late to my lectures."

"I'm frustrated when I'm teaching a twenty-eight-year-old what their parents should've taught them about how to be an adult."

These faculty members have gathered to discuss teaching young doctors who are often enigmas to them. Of course, generational tensions have always pulled at young and old—both thinking they have it right. Why can't those on the other side see things the way they do? The point of the discussion is not to just complain about "kids these days." Rather, it is to learn about the specific ways today's residents see things differently from their teachers. After all, they grew up in different worlds: Vietnam vs. 9/11 and Iraq; TVs that showed just four or five channels of programs

The form is always a **bright color.**

In any section left **unmarked,** the highest level of treatment must be provided.

HIPAA PERMITS DISCLOSURE TO HEALTH CARE PROFESSIONALS AS NECESSARY FOR TREATMENT

Physician Orders
for Life-Sustaining Treatment (POLST)

<u>First</u> follow these orders, <u>then</u> contact physician, NP, or PA. These medical orders are based on the person's current medical condition and preferences. Any section not completed does not invalidate the form and implies full treatment for that section.

Last Name/First/Middle Initial
Address
City/State/Zip

Date of Birth (mm/dd/yyyy)	Last 4 SSN	Gender
		M ☐ F ☐

A *Check One*	**CARDIOPULMONARY RESUSCITATION (CPR):** **Person has no pulse and is not breathing.** ☐ Attempt Resuscitation/CPR ☐ Do Not Attempt Resuscitation/DNR (<u>A</u>llow <u>N</u>atural <u>D</u>eath) When not in cardiopulmonary arrest, follow orders in **B, C** and **D**.
B *Check One*	**MEDICAL INTERVENTIONS:** **Person has pulse and/or is breathing.** ☐ **Comfort Measures Only** Use medication by any route, positioning, wound care and other measures to relieve pain and suffering. Use oxygen, suction and manual treatment of airway obstruction as needed for comfort. ***Do not transfer*** *to hospital for life-sustaining treatment.* ***Transfer*** *if comfort needs cannot be met in current location.* ☐ **Limited Additional Interventions** Includes care described above. Use medical treatment, IV fluids and cardiac monitor as indicated. Do not use intubation, advanced airway interventions, or mechanical ventilation. May consider less invasive airway support (e.g. CPAP, BiPAP). ***Transfer*** *to hospital if indicated.* *Avoid intensive care.* ☐ **Full Treatment** Includes care described above. Use intubation, advanced airway interventions, mechanical ventilation, and cardioversion as indicated. ***Transfer*** *to hospital if indicated. Includes intensive care.* *Additional Orders:* _____
C *Check One*	**ANTIBIOTICS** ☐ No antibiotics. Use other measures to relieve symptoms. ☐ Determine use or limitation of antibiotics when infection occurs. ☐ Use antibiotics if medically indicated. *Additional Orders:* _____

Decisions about the use of limitation of **antibiotics** may be decided in advance or on a case-by-case basis.

A **discussion** about treatment preferences is required when completing the POLST form.

D **ARTIFICIALLY ADMINISTERED NUTRITION:** Always offer food by mouth if feasible.

Check One
- [ ] No artificial nutrition by tube.
- [ ] Defined trial period of artificial nutrition by tube.
- [ ] Long-term artificial nutrition by tube.

Additional Orders: _____

E **REASON FOR ORDERS AND SIGNATURES**

My signature below indicates to the best of my knowledge that these orders are consistent with the person's current medical condition and preferences as indicated by the discussion with:

- [ ] Patient
- [ ] Health Care Representative
- [ ] Parent of Minor
- [ ] Court-Appointed Guardian
- [ ] Other _____

A physician must sign the POLST from, but the form may be completed by a nurse, social worker or other health care team member. In Oregon, it may also be signed by a nurse practitioner. The person who prepares the form is encouraged to sign the back of the POLST (not shown).

Print Primary Care Professional Name

Office Use Only

Print Signing Physician / NP / PA Name and Phone Number
( )

Physician / NP / PA Signature (mandatory) | Date

Copyright promotes the use of a standardized version of this form.

SEND FORM WITH PERSON WHENEVER TRANSFERRED OR DISCHARGED

© CENTER FOR ETHICS IN HEALTH CARE, Oregon Health & Science University, 3181 Sam Jackson Park Rd, UHN-86, Portland, OR 97239-3098 (503) 494-3965

The original form should **accompany the patient** on transfer and remain with the patient where they reside.

that had to be watched when they aired vs. a multimedia bath of interactive audio, video, text, and other data accessible almost anywhere and anytime; working dads and stay-at-home moms vs. blended families of parents and step-parents who work outside the home, and so on.

The differences in formative environments lead to different interpretations of words and actions today.

In a speech to the American Society for Surgery of the Hand, Peter J. Stern, M.D., shared a telling anecdote with his colleagues:

> Recently I asked my 83-year-old father and my 21-year-old daughter to use the following words in a sentence: crash, hard drive, virus, and mailbox. My father wrote: *During a hard drive to Boston, I contracted a virus, became delirious, and crashed into a mailbox.* My daughter wrote: *When I opened my mailbox, a virus caused my hard drive to crash.* I have no doubt that my dad and daughter have similar fundamental values, but in other ways they are generations apart.

Stern spoke of five traits that he said distinguish the generations of most faculty members (traditionalists born before 1946 and baby boomers born between the end of World War II and the mid-1960s) from the generations of most residents (generation X, 1965–1981, and millennials, born since 1981). Those traits are technology, loyalty, lifestyle, entrepreneurship, and diversity. Each has an effect on how faculty members teach and residents learn.

Computer and other electronic technology vastly increases the amount of information available, but the sheer volume of information may lead to more skimming than thinking. Traditionalists were more likely to work for one company until retirement, while today's economy displays much less loyalty from either employers or employees. The lifestyle of surgeons is evolving; with a growing sense that life outside the OR is important. Stern links entrepreneurship with innovation, and a greater comfort with change. And just as the nation is becoming more diverse, so is the OR, and that diversity brings increasing familiarity with different cultures and ways of working and communicating.

*   *   *

IN "LOSING MY MIND" (4-15), CHIEF WEBBER'S MENTOR HAS COME TO
Seattle Grace because he wants to have a friend with him as he prepares
to undergo a risky operation, in case he doesn't survive.

"I should have had a wife and a bunch of kids," the aging star surgeon
says. "So I wouldn't have to track you down to get someone to be at my
deathbed."

The consequences of personal sacrifices made by earlier generations
of surgeons help explain why younger surgeons want to rebalance career
and life.

AT A GATHERING OF OHSU FACULTY, PRESENTERS TRIED TO STEER THE
discussion away from whether the changes are for the better or worse . . .
and toward strategies for teaching across the generation gap.

For example, a common complaint from the faculty is that some residents and medical students dress inappropriately.

"When they come here for their interviews, they dress up, they hide
their tattoos, but then they slide back when they get here," one faculty
member says about how residents present a temporarily cleaned-up image
when they are applying.

The broad statement "dress professionally" doesn't always get the
results that faculty members are after. So one of the presenters recounted
her experience with using increasingly concrete and specific instructions
to remedy a communication breakdown. Students were told, "Cover up
your private areas." That statement turned out to be too vague for some,
so the next instructions were, "No cleavage. No visible thongs." Even that
rule did not always get the desired result. So finally, students were shown
pictures of how *not* to dress.

The clash of expectations is complicated by the fact that those expectations vary widely. On *Grey's Anatomy* Chief Webber is one of the few
surgeons who wears street clothes in the hospital; the rest wear their
scrubs everywhere in the hospital. One resident who transferred from
another program said that at his old hospital in New York City, wearing

scrubs would get you tossed out of lectures or conferences. Even within one hospital the rules change from one service to the next. So one day an intern can wear scrubs on rounds, but then when she transfers to the next service, scrubs may be forbidden on the patient floor.

As he stands at a computer in the Emergency Department, entering information on a new trauma patient, one senior resident recalls his first day as an intern. He was on a service known throughout the hospital for its demanding dress code. "White shirt and black slacks for men," he says. "Women were told they should look at the Brooks Brothers catalog." As they rounded on their patients, the brand-new intern was anxious about what the attending surgeon would think about his grasp of the medical facts. But the first feedback he got was not about the meaning of lab values or recommended drug dosages. "He suddenly grabs my tie to check it! Very strange."

After rounding with the attending, another resident remarks, "He said today that I have to learn how to tie a half-Windsor knot. Now you've seen the old school."

Of course, most patients will say that they are more concerned about whether their surgeon knows how to tie a suture knot on a blood vessel graft than a stylish knot on a necktie. Rather than being tightly linked to treatment, how surgeons dress outside the OR reflects broader attitudes in an institution, including how the attendings, residents, and students relate to each other and their patients.

That's partly why another senior resident backs the slacks and tie look. He says it shows that the surgeons respect both their patients and their profession. He admits that strict dress codes are out of sync with the generally casual attire of people in Portland. "Portlanders are sloppy dressers. Comfortable, but still sloppy," he says.

AN ETERNAL GRIPE BY INSTRUCTORS IS ABOUT STUDENTS AND RESIDENTS who show up late to lectures. Although almost never seen on *Grey's Anatomy,* classroom learning doesn't end with medical school graduation. Residents spend many hours each week in lecture halls, but not always as much time as the lecturers expect.

Of course, part of the problem is the competing demands of patient care. Residents certainly can't walk away from a patient who needs attention just because the clock says it's class time. And sometimes residents are trapped between the lecturers who want them in their seats and attending surgeons who want them in the hospital.

But there's another aspect of tardiness that is tied to differences between people who grew up in different times: learning styles. When many instructors were in school, learning meant listening to a lecture or reading a book. If you wanted to know what the instructor said in class, you had to be there or depend on a classmate willing to share notes. But now, class lectures are often recorded, available online whenever a student wants. PowerPoint files mean students no longer need to quickly scribble a copy of what an instructor draws on a chalkboard. And teachers from kindergarten on up are using a greater variety of teaching methods, so today's residents are used to learning in a variety of ways.

As a result, residents sometimes feel that sitting in a lecture hall may be a poor use of scarce time and attention.

ON A RAINY MONDAY MORNING, THE SURGERY RESIDENTS FILL A windowless lecture hall. The instructor, who is certainly a more accomplished surgeon than he is a speaker, drones through the details of guidelines for testing and categorizing tumors. The subject is of utmost importance to patients . . . some of whom will be told that, based on a surgeon's assessment, cutting out their cancer would be futile.

Despite the life or death subject, a number of the weary residents are nodding off. Even among those keeping their eyelids open, a number must be wondering: Is this the best way to learn the material? How much will have to be relearned later because the presentation didn't make a lasting impression?

AT THE FACULTY GATHERING, AN OLDER PHYSICIAN STRESSES THE IMPORtance of the lecture topics and the consequences if young doctors aren't there on time.

"If I don't learn infectious diseases, someone will pay," he points out.

"Yes," one presenter agrees, "but maybe there's a different way to teach the material. It doesn't always have to be just a lecture."

Residency originated with the belief that doing, rather than merely listening, is the key to mastering the practice of medicine. Lectures play a role, but that role is under review. And there are more and more efforts to imagine and then try out new ways of teaching critical skills, partly in order to develop ways of teaching and learning that occupy a middle ground between sitting in a classroom hearing the big picture and trying to distill lessons out of the haphazard experience of working in the hospital.

A SMALL GROUP OF INTERNS GATHERS AROUND A CONFERENCE ROOM TABLE. Vascular surgeon Erica Mitchell offers tips on how to hold an ultrasound probe in order to get the best image before plunging a needle into a patient's blood vessel.

"Always stand on the patient's right-hand side, so you get a consistent orientation," Mitchell says. Rather than simply listening, the interns are sharing portable ultrasound machines and synthetic models that mimic human tissue. This is a Vascular Skills Lab. The goal is to build up the proficiency of residents, without subjecting patients to their first fumbling attempts. Today's task is to practice getting vascular access, one of the most common tasks in a hospital.

Mitchell shows them how to adjust the gain and depth of the ghostly ultrasound image in order to get the best view.

"Why use ultrasound?" she asks. After all, doctors and nurses have been poking patients to get vascular access for many generations, long before ultrasound came on the scene. Mitchell then answers her question. "You get faster access and fewer mistakes. It's the standard of care now."

The interns try their hand at placing a simulated central line, a type of IV. They don't always get it the first time. A thin guide wire goes into to the vessel first, followed by a dilator that enlarges the opening enough for a catheter. At least one intern pushes the dilator into the model before confirming the placement of the guide wire. Then while trying to "see" into the model, she aims the ultrasound probe at the wrong blood vessel.

Somewhere there's a patient who should be glad he or she isn't enduring this kind of "practice" of medicine.

The mnemonic meant to help beginners follow the basic steps in order is EASE, which stands for exam, anesthesia (local to numb the area), stick (in the needle), ensure placement.

Vascular Fellow Aaron Partsafas runs down a checklist of steps for the interns to learn. "Before you stick, make sure you have everything ready. Think it through in advance. Position the patient to expose the vein," he tells them.

With the models, the ultrasound, the needles in their hands, this type of lesson engages the interns as no lecture could.

"Bounce the needle onto the surface of the vein," Partsafas suggests as he tells the interns about gaining access to the most commonly used veins, the femoral, the internal jugular, and the subclavian. "Then push through. The wire should slide in easily. If it's tough or the patient complains, you're going the wrong way."

Mitchell offers a little trick. "Standard catheter kits don't have tips that are visible on ultrasound, so score the tip with a knife, which makes it more reflective."

Practice makes a difference. Mitchell points out that someone who has done more than 50 catheterizations usually has half the complication rate of someone new to the task. Then as the interns experience the challenge of properly placing a needle into a vein, even a simulated one, Mitchell shows them a CT scan of what can go wrong.

The image on the screen is not from a musty old textbook. It's from the file of a patient currently in the hospital. The job was to access the femoral vein. But the needle went in too high up the leg. Then it punched through the vein. The incorrect placement of the needle meant the people on the case couldn't compress the vein against the thigh bone in order to stop the bleeding right away. The result: The patient spent two days in the ICU, received transfusions, underwent additional CT scans, and stayed in the hospital two days longer than planned. It's a real person, treated by people these interns know, in the hospital they work in every day . . . and the complication happened during the very type of procedure they are practicing. The lesson is concrete and immediate.

Mitchell wonders, though: Even if this lesson appears to be sinking in right now, how deeply is the memory burned in? To find an answer, in addition to teaching this skills lab, she is studying what they do here almost as if it were an experimental procedure. In a sense, it is; though rather than being a treatment that directly affects patients, the skills lab affects the surgeons who will be treating patients.

As Mitchell's research plan points out, the traditional "see one, do one, teach one" mantra of surgical training is fading. The problem is that with the 80-hour workweek and other limits on the time residents spend in the hospital, shorter hospital stays, and more outpatient procedures in community clinics, it is getting harder for surgery residents to see one of each of the many procedures they need to learn. And then growing concerns about residents practicing on patients, along with scrutiny from insurers who want to pay for only those surgeons actively involved in an operation, and the ever-increasing number of minimally invasive procedures and other new surgical techniques and devices; it is more and more difficult for residents to do one, much less teach one of the vast variety of skills they are expected to master.

The institutions and agencies responsible for guiding the training of surgery residents, such as the Accreditation Council for Graduate Medical Education (ACGME), are requiring residency programs to use new teaching methods to adjust to the changing world of surgery. But new standards for classes and teaching techniques have yet to be established. That's why the interns in this vascular skills lab are participating in a randomized controlled trial testing variations of the methods and timing of training.

Over several months, different groups of interns are learning basic vascular surgery skills in slightly different ways. The skills include vascular anastomosis (suturing together blood vessels, the essential skill needed to do cardiac bypass and many other operations), interpreting scans and other tests of blood flow, and the use of ultrasound to guide vascular access (placing catheters for IVs and other needs.) In part, this trial will try to find out how the training schedule affects learning; do weekly classes do the trick or does spreading the classes out to monthly sessions make a difference in how well the interns perform over the long term?

To know what kind of teaching works best, you have to have a way to test the residents. That's another challenge. Traditionally, the opinions and personal evaluations of senior surgeons have played a major part in rating residents. But the profession is trying to develop more objective measures. So this trial includes detailed score sheets that check off the skills to be mastered. Did the intern use the right clamps on the model blood vessels? Was the spacing between each stitch consistent? On broader measures, such as respect for tissue, instrument handling, and efficient work, the residents are scored on a 5-point scale from "frequently poor" to "consistently good."

"I carve out some of my own time to do this research," Mitchell says. "It's a passion."

MARCUS KRET, M.D.

Status: Intern

Where from: Colorado Springs. Medical school at Rosalind Franklin University of Medicine and Science, The Chicago Medical School.

Why did you want to become a surgeon?
"In medical school I always thought I'd do emergency medicine or cardiology. When I did my surgery rotation it seemed like the field with the most readily apparent and lasting effects on its patients; sort of an instant gratification type mentality, to oversimplify things."

What's the biggest difference between what you thought it would be like and the reality?
"The biggest difference for me is how much of the 'red tape' of modern medicine we get sucked into, especially as interns. I always assumed that I'd spend all of my time working with, counseling, and operating on patients. I never imagined how much paperwork I'd be overwhelmed with, for example trying to get someone's home health or nursing home set up. It's frightening to think how these elements are taking over medicine; that to pay the bills you need to spend so much time focused on checking boxes for insurance companies."

What do you want patients to know about what you do?

"Patients never seem to realize all of the work we do behind the scenes for them; arranging tests, talking to consultants, getting studies analyzed. Add to this the fact that we are doing this for between five and twenty other patients. Unfortunately, to the person in the hospital bed, I'm sure it seems that we spend five minutes a day with them and then leave.

"It also seems hard for patients to recognize the sacrifices we've made in our personal lives to do what we do. Even my own friends and family outside medicine have a difficult time realizing what working 80 hours per week leaves you for a personal life. My parents spent five days in Portland over Christmas and I probably spent a combined thirty-six hours with them during that week.

"I've also been asked numerous times by patients how great it feels to live in a big house and drive a nice car. They don't realize that with a salary of about $1,750 every two weeks, my hourly wage is not quite eleven dollars an hour."

What specialty are you most interested in?

Kret says he hasn't selected a specialty, though he jokes that, midway through his intern year, becoming a ski instructor looks appealing.

Additional Reading

Brooks Brothers. "Classic Tie Knots: Half-Windsor." Available at: www.brooks brothers.com/tieknots/half-windsor.tem. Accessed August 2009.

Hickman, Susan E.; Tolle, Susan W.; Brummel-Smith, Kenneth; Carley, Margaret Murphy. "Use of the Physician Orders for Life-Sustaining Treatment Program in Oregon Nursing Facilities: Beyond Resuscitation Status." *Journal of the American Geriatrics Society*, 52, no. 9 (2004): 1424–1429. Available at: www3.interscience .wiley.com/journal/118744147/abstract. Accessed August 2009.

Physician Orders for Life-Sustaining Treatment (POLST). For information about the paradigm program, see www.polst.org.

Stern, Peter J. "Generational Differences." Journal of Hand Surgery, 27, no. 2 (2002): 187–194. Available at: www.jhandsurg.org/article/PIIS0363502302505001/ fulltext. Accessed August 2009.

CHAPTER TWENTY-NINE

This M&M Isn't Sweet

In her first week as an intern, Laura Matsen begins to understand what she has gotten herself into.

"It's really, really hard. I'm realizing just how challenging this is," she says. It's not just the amount or the difficulty of the work, but also the weight of the responsibility. She diagnosed a clavicle fracture in a patient before he even got an X-ray. That felt good, but she missed something.

"I saw a bruise and felt that his clavicle is not continuous. I was so proud of myself for that. But I hadn't managed his blood pressure. In the middle of the night, the nurses called the Rapid Response Team. They had to take emergency measures to get his blood pressure under control. The nurses didn't like it. The Rapid Response Team didn't like it. The attending didn't like it. I didn't like it," she says. "Now I realize that I'm making errors, and it happens so fast. It's scary."

Loïc Fabricant is talking with a fellow intern about pain control.

"I've been 'the man' a couple of times using Toradol," Fabricant boasts with a smile. But then he admits that one time things did not go so well. Toradol, known generically as ketorolac, is a potent pain medication, but it can cause kidney failure. Once when he prescribed the drug, the patient's kidney function started to go south. Fortunately, he says, there was no permanent harm. "The patient did okay." But the case was a reminder of the responsibility that comes with the power to prescribe.

"YOU SEE THIS, O'MALLEY?" MIRANDA BAILEY SAYS AS SHE HOLDS UP A blade in "Grandma Got Run Over by a Reindeer" (2-12). "I make one mistake with this scalpel and this man's dead. My husband, he makes mistakes at his job all the time. As far as I know he's never killed anyone, but I have and you will."

IN A GRAND ROUNDS PRESENTATION, TRAUMA SURGEON RICHARD MULLINS echoes Bailey's words.

"Let's face it; we're in a business where people will die if you make mistakes. If you are a normal person, that's hard to take. The M&M process gives you an opportunity to work through your errors."

M&M stands for "morbidity and mortality"—disease or injury and death; they are always nearby in the hospital. In most cases, the inability to cure or rescue comes as no surprise. Age and disease and trauma often cannot be overcome. The M&M process is intended to openly confront the unexpected failures.

"PEOPLE DIE IN THIS HOSPITAL. ONCE A MONTH WE GATHER TO DISCUSS HOW our actions as physicians contributed to the deaths. This is a serious exercise," Miranda Bailey says in "Oh, the Guilt" (3-05). The episode features an examination of the death of patient Denny Duquette after a heart transplant. Preston Burke begins the presentation, but then some of the doctors in the audience turn their attention to chief resident Bailey. One of them accuses her of being sleep deprived and affected by the recent birth of her son.

"I sleep just fine, Dr. Savoy," Bailey responds.

"Really? Cause if a patient died due to my poor decision making, I'd lose a little sleep over it."

Chief Webber jumps in. "Let me remind everyone that our purpose here is not to place blame. This is a forum to discuss mistakes in patient care and learn from them."

M&M CAN FEEL LIKE A TRIAL TO THE PRESENTERS. IT'S THE CHIEF RESIDENTS of a service that deliver the outcomes of their teams to the audience. They display the total number of patients, the discharges, and the deaths, along with key facts on cases in which patients suffered complications.

"So there's no way to avoid that problem?" says a senior surgeon after a resident has explained a complication. "Is a one percent complication rate acceptable?"

"I would accept one percent," the resident replies.

When pressed on the choice of tools used in the procedure, the resident defends the choice but also says another option could work, too. The exchange illustrates a peculiar feature of many M&M conferences; while it is the chief residents who present the cases, the key choices and actions are often taken by attending surgeons. Those attendings sit in the audience and sometimes leave it to the resident to explain what they did.

In a physicians workroom, fourth-year resident David Cho is telling intern Tim Lee a few things about M&M.

"If you say too much, you will get called on it," Cho advises. "It's not good to say 'not sure,' when you are asked what would you do. Never criticize your attending directly; fifty percent of the time they will hang you out to dry. Use oblique references like 'it was decided' or 'the thinking at the time was.'"

"It's scary stuff," Lee says. "Scary to think I'm gonna be up there in five years."

IT SEEMS NATURAL THAT SURGEONS WOULD REVIEW CASES IN WHICH SOMEthing goes wrong, but in his grand rounds presentation about the M&M process, Richard Mullins points out the early proponents of accountability were demonized by their peers. Eventually though, surgeons began to set up forums to review their unexpected failures in hopes of reducing the likelihood the same problem would happen again.

M&M conferences are supposed to be sanctuaries where the surgeons can bluntly discuss problems. And as Mullins notes, the M&M process has no formal sanctions. Yet the aura of a trial remains. Standing in front of senior surgeons, trying to answer their questions about what could have been done differently, is a stressful experience. Indeed, in response to a survey of residents by Mullins and others, some residents said they did have some fear of retribution or damage to their reputations.

It seems that the discussion of complications and the medical literature would be educational. Each presentation outlines what happened and the possible explanations. Then there is a discussion of medical research on similar cases. Senior surgeons and residents probe for explanations and alternatives for next time.

In the discussion of an infection after a surgery, one surgeon says the hospital overuses the type of catheter implicated in this complication. But after all the back and forth, each surgeon takes away whatever he or she thinks is valuable; there is no formal follow-up. In fact, not everyone attends and not all of those in the room are paying close attention. It's late in the day and some eyelids droop low.

One resident who witnessed an unexpected death says that the M&M that followed was a disappointment. The case was presented by a resident who wasn't involved in the case. The facts weren't quite right. And the discussion didn't seem to deal with the central issues.

Mullins suggests a third purpose for M&M: Rather than either a courtroom or a classroom, it is a ritual.

"You realize that you are part of the tribe. Your participation confirms that you are part of the tribe of surgeons. It is a rite of passage, extremely unpleasant and difficult; but it makes you hardened and gets you ready to make difficult decisions of life and death. And you have to discuss your errors in front of your peers; it's a purification ceremony," he says.

The stress of M&M clearly affects some residents. They haltingly struggle through their case presentations, hesitatingly answering questions until the attendings cease asking more. One resident is chastised for not supplying a report in the format an attending expects. "I'm happy to jump through hoops. I just need to know where they are," the resident responds testily.

But then another resident steps up to the lectern. With an air of confidence he projects his first slide with the list of recent cases and complications.

"Tell me about R.L.," an attending asks, referring to one of the cases. One quick click of the computer mouse and the resident is narrating a new slide showing the key points of that case. Then he clicks back to the summary screen. "Why did you do an open procedure on that third case?" another attending asks. "I'm glad you asked," the resident smiles and pops up a slide about that case.

As he continues through his presentation, he demonstrates not only a clear grasp of the facts that the attendings want to know about, but also his mastery of the form of M&M. There's no doubt he is a full member of the surgeon tribe.

Additional Reading

Bosk, Charles L. *Forgive and Remember: Managing Medical Failure.* Chicago: University of Chicago Press, 2003. Surgeons often mention this book as a landmark examination of the culture of surgery. The 1st edition came out decades ago, but the echoes of that culture can be seen still.

Gore, D. C. "National Survey of Surgical Morbidity and Mortality Conferences." *American Journal of Surgery,* 191, no. 5 (2006): 708–714. Available at: www .ajsfulltextonline.com/article/S0002-9610(06)00068-7/abstract. Accessed August 2009.

Pierluissi, Edgar; Fischer, Melissa A.; Campbell, Andre R.; Landefeld, C. Seth. "Discussion of Medical Errors in Morbidity and Mortality Conferences." *Journal of the American Medical Association,* 290 (2003): 2838–2842. Available at: http:// jama.ama-assn.org/cgi/content/full/290/21/2838. Accessed August 2009.

Rosenfeld, J. C. "Using the Morbidity and Mortality Conference to Teach and Assess the ACGME General Competencies." *Journal of Surgical Education,* 62, no. 6 (2005): 664–669. Available at: www.journals.elsevierhealth.com/periodicals/ cursur/article/S0149-7944(05)00109-1/abstract. Accessed August 2009.

Wu, A.; Folkman, S.; McPhee, S.; Lo, B. "Do House Officers Learn from Their Mistakes?" *Quality and Safety in Health Care,* 12, no. 3 (2003): 221–226. Available at: www.pubmedcentral.nih.gov/articlerender.fcgi?tool=pubmed&pubmedid= 12792014. Accessed August 2009.

CHAPTER THIRTY

The Pause That Protects

In an effort to reduce mistakes like operating on the wrong patient or removing the wrong body part, almost all hospitals now require surgeons to pause before cutting. Indeed, the leading hospital accreditation agency advises patients preparing for surgery to "Ask your surgeon if they will take a 'time out' just before your surgery. This is done to make sure they are doing the right surgery on the right body part on the right person."

It would seem that surgeons, with all their years of training for tremendously complex operations, their experience, and their awareness of the consequences of errors, would not stumble on such simple points as cutting the wrong place on the wrong person. But surgeons are human. It can be the apparently simple errors that slip through when attention is focused on the most challenging aspects of an upcoming case.

A recent international study found that even after years of growing attention to preventable errors in surgery, hospitals that implemented a 19-item surgical safety checklist of procedures saw patients fare better. Overall, the death rate was cut in half, from 15 deaths per thousand surgeries to 8 deaths per thousand surgeries. Complications dropped from 110 per thousand to 70 per thousand. The focus of the checklist items is to "improve team communication and consistency of care."

As the authors of the study wrote,

> Surgical complications are a considerable cause of death and disability around the world. They are devastating to patients, costly to health care systems, and often preventable, though their prevention typically requires a change in systems and individual behavior. In this study, a checklist-based program was associated with a significant decline in the rate of complications and death from surgery in a diverse group of institutions around the world. Applied on a global basis, this checklist program has the potential to prevent large numbers of deaths and disabling complications, although further study is needed to determine the precise mechanism and durability of the effect in specific settings.

The Safe Surgery Saves Lives Study Group worked with the World Health Organization to implement a pilot program in eight hospitals in the United States, Canada, India, Jordan, New Zealand, the Philippines, Tanzania, and the United Kingdom.

For today's residents, checklists are part of the routine they've learned from their first days.

Before Renee Minjarez begins a vascular procedure, she clearly calls out the patient's name so that everyone on the team can hear, especially the circulating nurse, who has the patient's records in front of her.

"We are doing an endovascular repair of an abdominal aortic aneurysm," Minjarez says. After each person on the team agrees that the patient and procedure are correct, she proceeds with the preparations.

On another day, intern Ashley Stewart leads a pause before a different vascular service operation. She confirms the patient's name, and then she calls out, "We are doing a left great toe amputation."

"Right toe!" everyone else on the team hollers.

"*Right* great toe," she corrects herself. "Right great toe."

The correct toe was already exposed, so the chance of an actual error was essentially zero, but her slip of the tongue illustrates the point: People make mistakes. And a mistake in preparing for an amputation can be irreparable.

Sometimes though, the pauses seem perfunctory. While Minjarez and Stewart clearly called out the key information, at another vascular service operation the same day as Stewart's amputation procedure, a senior surgeon mumbled quietly through the pause without apparent enthusiasm for the requirement.

Another day, a transplant surgery team is checking into problems that an organ recipient was having. The attending surgeon, the one ultimately responsible for the operation, has not arrived in the OR. Senior residents frequently manage all the preparations before surgery, so that attendings can spend more time on other duties. The senior resident has the attending surgeon paged as she begins marking where she thinks the attending will want the first incision to be.

The attending arrives, makes a quick suggestion about shifting the incision line, and then turns away to make a telephone call. As the senior resident goes line by line through the script for the pause, the attending surgeon is talking on the phone, not really paying attention. When the surgery actually gets under way, her attention is focused and she's fully engaged, but if there had been any misinformation called out during the pause, she probably would not have heard it.

Sometimes the pause is forgotten until after the procedure is under way, leaving the surgeons to rush belatedly through the check of patient and procedure. "Shall we pause or something?" a senior resident asks when he realizes they have started cutting without going through the formal check.

And then there are some surgeons who openly disdain this requirement, apparently seeing it as merely an imposition by bureaucrats.

"Attention, everyone!" bellows the veteran surgeon when it is time for the pause. He calls out the patient's name and the procedure in a mocking, melodramatic tone. "Are we all in agreement?" he says with a huff. Then he tosses in a sarcastic reference to the often-ignored preflight announcements of airline flight attendants, "Until we reach 10,000 feet, turn off all electronic equipment."

The Safe Surgery Saves Lives Group found that while many hospitals were already doing some of the items on their checklist, none of the hospitals in the study was conducting formal team briefings either before or after a procedure. Planning and review does take place, but often the attending surgeon develops the plan on her own and then briefs the rest of the team as the procedure gets under way.

As the team prepares to operate on a liver cancer patient, the senior resident asks the attending surgeon how she wants to do things.

"Do you want to do the biopsy before or after removing the tumor?" the resident asks. "Do you want ultrasound now?"

"We may not need ultrasound. We may just see it," the attending surgeon says of the tumor.

"Are we going to do the biopsy before or after the resection?"

"Before, I want to know what I'm doing first."

John Hunter says he does not usually have a formal planning meeting with his surgery residents or others on the team before a procedure. He says the surgery fellow working with him would read the chart the night before the procedure and contact him with any questions.

OHSU "PAUSE" POSTER

Universal Protocol: Script for the Team Pause
Setting the Stage

1. The Circulator confirms pt ID band upon OR entry.
2. MUST OCCUR IMMEDIATELY PRIOR TO INCISION
3. The signed consent must be visible and used as a reference.
4. All team members must be present and actively respond to questions.
5. All Team **Pause** participants are documented on the PeriOperative Case Record.

The Script

Circulator: Attention, Everyone!

1. M.D.: This is _____ (Patient name). Circulator: Yes, I have confirmed this patient by name and birth date on the ID band.

2. M.D.: We are doing _____ (Procedure/Side/Site as stated on the consent).
   Circulator: Is the site marking visible? *(Must have concurrence from ALL present.)*

3. M.D.: We agree that the patient is in the correct position. *(Must have concurrence from ALL present.)*

4. M.D.: Do we have all implants, tissues, unique equipment, X-rays/studies available? *(Must have concurrence from ALL present.)*

5. M.D.: What pre-op antibiotics have been given? *(Response from Anesthesia provider)*

6. M.D.: Have all baseline counts been completed? *(Response from Scrub: YES, NO, NA).*

7. M.D.: Are we all in agreement? *(Must have concurrence from ALL present.)*

OHSU Policy Correct Site Universal Protocol.

Additional Reading

Haynes, Alex B.; Weiser, Thomas G.; Berry, William R.; Lipsitz, Stuart R.; Breizat, Abdel-Hadi S.; Dellinger, E. Patchen; et al. for the Safe Surgery Saves Lives Study Group. "A Surgical Safety Checklist to Reduce Morbidity and Mortality in a Global Population." *New England Journal of Medicine,* 360 (2009): 491–499. Available at: http://content.nejm.org/cgi/content/full/NEJMsa0810119. Accessed August 2009.

Joint Commission. "Speak Up: Help Avoid Mistakes in Your Surgery." April 2009. Available at: www.jointcommission.org/PatientSafety/SpeakUp/speak_up_ws.htm. Accessed August 2009.

World Health Organization. For information about the Safe Surgery Saves Lives Project, see www.who.int/patientsafety/safesurgery/en. Accessed August 2009.

Surgical Safety Checklist

World Health Organization · Patient Safety — A World Alliance for Safer Health Care

Before induction of anaesthesia

(with at least nurse and anaesthetist)

Has the patient confirmed his/her identity, site, procedure, and consent?
- [ ] Yes

Is the site marked?
- [ ] Yes
- [ ] Not applicable

Is the anaesthesia machine and medication check complete?
- [ ] Yes

Is the pulse oximeter on the patient and functioning?
- [ ] Yes

Does the patient have a:

Known allergy?
- [ ] No
- [ ] Yes

Difficult airway or aspiration risk?
- [ ] No
- [ ] Yes, and equipment/assistance available

Risk of >500ml blood loss (7ml/kg in children)?
- [ ] No
- [ ] Yes, and two IVs/central access and fluids planned

Before skin incision

(with nurse, anaesthetist and surgeon)

- [ ] Confirm all team members have introduced themselves by name and role.
- [ ] Confirm the patient's name, procedure, and where the incision will be made.

Has antibiotic prophylaxis been given within the last 60 minutes?
- [ ] Yes
- [ ] Not applicable

Anticipated Critical Events

To Surgeon:
- [ ] What are the critical or non-routine steps?
- [ ] How long will the case take?
- [ ] What is the anticipated blood loss?

To Anaesthetist:
- [ ] Are there any patient-specific concerns?

To Nursing Team:
- [ ] Has sterility (including indicator results) been confirmed?
- [ ] Are there equipment issues or any concerns?

Is essential imaging displayed?
- [ ] Yes
- [ ] Not applicable

Before patient leaves operating room

(with nurse, anaesthetist and surgeon)

Nurse Verbally Confirms:
- [ ] The name of the procedure
- [ ] Completion of instrument, sponge and needle counts
- [ ] Specimen labelling (read specimen labels aloud, including patient name)
- [ ] Whether there are any equipment problems to be addressed

To Surgeon, Anaesthetist and Nurse:
- [ ] What are the key concerns for recovery and management of this patient?

This checklist is not intended to be comprehensive. Additions and modifications to fit best practices are encouraged. Revised 1/09 © WHO, 2009.

CHAPTER THIRTY-ONE

Twenty-First-Century Charts

A prescribing error almost kills a patient in "Much Too Much" (2-10). Alex Karev orders too much sodium too fast for a patient. Although early in the episode Karev says that standard treatment to boost sodium levels in this kind of case is 300 cubic centimeters (cc) of a 3 percent hypertonic solution over a three-hour period, when a crisis hits, that's not what he tells the nurse to deliver.

The patient begins to act strangely and then the bedside monitors beep rapidly.

"Two of Ativan," Karev orders. He turns to Derek Shepherd, who has just walked into the room. "He started seizing."

"How much sodium did you give him?" Shepherd asks.

"500 ccs over four hours."

"Actually doctor you ordered 500 ccs per hour over four hours," nurse Olivia Harper corrects him.

"It's too fast. His brain is swelling," Shepherd says as he checks the patient's eyes.

In part to reduce errors, hospitals are moving away from bulging paper binders of medical information on each patient and toward electronic medical charting systems. As more providers put their records on computers, doctors should be able to call up background information on a new patient more quickly and easily.

An elderly woman arrived with air in the bile ducts of her liver. It's usually a life-threatening condition; so the emergency general surgery team went into action. They didn't know her history because they didn't have her medical records, so they took her right to the operating room. As it turned out, she did not need an operation. The hope is that this sort of scenario will become increasingly rare as more of our medical information is available through the computer systems of anyone providing us medical care.

The OHSU hospital flipped the switch on its inpatient electronic records system just as this class of interns started to work. So from the beginning they learned to document the care they provided and enter the medical orders for their patients on a computer.

On her first day, intern Laura Matsen had to turn down an invitation from surgeon John Mayberry to visit patients, because she needed to focus on getting vital information entered into the computer. Sometimes it seemed that the primary patient was the computer, not any of the people in the beds on the ward. Hour after hour is spent sitting in a windowless workroom staring at a computer screen or communicating with co-workers by telephone, pagers, and instant messaging. The dominant activity interrupted only briefly here and there by a quick dash to actually see a patient.

The morning of her second day finds Matsen again sitting at the computer, almost as though she had never left. Of course, interns have always been stuck with doing the necessary, but unglamorous, chores of hospital care. These days that includes mastering the computer.

For attendings and senior residents, the electronic system means relearning how to manage patient information and medical orders. Fourth-year resident David Cho spent the last two years doing research. So he was mostly out of the hospital during the transition from paper to the electronic record system, known as EPIC.

"It wasn't there two years ago. That's the most painful thing about coming back to the hospital. But I'll get used to it," Cho says.

Just like a parent asking a child for help programming the latest computerized gizmo, senior residents and attendings find themselves turning to interns for help navigating the new electronic waters of health records.

"Did you mean to order medication twice?" intern Jason Susong asks his senior resident, Karin Hardiman.

"Yes," she answers. "I couldn't figure out how to do it as a single order."

"Oh, I got called about it. I wasn't sure, so I held one of them. Want me to give it?"

"Yes."

"I can show you how to order it all at once," Susong offers. But he also gives her a warning.

"When you change an order, it automatically assumes you want to give a dose right away."

"That could be, uh, detrimental," Hardiman points out.

"And the VA computer system is the opposite way, so you have to figure it out," Susong says.

If you walk into a physicians workroom now, you will often see several doctors working at computer screens, silent except for the clicking of keyboards and mouse buttons. Until, that is, someone needs help again with the software.

"Okay, Jason, question: I'm getting this little 'stop sign' thing," Hardiman says.

Susong takes a look. With all the hours he, like every intern, puts in at the computer, he's seen this roadblock before.

"F-two gets you to the right place," he shows her.

"I'm not being crabby with you, I'm just wondering why we had to change to this system."

"Technology makes our lives better," Susong says sarcastically.

SEVERAL ROOMS IN A BUILDING NEAR THE HOSPITAL HAVE BEEN CONVERTED into computer classrooms. Every clinician is required to pass a course in using the electronic health record. The instructor runs through typical scenarios for admitting, treating, and discharging patients. He cautions the students to be careful with their passwords, of course. And he notes that everything is logged, in case there are questions later about who ordered treatments.

Despite the classes, getting comfortable with the new electronic system takes time.

"I'M ONE OF THE BIGGEST CRITICS OF EPIC, BUT THERE ARE SOME GOOD things," admits Surgery Residency Director Karen Deveney, in a meeting with the interns. "Like not having to rewrite orders and not running around to find charts. We can make it better by not entering unnecessary information. Don't just copy whole lab reports, just enter the values that are significant," she advises them.

Paper records certainly aren't perfect.

A man who crashed an off-road vehicle arrives from a rural hospital. Has his spine been checked? No one is sure. Was he defibrillated? The paper records that came along with the man are unclear. There seems to be an order for defibrillation, but it's not clear to the team here if it was entered as a precaution or as a record of an event.

Another patient comes into the hospital because her chronic condition suddenly worsened. Most of her recent care was provided by doctors in Arizona. Surgeon Jennifer Watters starts working the phones, trying to find out just what the diagnosis was and what treatments were provided. She has to stick close the telephone, waiting for a call back.

In these cases, complete electronic records might have improved patient care. But, in general, the changeover has led to grumbling.

"Honestly speaking, EPIC sucks," a senior resident tells interns. "But it's here to stay." He says they are working on ways to make the system better, but that the system's designers don't really seem to understand what they need.

One thing residents always need is more time. But the computer seems to suck away even more of their time than the old system of dictation and paper records.

"Things it used to take five minutes to document the old way, now take a half hour on EPIC," says a resident.

And then there are the quirks that any computer user encounters when trying to learn new software.

Intern Ashley Stewart sits at a computer terminal outside the room of a patient on the vascular service. She is trying to enter a medication order. On paper, she would have simply written "PRN Q4," which means give the medication as needed up to the prescribed dose every four hours. But entering "PRN Q4" into the computerized ordering system just gets her an error message. She tries inputting "Q4 PRN." No joy. Other variations also fail. She clicks on every box and option the system gives her. Time ticks by. Then finally she tries typing in "every 4 hours as needed." *Ta-da,* the computer accepts the order. She'll know next time, but it was a frustrating lesson.

"It used to be so easy to order labs," says vascular service fellow Aaron Partsafas. "We'd order a UA [urinalysis], micro, culture, and get to see the dipstick" (used to test the patient's urine). "With EPIC now, I'm not sure how to get to see the dipstick," he complains. "So now we run around like dipsticks."

While delays and software hiccups are annoying, there is deeper concern about how computers affect interaction with patients.

"On rounds, we used to all go into the patient rooms when there was only one paper chart," recalls chief resident Michael Englehart. "There was one person writing in the chart. Now everyone is pushing a computer dolly. They are not in the room, not actually seeing the patient."

David Cho echoes that thought. "EPIC separates us from patient care," he says. "Instead of writing a paper order and handing it off, we have to spend time at a computer, not at the bedside. Residents, instead of watching care and writing, have to try to remember everything, when they are documenting it later at the computer."

"I don't like the EPIC computer system," surgeon John Mayberry says. "Patients say they like dealing with surgeons better because we talk directly to them. They complain about seeing only the back of the head of their primary-care providers, while the doctor sits typing into the computer."

And although computers help prevent some errors, they can create new ones. For instance, just like many Internet browsers have multiple tabs, one for each open web page, this computer system can open multiple patient records. Early in the year, an intern is filling out discharge orders, only to realize that she is sending the wrong patient home. She quickly erases the erroneous orders and puts them on the correct page, but the incident shows how a feature that is convenient can also be hazardous.

Watters says she got a surprise recently when she got to work one day. "I came back from vacation to find a hundred verbal orders in my in-box to sign, that 'I' made," she says. Apparently, the system was linking her name to medical orders entered by others on her service while she was away.

Such complaints are familiar to Thomas Yackel, M.D. He is OHSU's chief health information officer.

"I do hear the complaints," Yackel says. "But they are comparing steady states; how it was with paper records versus how the electronic system is right now. They are not looking at how the electronic systems will evolve. Electronic health records are at the old WordPerfect stage; the days when users eagerly awaited new versions, because they had important new features." Now that computer word processing software has matured, few clamor for a return to typewriters.

"I'm skeptical about complaints that computers cut into face time with patients, based on the studies that have been done." Yackel adds that now more physicians are reviewing lab results and other information with patients by calling everything up on a bedside or examination room computer.

Just such an encounter takes place in vascular clinic one day, as resident Gordon Riha and surgeon Gregory Landry, M.D. visit with a woman who has had ongoing problems with inflammation of her arteries. They talk directly to the woman and aren't sucked into the computer, but then they turn the screen around and point out the trends revealed by her examinations. "The ABI [Ankle-Brachial Index] is stable at point nine," they show her. The ABI is one measure of peripheral artery disease.

"One nice thing about electronic medical records is the ability to go back and find old records," Landry tells the woman. "It was basically point five on both sides." Now it's better and seems to be staying that way.

Yackel says paper records had their own faults. "Patients say that in the paper days, the doctors looked at them, but didn't write things down, so they had to answer the same questions every time and with every doctor. Computers do change things, but that's not always bad."

The author of a commentary in a major medical journal wrote about his concern that electronic records systems may be turning patients into mere computer icons:

> The patient is still at the center, but more as an icon for another entity clothed in binary garments: the "iPatient." Often, emergency room personnel have already scanned, tested, and diagnosed, so that interns meet a fully formed iPatient long before seeing the real patient. The iPatient's blood counts and emanations are tracked and trended like a Dow Jones Index, and pop-up flags remind caregivers to feed or bleed. iPatients are handily discussed (or "card-flipped") in the bunker, while the real patients keep the beds warm and ensure that the folders bearing their names stay alive on the computer.

Yackel says he can agree with several of the observations in the article, but stresses that the issue is not the technology itself but rather how the technology is used.

"I appreciate that the author recognizes that it's not technology's fault—physicians are in control here, or should be. Are we teaching residents about bedside maneuvers or just complaining about them not doing it? He correctly identifies some of the root problems, including a reliance on younger faculty to do all the teaching and patient care, when it used to be different. Patients stayed in the hospital longer, there were fewer diagnostic tests that existed, there weren't work hour restrictions, and senior educators were given tenure, not productivity targets," Yackel responds.

He says the complaints he hears about electronic records systems echo the kinds of complaints that some physicians wrote about when the stethoscope was invented almost two centuries ago. Those physicians worried that using the stethoscope tube, instead of putting one's ear directly to the patient's chest, would put distance between doctor and patient.

"It's a tool, we have to figure out how to use it," Yackel says. "Everyone is going to computers," he adds. "We need to change sometime. Better to do it now, rather than wait."

Information technology staffers go out to meet with users in the clinics and hospital seeking feedback. "It'd be great if EPIC had a word search," one resident suggests to a computer expert who is visiting a physicians workroom. But in the crush of clinic duties, the computer expert is left on her own for much of the afternoon. The doctors are just too busy to chat.

She knows that clinicians grumble about the electronic records taking more of their time than the old paper records. She says sometimes the problem is that with paper records, doctors could skip things they didn't want to document, and there was no way a piece of paper could force them to completely fill in the information. The computer can be set to insist that doctors document required steps. For instance, before a patient gets an MRI scan, someone has to look for and ask about any metal that is either on the patient or implanted, because the powerful magnets of the scanner can wrench loose certain metals. The metal check was not always documented in paper records. Now the computer won't allow providers to proceed with an MRI without checking off the box about the metal check.

After the surgeons have a few months' experience with the electronic system, there are signs they are adjusting.

When Laura Matsen returns from a rotation at a community hospital that still uses paper records, she says, "It was weird to go back to handwriting. The chart was hard to read sometimes."

Even more-senior residents get used it or at least get tired of complaining.

"EPIC is getting slightly easier," says chief resident Michael Englehart. "I'm learning how to navigate it better. I still don't think it's a good system. It's still a pain. But occasionally now, I will say, 'That was cool.'"

Nevertheless, paper won't disappear anytime soon. Each resident always carries a printout of "The List." The list is a single page of tiny type that summarizes the condition and care of each patient on their service.

One afternoon, an intern is at a computer terminal looking up information on a woman who is donating her kidney to a patient.

"What're you doing?" asks Chief Resident David Cho.

"Looking up the woman."

"Isn't it on your past lists? Carry your old lists with you, at least a week's worth."

They quickly find the information she was hunting for on an old list. "See, wasn't that faster?" Cho says.

On another floor, intern Stewart panics. She can't find her list. She reacts as if she's misplaced her brain. Especially on long and busy days, when residents' fatigued minds are overwhelmed, the list, covered with scribbles of vital information, is indispensable.

Patting and searching all the pockets of her white coat, Stewart finally locates her list. And it's not just one sheet of paper, she has a heavy wad of folded lists with her . . . every list she's had for the entire rotation. Stewart sighs with relief.

Additional Reading

Frankel, R.; Altschuler, A.; George, S.; Kinsman, J.; Jimison, H.; Robertson, N. R.; Hsu, J. "Effects of Exam-Room Computing on Clinician-Patient Communication: A Longitudinal Qualitative Study." *Journal of General Internal Medicine,* 20, no. 8 (2005): 677–682. Available at: www.pubmedcentral.nih.gov/articlerender.fcgi?artid=1490186. Accessed August 2009.

Garrison, G. M.; Bernard, M. E.; Rasmussen, N. H. "21st-Century Health Care: The Effect of Computer Use by Physicians on Patient Satisfaction at a Family Medicine Clinic." *Family Medicine,* 34, no. 5 (2002): 362–368. Available at: www.ncbi.nlm.nih.gov/pubmed/12038718. Accessed August 2009.

Hsu, John; Huang, Jie; Fung, Vicki; Robertson, Nan; Jimison, Holly; Frankel, Richard. "Health Information Technology and Physician-Patient Interactions: Impact of Computers on Communication during Outpatient Primary Care Visits." *Journal of the American Medical Informatics Association,* 12 (2005): 474–480. Available at: www.jamia.org/cgi/content/abstract/12/4/474. Accessed August 2009.

Rouf, Emran; Whittle, Jeff; Lu, Na; Schwartz, Mark D. "Computers in the Exam Room: Differences in Physician–Patient Interaction May Be Due to Physician Experience." Journal of General Internal Medicine, 22, no. 1 (2007):43–48. Available at: www.pubmedcentral.nih.gov/articlerender.fcgi?artid=1824776. Accessed August 2009.

Verghese, Abraham. "Culture Shock—Patient as Icon, Icon as Patient." *New England Journal of Medicine,* 359, no. 26 (2008): 2748–2751. Available at: http://content.nejm.org/cgi/content/full/359/26/2748. Accessed August 2009.

CHAPTER THIRTY-TWO

Get Me off the Website

It's the middle of the day in the middle of the week when a bicyclist and a pedestrian meet in the middle of an intersection. It's the cyclist who ends up in a trauma bay.

In addition to the typical detective work of examining the patient's spine, looking for internal bleeding, and checking for broken bones, this patient tosses the team a curious request.

"Please help me get off the website," the man asks. Although the trauma team routinely sees an amazing range of people and behavior, the constant, repeated requests to "Please help me get off the website" raise some eyebrows.

Obviously the man is confused. There is concern about a head injury. But without any background information about the patient, no one really knows what is normal for him. It's possible he was concerned about "getting off the website" before the crash. Still, they want to get a scan of his head as soon as possible . . . if they can calm him enough to lie still.

"You're off the website, we logged you off," one of the doctors says, hoping to soothe the man.

They transfer him into the CT scanner that is just down the hall from the trauma bays. As the first scan begins to appear on the monitor a nurse says, "Ooh. Ouch."

The trauma attending sees the problem. "Oh, he's bleeding. Lots of subarachnoid bleeding."

Suddenly the patient starts trying to break loose from the soft restraints that hold him down. A team rushes into the scanning chamber to prevent him from lurching off the CT table. "I've never seen anyone act quite like this," says a nurse.

The patient continues to ask: "Please help me get off the website." And then the mantra changes slightly. "I'm stuck on two websites." A moment later comes, "Please take me off the website." The pleas come every 10 to 20 seconds. "Please take me off one website."

Back in a trauma bay the man again struggles, pulling off the collar that's meant to reduce the risk of making a neck or spinal cord injury worse.

The trauma team identifies him and gets his medication list trans-ferred over from another hospital. The man responds to his name. Maybe his mind is clearing a bit. But then he says what sounds like, "Please quack me." Slurred variations on the website request continue as a resident works to get access to a vein for a central IV line.

An hour passes, with moments of calm punctuated by the man's attempts to get loose from his restraints and pull off his neck brace. With other cases needing attention, everyone has left except for one nurse. "Please get me off one contract," is the latest request.

A neurosurgeon arrives to assess the man.

"How ya doing?"

"Not very good." It's one of the man's first rational responses. But then he says, "Please get this out of my system." It's not at all clear what he means.

"Do you have any heart problems?" asks the neurosurgeon.

"Yes." Another rational response.

Ninety minutes after the ambulance delivered him, the repeated pleas for help have slowed, but not stopped. "Please get me to headquarters," he asks a nurse.

Outside his trauma bay, pagers beep with an alert. A patient is coming in with injuries from a fall. That's the third one in a couple of hours.

A nurse remarks, "Another day when gravity is really strong."

CHAPTER THIRTY-THREE

Practice Makes Perfect

"Done! I'm done! I totally finished first. I'm done," Cristina Yang announces to everyone as she completes a simulated task in a laparoscopic surgery classroom in "The Name of the Game" (2-22).

"Forty-eight seconds!" Intern Loïc Fabricant matches the required time for a drill in the OHSU Fundamentals of Laparoscopic Surgery simulation lab.

Surgery training is following the lead of other professions in which errors can be catastrophic and opportunities for real experience are costly. Simulation is playing an ever-larger role.

"The successes in simulation come from these high reliability organizations in which the pilot sits in a flight simulator for hours, months, before actually getting into that 747 or the astronaut spends years in simulators before flying," says Donn Spight. He is the director of the Surgical Skills Program, which includes leading classes in simulated surgery.

The model of surgery residency training that was pioneered by William Stewart Halsted at the then-new Johns Hopkins Hospital over a century ago is undergoing a technological upgrade.

"The previous dogma in surgery was, 'See one. Do one. Teach one.' Now we are sort of accepting the fact that you can no longer 'See one. Do one. Teach one.' You have to see one, probably train one, then do one, then train some more, and then finally start to teach. You have to interject a stoplight in there in which training outside of the OR is important," Spight says.

Residents ultimately must hone their skills in the operating room, cutting and sewing patients. But the costs and risks of surgery are so high that alternative training methods are essential, especially in the initial stages of training.

"At this point the only way to do it is with simulation; activities that are not related to patient care," Spight says. "So I think that there is fundamentally a paradigm shift in the way the training is going to occur. And it's not just surgery, it's medicine, too. I think it's for the good."

"Oh. Stop. Stop," third-year resident Molly Cone, M.D., says to herself as a virtual tool threatens to slip from her grasp. Cone is working at the Laparoscopy Virtual Reality computer. The experience would be familiar to any video gamer; but the powerful computer simulator is several steps closer to reality.

"I feel a jolt a little bit when I touch something," Cone says. It looks hard. "It *is* hard." She says the simulator doesn't have exactly the same feel as the laparoscopic tools in the operating room, but it's close. "It's got pretty good feedback as far as the feel."

Fellow resident Stephen Noble, M.D., takes the next turn. An animated representation of a gallbladder looms large on the monitor screen. Behind it are the liver and the backdrop of the abdominal cavity. He's practicing a cholecystectomy, gallbladder removal, one of the most common laparoscopic procedures.

"It's pretty cool. You don't get to practice this much in real life," Noble says, as he picks virtual fat off the surface of the gallbladder.

The simulation shows bleeding when a blood vessel is cut. And in some simulations of colonoscopy examinations, for example, the simulated patient groans if handled too roughly.

Although sophisticated virtual reality machines are the closest you can get to the real thing outside of the OR, simulation doesn't always need to be high-tech to be effective. One of the best exercises for surgeons learning laparoscopic techniques uses a small board that has a grid of nine pegs. The task is to move little rubber rings from one peg to the next. It's not easy at first. Standing at a basic simulator, the resident grasps the handles of long tools that are just like the ones used in minimally invasive procedures in the OR. In this exercise, the business ends of the tools are grasping jaws. Just as in the OR, the resident views the action on a video monitor. The lack of depth perception adds to the difficulty of the task. Also, the resident has to get used to mirror-image movement. Because the long tool goes into the body through a narrow point, it pivots in the middle, like a seesaw; so moving the handle to the right moves the end of the tool to the left, and up is down. Students pick up a ring with the tool in one hand, transfer it to the tool in their other hand, and drop the ring onto another peg.

As crude as the ring and peg game is, it gives residents a work out and it works.

"There have been validated studies that really show that you can take a novice trainee, put them in this environment, and within a period of time have them reach the level of proficiency of at least a competent person in that field and approaching the level of an expert; just by getting the psychomotor skills in place," Spight points out.

"The key to efficiency is to hand it to yourself so that you don't have to make any unnecessary moves," Spight suggests to a resident. He tells him to use both hands at the same time. "Your hands are moving independently. As one drops the ring on a peg, the other is already picking up the next ring."

Little things count. If you can cut the time it takes to finish each suture, and then multiply that by all the sutures needed during one operation, the result can make a substantial difference in the amount of time a patient is on the operating table. Less time under anesthesia means less risk and more efficient use of operating rooms.

The procedures are stressful on novice surgeons.

"When I was doing my fellowship, I started losing sensation inside of my thumbs," Spight recalls. "My attending said I was squeezing the instruments too tightly, because I was so focused on what I was doing. But there's really no reason to squeeze. Just relax, and it resolves."

As duty hour limits reduce the amount of time residents spend in the OR, simulation can give them a head start, so they can make the best use of the OR experiences they do get. It can also help make sure that training programs provide a basic and standardized set of skills, something that haphazard experience in the hospital may not provide.

"You could take five graduating chief residents and ask them about a case, say, common bile duct exploration, ask those five people how many common bile duct explorations have you seen? And you might get an answer from zero to ten. But all of these people are going out in the world to practice surgery, in which there may come a time in which they are called upon to do a common bile duct exploration. So that really is a deficiency of the training program," Spight says.

Derek Shepherd practices a delicate procedure on a model of a patient's head in "The Becoming" (4-14). Spight looks forward to the day when such customized simulations are readily available.

"The Holy Grail would be to take a patient's data, to take a CT scan and put it into the simulator and reconstruct the data in three dimensions; and then actually do the operation on that patient. Everyone's anatomy is slightly different; the orientation of things is slightly different. You would be able to practice as many times as you want, for as long as you want, on the patient you are actually going to operate on."

Additional Reading

Berg, David A. "A Cost-Effective Approach to Establishing a Surgical Skills Laboratory." *Surgery,* 142, no. 5 (2007): 712–721. Available at: www.ncbi.nlm.nih.gov/pubmed/17981192. Accessed August 2009.

Fried, Gerald M.; Feldman, Liane S.; Vassiliou, Melina C.; Fraser, Shannon A.; Stanbridge, Donna; Ghitulescu, Gabriela;. Andrew, Christopher G. "Proving the Value of Simulation in Laparoscopic Surgery." *Annals of Surgery,* 240, no. 3 (2004): 518–528. Available at: www.pubmedcentral.nih.gov/articlerender.fcgi?to ol=pubmed&pubmedid=15319723. Accessed August 2009.

Gurusamy, K. S.; Aggarwal, R.; Palanivelu, L.; Davidson, B. R. "Virtual Reality Training for Surgical Trainees in Laparoscopic Surgery." *Cochrane Database of Systematic Reviews,* 1 (2009). Available at: www.cochrane.org/reviews/en/ab006575.html. Accessed August 2009.

Simulations. For video game surgery simulations, see http://nhsblogdoc.blogspot.com/2008/10/tomorrows-surgeons.html, www.gamespot.com/wii/adventure/traumacentersecondopinion/index.html, and www.wiinintendo.net/2008/01/17/wii-hones-surgical-skills.

CHAPTER THIRTY-FOUR

A Discharge

Sometimes the hardest part of treating a patient is finding the right place for him or her to go when you've done what you can in the hospital. That's one of the issues facing Laura Matsen. Although Matsen is working toward orthopedic surgery, her intern year includes a rotation on the neurosurgery service.

She's trying to keep an eye on almost 30 patients, all of them very sick. The attendings are usually in surgery and rarely on the floor. Because of the heavy load of very sick patients, neurosurgery gets two interns. Matsen says not only is it nice to be working as a team but it also means they can often trade off early and late hours. But today, Matsen is juggling the load by herself. Her teammate has ducked out to meet his fiancée at the airport. He sent Matsen a text of thanks: "If you ever need a kidney, I owe you!"

A woman recovering from a brain tumor operation has Matsen stymied. The tumor has altered her personality. She screams and sometimes threatens to bite. Although she has a very serious illness, she has physically recovered enough from her surgery to leave the hospital. "But we can't just send her home," Matsen says. "Her children want to have her at home or nearby. They don't want to just drop her at some institution. But they work and can't stay with her all day. The sniff [that is, SNF, or skilled nursing facility] won't take her."

At the moment, Matsen isn't sure how the case will be handled. "If I had just five patients, I would say, 'Let's spend hours on this.' But you can't, you can't. I have eleven [medical chart] notes to write. It's hard to do a good job on all of them."

A few hours later, Matsen gets some help. A care conference is called together. In a tiny office, a multidisciplinary team of doctors, nurses, and other staff crowd together. Matsen fills everyone in on the woman's case. She asks the group whether she should try to contact the woman's doctors. The patient's hometown is about an hour's drive from here. If a doctor there is willing to admit her to a local community hospital, she could at least be closer to her family, so they could spend more time with her.

Matsen says that based on the notes in the patient's electronic record, it appears that improvement is unlikely. She says the patient and her family seem to have unrealistic expectations about the treatment options that are available. But Matsen is just an intern after all, and the value of calling for a care conference becomes clear as the more experienced staffers point out that there may be ways to improve the woman's symptoms and help calm her outbursts.

A plan is laid out. They will contact the woman's health care insurance company and her regular physicians to get her into a hospital near her family.

"I'm really happy they organized this meeting," Matsen says. "The nurse suggested it. It was a real learning experience for me and changed my view of the options available and the likely future for this patient. Maybe she has a better chance of improving; I thought she'd be just as she is for the indefinite future. I've learned to contact other people for help earlier."

CHAPTER THIRTY-FIVE

The Bill

A young girl is suffering seizures in "The Self-Destruct Button" (1-07).

"Doctor, is she gonna need surgery?" her mother asks.

"I don't know yet," answers Derek Shepherd.

The girl's father raises a difficult issue. "It's just that my wife and I, we both work and I don't know if our insurance . . ."

"We know it can be very expensive," the mother interjects.

"I don't want you to worry about that," Shepherd brushes aside their concern.

When Joe, the bartender of the Emerald City Bar, is diagnosed with an aneurysm in his brain in "Raindrops Keep Falling on My Head" (2-01), Shepherd has the same advice.

"How much? How much does something like this cost?" Joe asks.

"I don't think you should worry about that right now," Shepherd replies.

"Hey, look, you guys say that you can kill me and bring me back, I believe you. You're doctors, but I own a bar. I don't got any insurance, so I'm not that concerned about the surgery so much as what I'm gonna do when I survive it. I need a number. Ten grand? Twenty? Thirty?"

"It's a couple hundred at least."

Grey's Anatomy viewers outside the United States must shake their heads in bewilderment that a man diagnosed with a brain aneurysm or the parents of a sick child would be worried about the cost of potentially life-saving treatment. After all, every other industrialized nation has universal health care coverage. But in U.S. hospitals, a patient's insurance status can be a life or death matter.

Federal law requires hospitals to provide emergency care in life-threatening situations. Hospitals routinely do much more than that, providing care for which they are never paid. Yet day after day, residents and others struggle to arrange ongoing care for patients who don't have generous insurance coverage.

"I'm looking for funding to get him into a sniff," intern Nathan Bronson, M.D., tells fellow intern Loïc Fabricant as they go over the patients they are managing on the neurosurgery service. Skilled nursing facilities (SNFs) provide more sophisticated care than a typical nursing home. Indeed, they offer the kind of support for healing patients that hospitals routinely did in earlier decades.

"He has no money. I need to get him some funding." Although Bronson has spent years studying human anatomy, medicine, and surgery, he is now facing problems not addressed in any of his textbooks.

"When you try to discharge patients, SNFs put up a brick wall. It seems like they are looking for any little thing. It's amazing how much time we spend trying to find a place for people who shouldn't be here," Fabricant comments.

Hospital bills are so maddeningly complicated and variable that no one, not even the surgeon performing an operation, knows in advance just what the final bill will be for a procedure and associated care. They know it's a lot and that many patients face tremendous financial challenges in addition to their medical problems.

"THERE'S A REHAB CENTER NOT TOO FAR FROM HERE. MEDICARE TAKES care of it. You can stay there. Food. Bed. Long as you need," Derek Shepherd tells a homeless patient in "These Ties That Bind" (5-08).

*   *   *

IF ONLY IT WERE THAT EASY IN THE REAL WORLD. BY THE WAY, IT APPEARS that Shepherd may have confused Medicare (which covers hospital treatment and some, but not all, other care for people over 65 and some others) with Medicaid (the state and federal program that pays for health care for certain categories of people who have little money.) And no doctor would tell a patient that he could stay as long as he needed, because the government health care financing programs, as well as most private plans, have all sorts of qualification procedures that can make doing your taxes seem like a breeze.

Later in the episode about Joe the bartender's brain surgery, George O'Malley tries some creative financing and runs into resistance from Chief Webber.

"We're operating on our patients. That's it," Webber says.

"I know, but," O'Malley pleads.

"I sympathize. I do. But solving Joe's finances is not my job, it's not your job, and it's sure as hell not the job I assigned you today."

"It just seems wrong to cut him open, sew him up, and just leave him, you know, left with nothing."

Indeed, it does seem wrong, yet it happens every day. O'Malley's solution is to assign the cost of the surgery to a research grant. While patients in clinical trials are usually not charged for experimental care, it is unlikely that a research grant would pay for treatment that is already under way.

Hospitals and doctors do provide some care without getting paid. A recent report on not-for-profit hospitals found that on average 7 percent of the hospital charges went unpaid. Another government report said that in 2004, U.S. hospitals provided more than $27 billion worth of care they were not compensated for. Some of that total is money that was owed, but wasn't paid. Sometimes though, hospitals and doctors agree in advance to forgo payment for certain care.

ON INAUGURATION DAY, CANCER SURGEON KEVIN BILLINGSLEY IS preparing to remove a suspected tumor from a woman. Scans up on the wall monitors show how the mass is pushing aside all the other organs in the woman's abdomen. It might not have grown this big if the woman had been treated earlier.

"I first saw this patient about two weeks ago, she had delayed treatment," Billingsley says. "Her biggest concern was not, 'Am I going to die from this cancer,' but, 'Is this going to bankrupt me and my family?' "

The patient, Diane Hinds, later recalls the events leading up to her surgery. She had been feeling rundown for several months. She thought her swelling midsection was just weight gain. She didn't go to see a doctor. Her husband's job doesn't pay much and doesn't include any health care insurance. Eventually the swelling got to be too much. She went to a hospital emergency room. After a day of tests and examinations she was told that she had a large mass that might be cancer. The bill that came with that frightening news was $6,000.

No one would treat her as long as she couldn't pay. She applied for Medicaid and other programs without success.

"I had gone to every place that I could think of to get some kind of assistance. I had just sort of accepted the inevitable. And I told my family the same thing." She had recently watched her brother die of cancer despite nearly $1 million worth of treatment. "There's no way I could ever pay for it, and even if I could, I would bankrupt my whole family. I'm sixty-four and I just thought, 'Why bother?' That's the way I felt. I was pretty down and out."

Her oncologist sent her to see Billingsley. She listened to his assessment and proposed treatment. She declined.

"He couldn't understand why I would turn down a chance to have my life saved. I said, 'I don't have insurance. I don't have that kind of money.' He came right out and told me, 'My job is as a surgeon.' I said, 'I realize that. I just want you to know where I'm coming from. I'm not against medicine, I'm not afraid of the surgery or anything, but let's be practical here with the issue of paying for it.' "

Billingsley referred her to administrators at OHSU who reviewed her situation. She submitted her financial and other information. When the financial assistance staff determined that she did not qualify for Medicaid or other coverage and couldn't afford to pay for treatment, the hospital agreed to write off almost all of the cost of her care. On average, the hospital says it provides $15 to $20 million worth of charity care each year and also writes off almost $20 million in bad debts. It adds up to about 5 percent of the net patient revenue.

So Hinds got her surgery. And there was more good news: The mass was not a tumor after all. It was a hematoma, a collection of clotted blood. It was still a threat as it squeezed her pancreas, spleen, and other organs to the side, but now it's gone, and Hinds doesn't have to worry about lingering cancer cells. She says the recovery has been slow and steady.

Despite everything she's been through, she marvels at how Billingsley and the hospital treated her even though she couldn't pay them.

"How I got so fortunate, I don't know," she says.

During the procedure, a computer monitor at the nurse's desk was showing coverage of the new president walking to the White House. In the OR, there were wishes that someday they would no longer see patients delaying care and suffering because they couldn't afford to get treatment.

SURGEONS FREQUENTLY SWING INTO ACTION TO DEAL WITH INJURIES AND other problems that might have been prevented.

On a summer night, a confused man is brought to the Emergency Department with trauma injuries. As the trauma team tries to piece together what happened, they discover that the man had not been taking all his medications. He has symptoms of Alzheimer dementia. He was prescribed the drug donepezil. It can temporarily improve thinking and memory for some Alzheimer patients. But the drug wasn't covered by the man's insurance. Meanwhile he was taking painkillers that were covered, and drinking alcohol.

The trauma surgeons are not surprised he got hurt, but they are dismayed that insurance issues may have left him vulnerable.

"A patient with Alzheimer's taking pills, oxycodone, and alcohol. That's not good. We need to get him some help."

But it's not the kind of help a scalpel or suture can offer.

Grey's Anatomy has incorporated health care financing nightmares into a number of episodes. In one of the first episodes of the series, Izzie

Stevens sneaks supplies out of the hospital to stitch a wound on a woman who has no insurance because she is in the country illegally. In the opening episodes of the fifth season, the surgeons face a different payment problem. The patient had recently canceled his policy because the premiums were too expensive, then he was in a car crash. His coverage ended at midnight. In the OR, the team pretends they can't read the clock right, so the log will indicate that the procedure was completed before midnight. Of course, fudging the time of the operation, which is technically insurance fraud, wouldn't do anything about coverage of subsequent care, which may end up costing more than the initial procedure.

In an ethics skills lab, second-year residents get into a debate about whether and how they should consider the costs of treatments.

"You have to worry about the resources," one resident says.

"Right now, there are no limits," the discussion leader points out.

Another resident says he had a case recently in which the patient was receiving massive blood transfusions. The transfusions did not seem to be working. It seemed to be just a waste of resources. "We said, 'We're gonna give it another hour and we're just going to stop,'" the resident says. However, they didn't know what the family's reaction would be. Before the hour was up, the family agreed to halt the transfusion, avoiding a potential conflict.

"We're in a health care crisis. It's going to come up," says another resident, referring to the ever-growing size of the national bill for health care. It's already more than $2.5 billion a year or almost $8,500 for each man, woman, and child in the country. Within a few years, health care is expected to make up 20 percent of the U.S. economy.

Despite the huge price tag for the nation, the burden falls unequally. Some people delay treatment or are sent into bankruptcy, whereas others with generous insurance may have little awareness of the amount of money changing hands.

"People don't want to pay for health care, but they want an MRI for their headache, they want everything," notes one surgeon in the ethics discussion.

Sometimes there is a temptation to blame the patient, at least in part. "The ones I have the hardest time with are the ones with no health insurance and they've been in the hospital for a year because of problems from alcoholism," admits one resident. She sees patients in the ICU who can't breathe without a machine, depend on IV nutrition and kidney dialysis. And they will never recover enough to get off the machines. "What do you tell someone like that? They could stay like that forever."

"We need a national discussion," says another.

The leader asks, "What's the difference if it's due to cancer or because the patient drank and did it to himself?"

"Isn't it funny that a discussion of ethics always seems to turn into a discussion of finances?"

"It's an issue of limited resources."

"Does that make the decision only about ethics?"

"Most of the time we aren't thinking about the money; we're thinking, 'This is futile.' "

"Ethics is right or wrong, but it intersects with resources."

These surgery residents are on the frontlines, along with others in the hospital, seeing how health care policies and financing affect and complicate their duty to care for their patients. They struggle with what their role should be.

ANOTHER MANIFESTATION OF RISING HEALTH CARE COSTS IS THE NUMBER of people who travel to other countries to get surgery at prices that are just a fraction of those charged in the United States. One estimate is that more than 750,000 Americans go outside the country for treatment each year. Often they get good care . . . and don't have to exhaust their savings. But sometimes things don't go well.

In "Sympathy for the Devil" (5-12), a short man went to China to get surgery to lengthen the bones in his legs. There were complications after he returned home, and Callie Torres ended up having to actually shorten his legs in order to repair the problem. In "The Self-Destruct Button" (1-07) a young woman sneaks off to Mexico to have a gastric bypass procedure in order to lose weight.

"Unfortunately, there were complications with the bypass," Miranda Bailey tells the girl's mother.

"What do you mean?"

"She has what looks like an abscess under her diaphragm, and edema, which is a swelling of the bowel wall. I can't say for certain she'll recover completely."

Surgeon Robert Martindale sees similar cases far too often.

"I've had six or seven patients nearly die in the past year. One woman ran up a bill of more than five hundred thousand dollars," he says. Her attempt to save some money failed miserably. "We are the hospital of last resort. Their insurance won't cover treating the complications, because the original surgery wasn't authorized. Many of the procedures cost two or three hundred thousand dollars. But if we don't take these cases, they'll die."

Additional Reading

Agency for Healthcare Research and Quality. "Serving the Uninsured: Safety-Net Hospitals, 2003." HCUP Fact Book No. 8. Available at: www.ahrq.gov/data/hcup/factbk8/factbk8a.htm. Accessed August 2009.

Centers for Medicare & Medicaid Services. "National Health Expenditure Data." 2009. Available at: www.cms.hhs.gov/NationalHealthExpendData. Accessed August 2009.

Horowitz, Michael D.; Rosensweig, Jeffrey A.; Jones, Christopher A. "Medical Tourism: Globalization of the Healthcare Marketplace." *Medscape,* November 13, 2007. Available at: www.medscape.com/viewarticle/564406. Accessed August 2009.

Internal Revenue Service. "IRS Exempt Organizations Hospital Study." February 2009. Available at: www.irs.gov/pub/irs-tege/execsum_hospprojrept.pdf. Accessed August 2009.

Oregon Health & Science University. "Financial Assistance General Operating Policy." Available at: www.ohsu.edu/health/page.cfm?id=9999. Accessed August 2009.

CHAPTER THIRTY-SIX

Planning for the Worst

Seattle Grace has dealt with everything from an unexploded bazooka shell lodged inside a patient to a mass casualty event from a ferry crash to a massive plumbing failure in the OR wing. Emergencies happen. Real hospitals expect them to happen and plan for them.

Robert G. Hendrickson, M.D., co-chair of the OHSU Emergency Management Committee, says the hospital does a formal "hazard vulnerability analysis."

"We do it once a year. It basically has to do with what sort of threats would the university and the hospital face," he says. General responses are prepared. Key people are assigned specific tasks in advance, so that when a crisis hits, people know where to go and what job to do.

By contrast, it seems Chief Webber and his team at Seattle Grace Hospital try to fly through crises by the seat of their pants.

A Seattle ferry crash creates havoc in "Walk on Water" (3-15).

"We just received word of a mass casualty incident nearby. All available Level One trauma centers have been asked to respond. I need to send a team into the field immediately," Chief Webber says.

"Is this a part of the exercise? Are we supposed to act appropriately, um, tense?" asks Cristina Yang.

"This is not an exercise or a drill, Yang. This is an emergent situation and I need all hands on deck," Webber replies.

"Seriously?" asks Izzie Stevens.

"What happened?" Miranda Bailey chimes in.

"I don't have details, just orders," Webber barks.

In this chaotic atmosphere, Bailey and several of the interns pile into an ambulance to go to the scene. And even though Bailey refers to a "protocol," it doesn't seem that the interns have been trained in what to do or have been assigned specific duties at such a mass casualty event.

"Where should we start first?" asks Meredith Grey.

Stevens presses for an answer. "Dr. Bailey?"

"Ok, um, I don't have time to hold your hands. You know the protocol. Go do it," Bailey snaps back.

"Do what?" asks Alex Karev.

Bailey's vague guidance: "Go help people."

Hendrickson says they have a specific plan and drill for exactly this kind of disaster.

"Let's say there's a plane crash at the airport and there may be a hundred trauma patients coming. We would immediately open up the emergency operations center. The incident commander would communicate with the chief surgeon of the day. The surgeon would initiate a call-in plan. The emergency operations center would cancel all elective surgeries. They would start calling anyone who is coming in to get an elective surgery and they would cancel those so they could free up the OR. They would communicate with the OR so that surgeons would finish any surgeries as quickly as possible. No one would stop a surgery prematurely, of course," he says.

One thing the hospital probably would not do is send surgeons to the disaster site, unless there was a need to perform an amputation or other procedure on-site. First responders from local fire or ambulance operations take that on-scene responsibility. Hendrickson says that when he saw surgeons being sent to do triage at the ferry crash scene on *Grey's Anatomy* a question popped into his mind.

"I was wondering who was back in the OR operating on these poor folks. Paramedics do triage every day. They get formal training on it yearly; education and training on mass casualty triage. That's what they do. Surgeons really have no place at the scene doing that at all. They don't have that skill set. They are really good at doing surgery and making those surgical decisions and triaging surgical patients. They are the only people in the hospital who can perform trauma surgery. Why in the world would you send them away from the place where they can do surgery?"

There are rare circumstances in which surgeons do go into the field to treat a patient. Hendrickson says he and a trauma surgeon were called to a factory accident where a worker's arm was pinned in a newspaper printing press. Hendrickson helped treat the man while the surgeon prepared to amputate the man's arm. Fortunately, the man was eventually freed without the loss of his arm. The scenario is somewhat like what Izzie Stevens faced at the ferry crash: trying to a treat a man trapped under a car. But in reality, a surgeon would not be the first responder at the scene.

A surgeon's place is in the OR. "That's where we want them. That's where they do the most good for victims," Hendrickson says.

Just as the scriptwriters have surgeons perform duties that in real hospitals are done by nurses, radiologists, pathologists, and other specialists—partly in order to avoid cluttering the plot with additional characters—the residents and attendings on *Grey's Anatomy* perform tasks during emergency situations that are well outside their training.

"The way most television shows and movies depict it, it's one physician making all of these huge decisions about the hospital, about how they're going to send doctors to the scene, etc. And quite frankly, one of the keys to disaster management and response is to let people do what they have been trained to do and what they do on a regular basis. When a disaster happens, you don't want a physician making decisions about the stability of the hospital after an earthquake, for example. You have a facilities department person who is an expert in that, and they make that decision," Hendrickson points out.

"When there is a disaster we have an incident command center. And there is a whole, very structured response. There is an incident commander. There are several deputies underneath, all of them making specific decisions."

As Chief of Surgery, Richard Webber would be responsible for managing surgeons and ORs, not acting as the hospital CEO, facilities manager, chief nurse, and so on all rolled into one.

"Frankly, when it comes to disasters, the best way to respond is always to let people do what they do normally. Doctors diagnose and treat diseases. But that's all they should do. They shouldn't really be making the big hospitalwide decisions, unless they have specific training," Hendrickson says.

As friends and family members of people missing in the ferry crash on *Grey's Anatomy* crowded the hospital clinic seeking answers, instead of turning to a community relations specialist, Chief Webber tossed the assignment to intern Alex Karev.

"Alex, go to the clinic. The victims' families are there. They need answers," he ordered.

It is not surprising that Karev was flustered and family members were frustrated. He didn't know what to do. He appealed to Chief Webber for help.

"Chief, we've got a mob scene in the clinic of people looking for missing family members and nothing but a two-hour-old list of patients," Karev pleads.

"No one has any more information than you do. The police are asking us questions. Search and rescue can't track it. We'll have to do it ourselves," Webber shoots back.

"Is there some kind of system that . . . ?"

"You're the system, Karev. Figure it out," Webber says as he turns to leave.

Of course, in real hospitals there is a system. Communications staffers respond to media and other public inquiries. No competent hospital administrator would think of tossing the job to an intern. Karev's solution to the information vacuum demonstrates why: He posts photographs of the dead and injured on a wall for everyone to see. Although faces of unidentified victims might be released after every other attempt to identify them has been exhausted, premature disclosure could violate patient privacy standards, emotionally traumatize family members, and land a hospital in trouble with state and federal regulators.

LATE ONE EVENING, INTERN MARCUS KRET GOES DOWN TO THE CAFETERIA. As so often happens, as soon as he sits down with his food, his pager goes off. A trauma patient is due in 15 minutes. As he shovels food in his mouth, Kret glances at a TV on the wall. It is showing live coverage of a train crash that has killed a couple of dozen passengers and injured at least 100.

If a crash like that happened nearby, Kret would be in the thick of the action in the Emergency Department.

"When I was in medical school, I thought it'd be cool to be in on a big event; but the more time I spend in the hospital, well, now I'm not so eager," he says as he finishes eating, glad he has just one trauma to deal with right now.

ON GREY'S ANATOMY PEOPLE RESPOND TO CRISES AS THOUGH IT WERE THE first time anything like that had happened, when in reality, even if it were the first time that particular hospital dealt with a certain kind of crisis, each hospital learns from the experiences of other health care systems around the country and the world. That's not to say that there isn't confusion, chaos, and failure in disaster responses, but hospitals are required to have plans, make duty assignments, and perform drills.

In one statement, the Joint Commission (formerly the Joint Commission on Accreditation of Healthcare Organizations) has specific guidelines that hospitals are expected to meet:

An emergency in a health care organization can suddenly and significantly affect demand for its services or its ability to provide those services. Therefore, the organization needs to engage in planning activities that prepare it to form its Emergency Operations Plan. These activities include identifying risks, prioritizing likely emergencies, attempting to mitigate them when possible, and considering its poten-

tial emergencies in developing strategies for preparedness. Because
some emergencies that impact an organization originate in the community, the organization needs to take advantage of opportunities where
possible to collaborate with relevant parties in the community.

Also, the Federal Emergency Management Agency (FEMA) has
guidelines for health care institutions. "Hospitals and healthcare systems
should work towards adopting NIMS (National Incident Management
System) throughout their organization," one FEMA statement says. The
federal plans were strengthened, expanded, and updated after both the
September 11, 2001, terrorist attacks and after Hurricane Katrina.

"Make no mistake: disasters are disasters, and they always will be, but
there is a tremendous amount of planning that goes into the response. No,
everything does not go as planned, but certainly something like having a
surgical resident be the public information officer is completely unheard
of. That surgery resident would be doing surgeries or would be in the ER
evaluating people who might need surgery," Hendrickson emphasizes.

Hendrickson is a fellow of the American College of Emergency Physicians, which also has disaster response standards and resources.

ANOTHER SET OF *GREY'S ANATOMY* EPISODES—"IT'S THE END OF THE
WORLD" (2-16) AND "As We Know It" (2-17)—revolved around a patient
with an unexploded bazooka round lodged in his body.

Preston Burke is about to begin operating on the patient when Alex
Karev tells him the ammunition is live. He turns to Meredith Grey.

"I want you to walk out of this room. Walk, do not run. Go and tell
the charge nurse that we have a Code Black," he says quietly.

"I'm sorry, Code Black?" she responds, apparently unaware of the hospital's emergency categories.

"Code Black," Burke affirms. "Tell him that I am sure. And then tell
him to call the bomb squad."

Hendrickson says that he wouldn't take a patient who might explode
into an OR, but if the ammunition was discovered too late, as happened
in this *Grey's Anatomy* episode, he would evacuate the rooms around the

area, including on the floors above and below, just as they did on the show.

"If the person did need surgery, it's possible to do that, but I personally would never risk several surgeons, nurses, techs, and an anesthesiologist's life. I wouldn't put them in that situation, where there's unexploded ordnance sitting there. I would have the bomb squad deal with it first. If it's possible to make it so that it's not going to explode, then I would have the surgeons take a look at it," he says.

Certainly bomb threats are something hospitals do have to deal with.

"That scenario is very bizarre, but we frequently get unusual packages. In fact, last year I remember we had a package sitting in the hallway with wires sticking out of it," Hendrickson says. It turned out to be some computer equipment an engineer had forgotten.

"But someone stumbled on this bag, unattended, with wires sticking out of it. So we had a facilities person go to the scene and determine whether it was near a support structure or not. The people on the floor above and the floor below were evacuated. We had the bomb squad come and look at the package and then they made the decisions about whether to move it or try to disarm it or something else."

He never considered asking the chief of surgery how to deal with the suspicious package.

Bombs and mass casualty events are rare, but hospitals do have to deal with more mundane disruptions that interfere with surgeries. In "Here Comes the Flood" (5-03), Seattle Grace operating rooms are knocked out of commission by leaky plumbing. Real hospitals have written procedures for dealing with water failures or other breakdowns to minimize and manage the effects on patient care. If there aren't enough functional operating rooms for the surgeries that can't wait, then patients will be sent by ambulance to other hospitals.

Some critical systems have backups. If oxygen lines fail, for example, there are portable oxygen tanks on hand. Hendrickson says that in order to reduce the likelihood his hospital could lose telephone service, there are two totally separate systems that come to the campus from different directions. That way if an earthquake, landslide, or other disaster knocked out one trunk line, they could switch all calls to the other system, without users even noticing.

Additional Reading

American College of Emergency Physicians. "Disaster Preparedness and Response." Available at: www.acep.org/practres.aspx?id=40474. Accessed August 2009.

Federal Emergency Management Agency (FEMA). For general emergency information, see www.fema.gov/emergency/nims. For hospital and healthcare NIMS implementation information, see www.fema.gov/pdf/emergency/nims/imp_act_hos.pdf and www.fema.gov/good_guidance/download/10060.

Joint Commission (formerly the Joint Commission on Accreditation of Healthcare Organizations). For FAQs on emergency management, see www.jointcommission.org/AccreditationPrograms/CriticalAccessHospitals/Standards/09_FAQs/EM/Emergency_Management.htm. For hospital emergency management accreditation programs, see www.jointcommission.org/NR/rdonlyres/DCA586BD-1915-49AD-AC6E-C88F6AEA706D/0/HAP_EM.pdf.

CHAPTER THIRTY-SEVEN

Reputations

Residents are watched constantly. In addition to the many formal tests that residents must pass on their way to becoming practicing surgeons, they are always being monitored by attendings and chief residents.

"SO HOW WOULD YOU PROCEED, DR. GREY?" DEREK SHEPHERD ASKS LEXIE Grey as they review scans of a patient in "The Heart of the Matter" (4-04).

"Oh, uh . . . you won't be able to operate unless you realign his spine, would you?" she responds.

"And how would you do that?"

"Traction halo?"

"Very impressive, Dr. Grey. Your intern year's off to a good start," Shepherd says.

DURING MORNING ROUNDS, THE SENIOR RESIDENT ASKS ONE OF HIS JUNIORS to sum up a patient's feeding status following surgery.

"She is on twenty milliliters now. We'll leave it there until after her esophagram."

"Where is the tube?" the senior asks.

"In the bowel."

"Is that before or after the esophagus?"

"After."

"So it wouldn't affect the esophagram."

"Okay, so we'll increase it slowly."

"Would you starve your mom?"

"Well, depends," the junior jokes. "No."

In a physicians workroom, a chief resident sits with an intern to practice reading abdominal CT scans.

"Okay, where are we?" the chief asks. They run down a list of anatomical features seen in grayscale cross-section on the screen.

"What's that?"

"The esophagus."

"Sure?"

"Yes."

"Good. What's that?"

"Pericardium."

"What's that?"

"Common bile duct."

"Are you sure? Follow it. See the branch?"

"What's that?"

"Superior vena cava."

The chief points to the actual location of the superior vena cava.

"Go home, look it up and then page me tonight," the chief says. "I don't want you to try to memorize it. You won't be able to. It has to make sense, so you can look at it, and it makes sense by following the connections."

Each interaction—in the OR, during rounds or teaching time—is part of the ongoing evaluation of each resident. It involves much more than facts. When one intern breaks away to do something for an attending, the chief resident is not pleased. "Your first responsibility is to the team. Don't go off to do something for the attending unless you are ordered to or really have to," he says. Later the same intern interrupts him. "Excuse me, I'm getting paged by the nurses." As soon as the intern leaves the room, the chief rolls his eyes, "See? No sense of prioritization."

A few days later, the interns rotate to new services. The chemistry between this chief resident and the new intern is clearly different. The new intern is more assertive, and they debate cases back and forth. This intern, like the one before, makes mistakes; they all do.

"Have you been checking everybody's hypercoagulation panels?" the chief resident asks.

"No, I forgot," the new intern admits.

"Get on that."

What's different is how this intern handles the problem and the critique. The chief says he and the other senior resident on the service were both busy in the OR on the intern's first day on the service. "He was all alone and some things were missed. That first day was rough. I got admonished by attendings," the chief recalls. Still, the chief shows more confidence in this intern. "With some interns I say 'Call me all the time.' With others, I trust them more. Sometimes I can tell within hours how a new intern is going to work out. It's rougher in July when they are all new."

"We have to feel each other out," a chief resident says about the interns that rotate through his service. "Reputations travel fast, especially when they are bad. We check with the rotation before and ask, 'How's the new guy? Sweet or oh, no! "

Interns are not expected to know everything. Indeed, chiefs and attendings watch out for cocky interns and other residents who seem to be overconfident.

"The most dangerous residents are the ones who think that they're really good," says Robert Martindale. "The ones who don't think they're very good are cautious, but the ones who think they're good are the ones I watch and stay with."

He has firm opinions about residents on his service, good and bad.

"She loves what she's doing and it shows. She's efficient," he says of one. But another resident doesn't get a glowing review. "He's not that strong, see how fast he backed off? He's always looking for something or someone to blame. He complains if the equipment is not exactly right. He'll be okay. He'll be an average surgeon."

During one procedure, Martindale is watching the resident. He isn't satisfied with how things are going and jumps in to take control of the operation. "If I hadn't stepped in, they would have been struggling with it forever," he says later.

But the judgments of the attending surgeons are not always unanimous. Another attending who was watching the operation sees things differently. "He is quite capable. I feel sorry for the resident," the second attending says after Martindale takes over the operation.

While missteps are expected early in residency, as the years pass, reputations are harder to change.

"Reputations form by the third year," Martindale says, "though I do see some that make a turnaround after starting with a bad reputation. They have to realize what they don't know."

Residents know they have reputations and that the reputations have consequences.

"Once you get labeled it's hard to get away from it," says a resident. For example, "there was a resident who was always asking for time off and already arrived a week and a half late because of a car crash while moving. Maybe it wasn't all this person's fault, but the resident got a reputation."

As you would expect of surgeons, their comments about residents and students are not always diplomatic.

"If you gave him a connect-the-dots diagram, he'd do okay, but give him a blank sheet of paper and all you get back is scribbling," one attending says of a student he doubts will do well.

"It's weird sometimes when we overhear senior residents talking about other interns," says intern Nick Tadros. "They may be bad mouthing them, and we're like, "Hey, I'm right here. You're talking about my friends.'"

They may know more about the reputations of their fellows than about their own.

"You often don't have an idea of how well you're doing, despite the ongoing evaluations," says intern Ryan Gertz. "There's not always feedback. I got my sutures criticized once. Then later I found out they thought I'd actually done well."

Sometimes they do know what their seniors think of them and the word may even be good. When intern Jason Susong wrapped up his liver transplant rotation, he got a hug from attending surgeon Susan Orloff.

"Can I page you?" Orloff asks before he leaves.

"Any time."

"You did a great job."

INDEX

ABOUT THE AUTHOR

Andrew Holtz, M.P.H. is an independent health journalist based in Portland, Oregon.

His first book, *The Medical Science of House, M.D.* was published by Berkley in October 2006. He writes the ScriptDoctor column on medicine in the media for *Oncology Times*.

Holtz began reporting for CNN in 1980. He spent 17 years at CNN, including a decade as a medical correspondent.

In addition to his years as a CNN correspondent, Holtz has reported stories and produced programs for PBS, Oregon Public Broadcasting, and international TV networks. His work has appeared in Harvard University's *Nieman Reports, TV Week,* and on websites such as TheScientist (the-scientist.com). In 1998–1999 he was a Media Fellow of the Kaiser Family Foundation.

Holtz is on the Board of Directors of the Association of Health Care Journalists (AHCJ) and the Center for Excellence in Health Care Journalism. He was AHCJ Board President from 2000 to 2004 and was Interim Executive Director during 2004–2005. AHCJ represents more than 1,000 journalists who cover health, medicine, and the business of health care. The center produces educational conferences and other training and development materials for journalists.

Holtz has an appointment as a Clinical Instructor at the Oregon Health & Science University (OHSU).

Holtz is a member and former chair of the Multnomah County Bicycle and Pedestrian Citizen Advisory committee and is active in community efforts to make neighborhoods friendlier to walking, cycling, and other physical activity. He has a B.A. in Broadcast Communication from Stanford University and a masters degree in Public Health from the Oregon M.P.H. program at Portland State University.

Holtz is married and has two children.